The Monographs

A comprehensive manual on all you need
to know to become an expert Deductionist

Ben Cardall

Paperback ISBN 978-1-78092-850-0
ePub ISBN 978-1-78092-851-7
PDF ISBN 978-1-78092-852-4

Published in the UK by MX Publishing
335 Princess Park Manor, Royal Drive,
London, N11 3GX
www.mxpublishing.co.uk
Cover design by www.staunch.com

CONTENTS

ABOUT THE AUTHOR BEN CARDALL

I grew up in the middle of England; in a place called Stoke on Trent; in a quaint little village. During high school is when I was first introduced to the wonderful canon that quickly turned into my life's obsession! Not to tell too much of a horrible tale but it all began when I was reading *the speckled band* and *a study in scarlet* during my English class. I was admittedly fascinated right from the get go but it wasn't until I discovered that my girlfriend at the time had cheated on me with my best friend that I vowed I would never be lied to again and I sought the real lessons that can be learned from the canon. This was at the age of 15 and I have been studying every day since.

I learned more valuable lessons, in particular about human behavior, from high school that made particular reference to the powers of modelling/mirroring techniques written in popular body language books. Termed as one of the more popular kids just because I spoke how different groups spoke and spoke about what they spoke about. The foundations of memory palace work began at this point as my high school forms the basis for my palace itself. It was at the age of 19 that a neuroscientist friend diagnosed me (as much as a friend can officially diagnose anyone) with Ataraxia. This is a condition to do with emotions and means that I don't process them properly or understand many decisions based on them and is characterized by freedom from preoccupation with them. This in turn helps with my ability to be able to deduce the most from a scene with ease as I find it easier than most to be able to switch off that emotional side of my brain.

The age of 21 and I begin to perform magic and mentalism as a paid job. I always remained more fascinated with the people and what I could read in them rather than any "tricks" I was doing. I began to actually do the things that I was telling my audience I was doing. In mentalism/magic you expect the performer to lie to you. It is that unwritten code. I began to perform lie detection routines where I would genuinely detect the lie or memory stunts where I was doing the actual memory work. There were very few people in the world working this way. This went hand in hand with the deduction I was performing which always encouraged me to learn more and store anything I kept in my palace.

It is with this I developed the accolade locally and amongst friends/peers as a 'Rock and Roll Sherlock Holmes', which I was honored to have. I now spend my time between my family and my work in the field of deduction and my jobs as a performer. I have been at this for 14 years now as I enter my 29th year of being alive and my love for Holmes and the skill set grows with each minute that I study and practice. I consider myself to be a true Sherlockian as there is never a hiatus for me. I watch the DVD's on a rainy day; I fall asleep to the audiobooks and it makes me laugh when I am sad and better when I am ill! It is my way of life that I am truly grateful to get to share with you as part of this book! So, thank you intrepid reader for having the courage to take the time and do the work that is set out in this book.

DEVELOPING YOUR DEDUCTIVE EYE

"My mind," he said, "rebels at stagnation. Give me problems, give me work, give me the most abstruse cryptogram or the most intricate analysis, and I am in my own proper atmosphere. I can dispense then with artificial stimulants. But I abhor the dull routine of existence. I crave for mental exaltation. That is why I have chosen my own particular profession, or rather created it, for I am the only one in the world."

Sherlock Holmes - The Sign Of Four 1890

First of all, I am no expert. I am a Sherlockian by heart and by nature who has spent the better part of his life exploring the reality of these skills and how to learn them. I use deduction as part of my work as a mentalist. I utilize these skills to show my audiences that I can know more about them than I really should.

So who is Sherlock Holmes in terms of what this book is about?

Sherlock Holmes was a man who could read you, completely, and without failure. He was a man, who could read the clues in your eyebrows and your collar, all the way down to the tan on your wrists and the mud speckled on your boots. He knew if you were lying; knew how you were feeling and even in some instances, knew what you were thinking and could predict your movements based on what he could deduce. So why is it that we as a culture have been fascinated with this for many, many years? I believe it to be due to the fact that it is the ultimate tool. We would all like to know what the rest of the people around us were thinking and why? We could use this tool in business meetings; when out with friends; if someone has wronged us in some way. Anything.

5

You can't take two steps into thinking of the Holmesian skill set without talking about Dr Joseph Bell. The man who was partly the inspiration for Sherlock Holmes' skill set because he actually could do it. A Pioneer of the method, if you will. Joseph Bell was Arthur Conan Doyle's medical professor. It was said that in his surgery he could diagnose the people waiting without them even having to say a word. The brilliant doctor observed the way a person moved. He saw that a sailor would move differently to a soldier or a builder and have the marks on his body and hands to corroborate his thoughts and deductions. Originally learning his skills of observation from his great grandfather Benjamin, he elevated them to such a degree as to be considered one the most brilliant men of his time. Thanks to these observations he was able to know an awful lot about his patients before they had even opened their mouths, thus enabling his diagnosis to be that much more accurate.

These traits and attributes of the eccentric doctor can be found in Holmes' wheelhouse. So why do I mention them? Simply to highlight the point that these skills are not entirely fictional and can therefore be obtained by anyone given enough diligence and training. It is a largely heralded belief that if something appears as part of a fictional book then it is a work of pure fiction.

Not so. Take the work of Edmond Locard. A man not known for his deductive traits, but he wasn't known as the Sherlock Holmes of France for no reason whatsoever. Working primarily between the 1930's and 40's, a pioneer in the field of forensic science, he took some of the ideas put forward in the cannon to develop some forensic approaches to police work. Some of which have forged the foundation of modern day forensic work. He gave birth to what is known as Locard's exchange principle; The basic idea being that every contact will leave a trace; an idea that we can look at in our deductive work a little later in the book.

Jerome Caminada was a Manchester based policeman who rose to prominence in the force around the same time as the great detective was gaining popularity. A man well versed in logical reasoning and forensic approaches and not to mention a vast base of disguises that he used. Such an incredible expert was he that over the course of his career he had arrested over 1,225 criminals and shut down over 400 public houses. Even down to the baffling cases he solved such as a cab mystery involving a body found in a moving cab. Even down to a 20yr long feud he had with Bob Horridge, a career criminal at that time.

My point in telling you all this is simply that the only thing that will stop you achieving such incredible mental powers is yourself. These exercises will be a lot like press-ups, in that you will only feel the benefit of them the more that you do them.

Deduction and the other uctions!

When we speak of deduction and what that means as a process there are those who know what you mean purely by extension and there are those who bring up induction and that it is more akin to the actual process that was used in the tales from the canon. Even fewer people know of the theory of abduction. No, I am not talking of a fancy way to steal people but a logical approach to problem solving.

Charles Sanders Peirce is sometimes known as being "The Father of Pragmatism; A master in philosophy, mathematics and science, as well as a keen logician. He popularized several ideas in his work with mathematics and the epic problems he faced.

So he classed deductive reasoning as the following. "This process allows you to derive an answer form a source where the answer is a formal and logical consequence of the source".

In other words, the consequences of what is assumed. So for example, a spinster is an ageing, unmarried woman who lives alone. We can therefore deduce that this woman who has described herself as a spinster is ageing, unmarried and lives alone.

Inductive reasoning only differs slightly. You infer the answer from the source where the answer does not necessarily follow on from the source. The source gives us very good basis to infer the answer to be true but it does not guarantee it. For example if all chips/French fries we have seen are entirely unhealthy we can therefore inductively believe that all chips are unhealthy. We have good reason for this to be true but it doesn't guarantee the outcome. I point you in the direction of sweet potato fries and Tefal Acti fryers.

Abductive reasoning, again only differs slightly to inductive reasoning. This process allows you to infer the source as an explanation of the answer. So abductive reasoning and deductive reasoning differ in the direction of the process used. Holmes himself alludes to this process when he was quoted as saying:

'In solving a problem of this sort, the grand thing is to be able to reason backwards. That is a very useful accomplishment, and a very easy one, but people do not practice it much. In the every-day affairs of life it is more useful to reason forwards, and so the other comes to be neglected. There are fifty who can reason synthetically for every one who can reason analytically...Let me see if I can make it clearer. Most people, if you describe a train of events to them, will tell you what the result would be. They can put those events together in their minds, and argue from them that something will come to pass. There are few people, however, who, if you told them a result, would be able to evolve from their own inner consciousness what the steps were which led up to that result. This power is what I mean when I talk of reasoning backwards, or analytically."

However, with all this in mind, I consider deduction to be a phrase that could appear in the urban dictionary online. This is because when you mention this term in the right context and not in math's class or profit and loss for business', everyone knows what it is you are talking about. So from my own personal standpoint, so long as you know what you are doing and talking about and the right process to tackle what problem then you are on to a winner and don't necessarily need to know or argue over the correct terminology. Though being aware of how to utilize it is paramount so please don't confuse that message for apathy, it isn't.

So when we look at the idea of using deductive prowess in the 21st century let's take a look at the parallels between the culture of today and the 1890's. There is so much that is different, let's face it, but quite a large number of the initial principles remain the same. The roads were different, the shoes were different, the clothes were different, the jobs and the trinkets that one would carry. So much of what could immediately be deduced changes only slightly when using Locard's exchange principle. There would be no mud flicked on to someone's shoes or trousers thanks to a handsome cab wheel, Pocket watch marks of pawnbrokers and the like are now a thing of the past. These things are now exchanged for other forms of the same things, these ideas and many others as well so whilst there are many transferrable issues, if you don't spend your time concerned with 1890's deduction and focus on the 21st century then you will have much more success. You cannot, I believe, have an item in your possession for so long without impressing upon it some personal quality from your life, be that the large batch of change you carry in the same pocket as your phone that doesn't have a case, or the mix of cement that stuck to the side of your new shoes as you were leaving work for date night with your wife. To be able to do this successfully every time and with ease requires a state of mind and a way of thinking that must be continually worked toward. What this chapter will contain is exactly how to cultivate this way of thinking and seeing the world, as well as a considerable number of ways to practice and hone your observational skills as well.

This is a way of looking at the world which can be taught but for some it will come easier than others. Do not be put off by this though as it doesn't mean that it will be any harder to grasp, only that some things will require a little more practice than others in order to get to a sufficient level. It is in this way a lot like learning to drive. At first when you get in you think about where the key goes and whether you are in neutral or not. Then you check your mirrors and put your seatbelt on; as you pull away you are checking for hazards as you slide from first into second gear. After driving for a few months you simply get in and go. With deduction in mind you may see someone's grass covered shoe but only one side. Then you see the accompanying stain on their knee and equate it to a fall .Next you see the football/soccer boots in their kit bag and think this obviously happened in a game and the more action on the shoe indicates the more dominant side of their body so you know which side of the field they play on. No goalkeeper gloves in the kit bag too. The furrowed eyebrows and clenched fists indicate a clear loss, he is bottling up anger as well which would suggest poor refereeing decisions. All this after a while will happen in a split second and you will just know that this hypothetical person is a right footed midfielder, who has just lost the big game by having one of their goals disallowed. It will be easier to explain what you know than how you know it because you will be seeing the world in this way by then.

'It was easier to know it than to explain why I know it. If you were asked to prove that two and two made four, you might find some difficulty, and yet you are quite sure of the fact.'

Sherlock Holmes - A Study In Scarlet 1887

So, how then do you begin? We all must start somewhere so where is the best place? Could you announce the number of stairs you have in your house right now, irrespective of how many times you have used them? Probably not, well that is all about to change. We begin with two exercises that will begin to clear the emotions from your head and open your observations. We all have emotions and form our opinions on things that we like and we don't like based on these opinions and our thoughts and feelings on the topics at hand. This is part of the reason Mr. Holmes informs us that our emotions can be antagonistic to clear reasoning. These emotions can colour our opinions of anything that we need to deduce about and stop us from getting at the truth of the matter. They make us fall foul of things like confirmation bias and versions of inattentional blindness. Let us say, for example, that you had a particularly bad run in with a tall bearded fellow, who is covered in tattoos He was in a rock bar, showed typical signs of angry personality i.e not willing to listen to reason, only interested in talking with their fists, the worst kind of narrow minded person you could ever hope to meet. The worse this run in was, then invariably the worse your opinions on this ilk would be.

(You see this man, mercilessly looking down at something on the floor? What could it be? A gun? His victim?)

Continuing on down this hypothetical rabbit hole, you then come to aid the local police force in their murder investigation. The person who stands trial is exactly this type of person to look at, tall, hairy and covered in tattoos. You have to examine the evidence to help him clear his name as he is protesting his innocence. Your emotions at this point would then entangle you to such a degree that you wouldn't be able to read their body language and emotions properly; you wouldn't be able to read the evidence and the crime scene properly. Your emotions would feed the confirmation bias and only look for things that support your original theory of how all of these people are. Your inattentional blindness would be fed in the sense that you would not see evidence that aids what you were hired for in the first place. This is how they become antagonistic to clear reasoning.

(Nope, he's hugging his son. There was even a bit of his son's hand on the other photo)

Unless you learn to quiet that emotional voice in your head, which informs you of your opinions and models of everything in the world, you will truly miss a lot of relevant data. If not all of it at times. This will prevent you from obtaining a high degree of accuracy in your deductions. Unless you quiet that voice all people who dress in black and have tattoos will be heavy metal fans; all women who wear revealing clothing will be trampy; all builders will be inarticulate and unintelligible and so on. You don't want to see the world in your models of it when you are reading everything as a Deductionist. Let the truth of what is there speak for itself. This doesn't mean that you have to be a cold-hearted person who has no feelings whatsoever. It just means that you have learnt how and when to quiet that voice in your head. Before this becomes something strictly about what other people have said i will mention the infamous Bruce Lee and one very poignant statement he made. His was regarding the art of combat but we can take the same meaning here:

'It is like a finger pointing away to the moon, don't concentrate on the finger or you will miss all that heavenly glory.'

Simply put, if you concentrate on your own models of what is around you then you will miss all the heavenly glory of the truth in what you see in the people in front of you. This will begin a very powerful development of being able to quiet your mind to do the work that is needed of a Deductionist. Now then, to open your observations I would like you to begin practicing this game. Start with one room of your house, preferably one that you and others frequent a lot. If you live on your own then use a room at your place of work or even a corner of a restaurant if you are currently unemployed. You are then going to take a mental picture of the scene and take in as much detail of it as you can. You can spend as long on this or as little as you'd like. Now then, when you leave, the other people who will use this room will come in and mess up the scene you have stored in your head for use at a later date. When you arrive back at this place, which should be later that same day (if you leave it any longer, too much will have happened for you be able to backtrack all of it) you then compare what you see in front of you to what you have memorised and then begin to deduce the details. You see a cup on the living room table that wasn't in the room before but has moved and has been filled with something else. Why? A TV magazine by the sofa. Why? A freshly made bum print on the chair. Whose is it and why? All of these questions you will be able to answer as you know the people who frequent the room so you can extrapolate the details based on this. You know everyone has their favourite cup they like to drink out of, so you know who has had what, but why was it moved? What is it now in front of? The TV magazine, poses new questions and the bum print also. This scenery points to the idea of a live- in partner with poor eyesight who attempted to record their favourite shows and then took a load off after a hard day doing whatever they were doing. The more detail you can observe in a room then the more detail you can reason backwards from.

"In solving a problem of this sort, the grand thing is to be able to reason backwards. That is a very useful accomplishment and a very easy one, but people do not practise it much. In the every-day affairs of life it is more useful to reason forwards and so the other comes to be neglected. There are fifty who can reason synthetically for one who can reason analytically...Let me see if I can make it clearer. Most people, if you describe a train of events to them, will tell you what the result would be. They can put those events together in their minds, and argue from them that something will come to pass. There are few people, however, who, if you told them a result, would be able to evolve from their own inner consciousness what the steps were which led up to that result. This power is what I mean when I talk of reasoning backwards, or analytically."

Sherlock Holmes - A Study in Scarlet 1887

The more often you perform this task the more your brain will become accustomed to taking in all kinds of information in this fashion and then allowing you to be able to draw on it. Your ability to observe and then store the details will grow and grow. Until you will be able to come home from work one day and not have to ask how their day was, you will know by the evidence that is presented for you. It is all out there. You just have to observe it and then reason from what you see. You will get to the stage when you can up the game to the next level, which is when you will need the help and aid of someone else. Choose a room that you are in and take a mental picture of it as you did with the exercise listed before. Your imaginative capacities are needed greatly with this exercise and not in the sense of creating things in your head but to really picture something that you have seen clearly will rely heavily on your imagination. After you are confident that you have stored everything in your mind correctly, you will leave the room and the remaining person will change only one thing about the room whilst you are out. Upon your return it will be up to you to figure out what that one thing is. It can be anything. From an ornament that has moved to swapping two books around on a bookshelf. It just depends on how hard you want to play and much you want to develop your observational skill. Once you get to a point where you have experienced success with this, you then add a room and begin again. Keep going with this until you are doing this with your whole house. This will help you to be able to take in large amounts of information at once whilst being able to hone in on the details, as 'the little things are often the most important'. For example if you were to walk up to me you would be able to know what one of my favourite pastimes is and, best of all, you would have a very close idea as to the name of my partner. All this from careful observation and well placed reasoning.

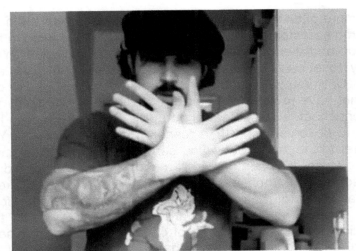

As you can see, there are three very important points you can reason back from here. I am a big built man, covered in tattoos of a Chinese origin, In particular, I have a tattoo of initials on the ring finger of my left hand, which may not be clear enough on the photo so I will tell you that the initials are CH. From these three obvious deductions you should be able to reason backwards and pull out a lot of detail about me already, including possibly what my partners name is.

Answers will be given afterwards so don't read on, test yourself first.

- Toned point to diligence and hard work. Can only be achieved properly through diet and exercise so commitment and focused based.
- Tattoos are predominantly Chinese, combined with the fitness dynamic which is clearly a big part suggests fascination with the culture and possibly some form of martial arts training.
- The tattooed finger is indicative of a serious relationship as it's on the ring finger of the left hand and we can take this to be metaphorical.
- We know he is straight so it will be a female name and how many female names do you know beginning with the letter C?

That is a lot of information that you can build on, we have just merely glazed over the aesthetics for you here. From sight, as in not having to talk to him at all, you would have a pretty solid idea of just what kind of a person he is, his preferences and passions in life, and the fact he is in a long term committed relationship.

- Ben is extremely focused and task driven,
- Trained in china at the shaolin temple for 6 months and can speak a little of the language as well

- His partners name is Charlotte.

So think about this. You would be able to walk up to me and tell me so much about myself through using only your observational skill and your ability to rationalize the information backwards from this point. You will not have formed any preconceived notions of who I am based on being tattoo ridden or anything else and consequently you will have been able to give one hell of a powerfully direct reading from what is essentially nothing. No questions and no fishing for any information this is pure cognitive awesomeness!

These exercises will help you to get well on your way to deductive success. The more you practice them the more you will attain what is in my opinion a higher understanding of the methods in play here. From earlier on in the chapter I mentioned that you would just know what the information meant instead of you having to go through a breakdown of it in your head. You want to be able to carry out your deductions with speed and accuracy, which means that you need to process as you go. If you spend too much time critically analyzing the information in front of you then you will make mistakes and you will slow down.

'A good martial artist does not become tense, but ready. Not thinking, yet not dreaming. Ready for whatever may come. When the opponent expands, I contract; and when he contracts, I expand. And when there is an opportunity, "I" do not hit, "it" hits all by itself.'

Bruce Lee

Which is again something we can learn from. Relaxation will open up your observation to much more around you as too much critiquing will lead to a tunnel vision effect of only the things that you see in front of you. Then when the time comes if you have done the work and the research then 'it' as in your deductive mind will hit all by itself and the answers will be presented for you. Now when you reach this time it is slightly odd as it does feel like your intuitive capabilities are taking over. What this is, in essence, is the beginnings of mastery of your technique. Practice all the techniques and all of the methods that are divulged in this chapter for developing the correct mindset and the correct thinking pattern for deductive capabilities. It does not really fall into the realm of guesswork here as there is a method to what you are doing. It is just happening all by itself which is why it is difficult to describe to anyone else how you knew what you know.

All of the exercises in this chapter are designed with one purpose in mind and that is too broaden the spectrum of your thinking; to find that all kinds of information about someone can be seen if only you look and put the work in to see it. Some of them are quite niche and difficult to get your head around and others are fairly simplistic but either way they will give you the tools you need to attain a very sharp mind, capable of detecting and observing things that others simply are not.

THE NAMELESS STAFF

This game can be played at any time and any place. If you want to really test yourself it is best to do this with the aid of someone else, though it is just as easy to complete the task by yourself. It is a fairly simple exercise taking advantage of the fact that in most customer service based jobs they will give you their name or it will be on their name badge.

Go into the shop and do whatever it is that you went in there to do and then on the way out you are to name every worker in there. At the very least name the ones that you encountered. This becomes a challenging game as you are going in to the shop with a purpose of some kind, even if it is only to buy milk.

If you spend too much time in your head trying to take note of everyone's name then you may struggle to remember why you went in there in the first place. It is designed to basically force you into observational approach. There will be other people ferrying around the shop, possibly even wearing similar coloured clothes to the uniform.

It is therefore best to remain as receptive as you can to the world around you. If you are consciously trying to make yourself aware of and complete 2 mental tasks at the same time, it can prove to be quite problematic. It is not too dissimilar to trying to process and take part in a conversation and read a story at the same time. Relax, quiet the inner voices (for want of a better phrase), pay attention and let the details sink in. After you leave you then go over what you have just seen in your head, (much like you did when making a mental picture of that particular room you frequent), and then back track the journey you have just taken in order to answer the questions. It is these little details that we often take for granted and it is here where you will really find the challenge.

You have just been in here to order your food and you sat

down to eat it. As you leave, the person you are with turns around and asks you," *What was the name of the manager in the background, the little lady with her hair tied back?*"

The information would have been there for you to observe but did you truly see it? We would hazard a guess that a few of you did not even spot her in the picture at first glance. You can see how this game will force you into paying attention. The little things can often be the most important! Holmes knew it and now so do you.

HOT AND COLD

Again a very simple game in its nature but will force you into a rather taxing state of mind and observation. You will again need the aid of a willing participant to take an object from their pockets and to hide it somewhere in a room. You need to ask your participant to only think of whether you are hotter or colder in relation to the hidden object. In how you frame this you will need to make them aware that warmth is to be viewed as positivity and cold as negativity.

They will be giving off directional cues from their entire body which is why you need to be able to observe the whole at one time. Move slowly but with purpose and keep your eyes focused on them the entire time. Hips will give clear directional cues here as well pupillary movements. This will again force you to behave in the correct manner in order to achieve success in this game. If you concentrate too much on one particular part of the person you are reading, you may miss the heavenly glory of other tells.

MODERN TWISTS

You can use your newfound skills to achieve greatness in other areas as well. This is as much about exercising your mind as it is about your deductive attributes. So, here are a few age-old games where you can use these skills you have learnt in this book to help you achieve more success with your training.

Take the classic memory game of pairs in which numbered cards are laid out in a 4x4 or 6x6 square. Each one is turned over in turn and you have to memorise what you seen and try and find as many of the pairs as you can. So when you see what is on the back of card number 1 you attach that image to a tie. So that when the other images come up that corresponds with the image on the back of the first card you will know for sure where it is. Never lose at this game again.

You can turn every celebration where gifts are given or received into a chance to work on your skill. Ask someone in your close family circle to get you a random present so that you may try and figure out what it is before the day that you are to open it. They can spend as much or as little as they like. You will have physical clues such as the shape, sound and malleability but more importantly you will have the person from whom to draw inferences. A fairly sound inference for me to draw here as the author is that if you know someone well enough for them to get you a gift or to receive one, then you will have an idea as to how they think, their job and therefore possible income allowance. This places certain gift choices inside the remit of possibility or outside. This is a great game and a challenging game. You will need to draw on all of your memories of past conversations, their likes and dislikes. Keep your observational eyes open as they may unknowingly let clues slip in receipts that they leave protruding from their coat pockets or email notifications on their phone for example.

There are those that will be using this type of skill to improve their mentalist demonstrations. For those people I give you this exercise to practice the classic but very niche market tool of sound and pen reading. This is extremely useful for knowing information that you couldn't possibly know and that you shouldn't possibly know. Pen reading works on the movements the pen makes as it writes in the hand of the owner. There is no real technique for me to describe here for you other than you need to practice it. What I have found though is at the start you will need a person kind enough to be helping you out with this, to go slowly, like a letter at a time when writing a secret down. Then you can guess each letter. Treat this as building blocks. Once you are capable of doing one letter then build it up to two letters and then up and up until you can read words at a time. After you can complete this task sufficiently well you will then ask the person to begin upping their pace until they are writing at normal speed.

There are a few things to be aware of when doing this though and that is that some people (based on their unique personality characteristics) will write certain letters in certain ways. Capital E's can be written with curves to them so they look like a backwards three. Lower case A's can be written like 'a' instead of the standard version like @-only without the circle (apologies as this is difficult to do on a keyboard). The letter Z can also be written as in the following photo:

It just depends on their handwriting style which, with even a cursory knowledge of graphological traits, could give you a direct reading as well as the information that you couldn't possibly know.

Sound reading is essentially the same thing but you are going to listen to what the pen does on the paper instead of watch. It is wise that you follow the same learning curve as stated beforehand. You can stack the odds slightly more in your favour as well if you get the opportunity to have them write something down on a sheet of artist paper with a marker pen so it will make a louder noise.

Right then. To elaborate on what will follow, I consider this an in depth look at something that isn't widely known about. These are methods for being able to deduce and glean information by observing the actions of those around you. All sorts of information that will hone your deductive skill and cognitive prowess, as well as fine-tune your rational mind.

So why has this not been focused on or expanded on? In my honest opinion it is because it is bloody hard work to be able to practice, other than actually using it. However when you weigh up what you get out of it in the end, against the work that goes in, it is worth every second spent and then some.

I mean just think about it for a second. Let's put this in the context of a magic trick. Say to a spectator that they are to write down a word on a sheet of paper or a business card. You use whatever lines you use to get them to be okay and accept the writing down of it. You make sure they know that you haven't influenced them. You can't peak at what they have written, there are no mirrors reflecting, there are no confederates in the room and yet you can still know what they have written. In short, using these techniques and methods it will allow you to know anything that is written down on a piece of paper/card/hand whatever can be done at any distance (given the power of your own eyesight though), can be done in any setting, with anything, if you're multi-lingual then there is another avenue to look at.

PRACTICE MAKES MORE PRACTICE

You only get out that which you put into it. You will reap what you sew. If you only do a couple of press-ups every now and again then you will feel no fitness benefit from this, but regular

24

work and you will reap the rewards. Bruce lee put it best when he said:

"I fear not the man who has practiced 10,000 kicks once but who has practiced a single kick 10,000 times"

You know what I mean with all this philosophy nonsense though. To begin I would find a patient friend/partner/talented poodle to go through this first exercise with you. Get an a5 artist sketchbook and a marker and have them write down the numbers 0-9 and then have a look at them and note the formation of each as best you can. Give them the pad back and ask them to write down a number, watch the pen/hand and note the formation. Compare this with how you know each number is formed and you will have your answer. Best way I can describe this in the written word is that if you see a straight horizontal line followed by a longer diagonal line then the number can't be a 0,2,3,4,5,6,8,9 could possibly be a 1 in most cases this will be a 7.

Practice this over and over until you can comfortably guess a pseudo pin number with ease and when the writing is at normal speed. You then repeat this method but with your eyes shut. Until you achieve the same standard. You will more than likely have to repay this helper of yours for their time in some fashion however it will pay dividends with this new skill you are developing. Once you have achieved this level in both sound and pen reading you begin to decrease the size of the paper and then add distance between you and your helper.

How then I hear you cry could you practice on your own? I am making the fairly obvious deduction that, given the century we live in most people will know how to send a short video via email or a messenger service. Ask your friends to send you a video of them writing down a word/number, place whatever limits in that you need to based on the standard of your pen reading at that time (quiet room, stand back from the camera, fill the paper with your word) and then tell them you are going to try and "read their body language" to figure out what they have written. You could just tell them what you are doing but keep your friends to as few as possible, lest your secrets escape into the wilderness of society. Your friends will already know you to be a quirky creative creature, given your current vocation in training to become a multi faceted Deductionist of excellent repute and they will 9 times out of 10 happily comply because a) they are your friends and b) this isn't an everyday request and will be fun to get involved with.

Once you have mastered numbers, then you move on to letters in the exact same process as numbers, with one slight difference, do capital letters first and then move on to lowercase letters. I have suggested this approach to maintain a steady increase in your success and so you won't over face yourself on failure. This way you incur the best learning curve possible with a new skill such as this. Now then, once you have reached this sufficient level of capability with the sound and the pen reading you would be wise to then vary your practice, going from business cards to paper, to napkins and post it notes and everything in between. There is one other considered way for you to practice your sound reading on your own and that is to use your laptop or mobile phone to record yourself and a few others writing the numbers 0-9 and the alphabet in both capital and lower case. This way, when listening to your own writing you will become more aware of the formation of letters. From the other people you will get chance to practice your skills with new formations and practice. Once you make your recordings (1 per letter/number) import them into your music library on your laptop so you can put them onto your phone. From then it is a simple matter of selecting shuffle and hitting play, then seeing if you can figure out what it is that you hear.

I have sighted many ways for you to practice and better your skills in this field and I also highly recommend that this is something that you keep at with consistent practice. Therefore it should be more than enough to keep you going.

ULTERIOR MOTIVES

In short what I mean by this is other ways that you can use the ideas behind pen/sound reading. Mobile phones that have a lock code can be figured out via a similar approach. It will all depend on how familiar you are with the models that are available. Here are 2 examples;

The left is an iPhone and the right being a Samsung s4. Now in short, you follow where the fingers go, then you will be able to figure out the code that has been typed in. Samsung's occasionally use a graphic as the code, a single line drawn around some numbers. The finger will not leave the screen. Thus making it much easier to figure out. 9 times out of 10 it is an initial anyway.

All this may seem irrelevant and I shouldn't have to remind you of this but I will.

"My name is Sherlock Holmes. It is my business to know what other people do not know."

— **Arthur Conan Doyle, The Adventure of the Blue Carbuncle**

Whichever way you obtain this information will depend upon what you are using it for. In the end it will all lead to the same cerebral skill that you can use in a variety of fantastic situations.

LOGIC PUZZLE PRACTICE

To be able to think laterally based on a specific set of information that you have in front of you is a much needed skill in this line of work. So I will give you a few to sink your teeth in to here but I encourage you to source more material on this topic.

Answers are provided but do yourself a favour and do not cheat yourself.

Puzzle 1: A woman enters a field and immediately dies. Her backpack is empty.

What happened?

Puzzle 2: A man is writing for his job. There is a thunderstorm outside. He dies as a consequence. How?

Puzzle 3: John leaves home, when he tries to come back a man in a mask blocks his path.

- what is John up to?

- what is the masked man's job?

- where would John's safe place be?

These will tax the way you approach problem solving in this area. All the information given will allow you to solve the problems. For the true students here, the answers are about to follow:

1. The cause of death is a failed parachute attempt.

2. The person is a skywriter and it was their plane that was hit by thunder.

3. John is playing Baseball, which would make the masked man a catcher. John's safe place would therefore be 3rd place.

You will now have some of the foundations and building blocks of training and practice in this field. It is an ongoing field of study. You will need to master a new way to think and approach problems and people for deduction. You are training yourself to observe mass amounts of information at any one time to be drawn on whenever you need it and how to engage your imagination and make use of this unique and wildly overlooked piece of brain power. This is a remarkable starting point for building a solid foundation on for becoming an expert Deductionist.

These aren't the only exercises to practice. There are exercises in the other chapters however I did not want this to turn into a book purely on how to practice and what to practice and why. There are a lot of bases to be covered and to do it all inside one book is a huge undertaking.

Keep this very important message in mind though with everything you are learning from this book. The deductions you reach are to be derived from context of the situations therein. Confirm your work and thoughts because a scratch of the nose could always be just a scratch of the nose and it is up to you to figure out which of these they are.

So have fun with these games! I still do!

MOULDING YOUR CLAY INTO BRICKS☐THE FINE ART OF STORING WHAT YOU HAVE LEARNT

"I consider that a man's brain originally is like a little empty attic, and you have to stock it with such furniture as you choose. A fool takes in all the lumber of every sort that he comes across, so that the knowledge, which might be useful to him, gets crowded out, or at best is jumbled up with a lot of other things, so that he has a difficulty in laying his hands upon it. Now the skillful workman is very careful indeed as to what he takes into his brain-attic. He will have nothing but the tools which may help him in doing his work, but of these he has a large assortment, and all in the most perfect order. It is a mistake to think that that little room has elastic walls and can distend to any extent. Depend upon it there comes a time when for every addition of knowledge you forget something that you knew before. It is of the highest importance, therefore, not to have useless facts elbowing out the useful ones."

A Study in Scarlet 1887

This is where it starts to get thoroughly interesting. I know what you are going to say though and yes it has been just that already but memory and training are where the fun really starts. This chapter will describe the many tools and training methods to developing a near perfect memory and eventually build to the guide of how to construct your own working palace. You will also find exercises to train your memory and observational skills to Holmesian like dexterity. Take heed of the games in this next chapter and you will notice and observe and retain anything and everything you choose to.

It will be taken in building blocks though; not everyone can just jump straight into memorizing great volumes at once. I am also aware that a considerable number of you will be reading this chapter with a few of these techniques already under your belt but for the sake of everyone we will all start together from the beginning.

Firstly what needs to be addressed then is the confidence you have in your own mental capacity and retentive capabilities during the whole time you undergo your training and practice. It is not advised that your arrogance grow but rather to know that, once you have done the work and gone through the necessary techniques in order to memorise whatever it is that you want to learn, you are confident enough to recall it and not second guess yourself. This is because the minute you begin to walk down that route the battle has pretty much been lost and the images you have committed to in your head will not be anywhere near as potent. I am sure we have all been in that situation or something similar where you're going to bed and locking all your doors on the way up and then your wife/husband/partner whatever says to you something like 'did you lock the back door' and even if it is just a split second where you have to double check in your head whether you did do it or not, then the memory strength can begin to crumble the longer you dwell, and this is with only having completed the task a few minutes before hand. Confidence is key! Do not let that seed of doubt creep in there and begin to tear at the foundations of your 'attic'.

Conversely I am not here to encourage complacency either. As previously stated, you cannot expect to half arse the work and reap the rewards no matter how confident you are. The reason I am so adamant to encourage the seed of confidence, is because it will then branch out into other positive areas. This is due to the fact that you will experience benefits from the test you passed or the anniversary you remembered or even the crime you solved and, thanks to this feeling, your abilities will grow and grow and keep having the same effect on each other.

There has been a study related to this effect done by scientists

32

at Brandeis University and funded by the National Institute of Ageing to see how confidence in one's own mnemonic capabilities could have positive effects at a later stage in life, such as staving off cognitive deterioration and benefits to overall self- esteem and one's own sense of self-control. Their results clearly showed that the contenders with greater belief in themselves did better on all memorization testing.

http://www.sciencedaily.com/releases/2006/03/060307220219.htm

Details of the study can be found at the link above. So remember to practice these techniques until you have mastered them and then continue to practice some more. Once you have done the work, you can then have faith in your own abilities and reap the rewards that you so richly deserve.

There are 2 exercises I recommend for building confidence. They are both insultingly simple and use the same props. You need to get yourself a giant pile of coins. As many as you can and in as many different denominations as your country will allow. Take a handful of them and drop them on the floor; Wait for all the coins to stop rattling and come to a standstill; Turn and look at them for a few seconds and then turn back; Count through how many coins you saw in your head and then check your work.

The initial reaction will be to turn around and double check, which is where your confidence will come in. In order to achieve success with this, you need to turn the picture of the coins on the floor into separate manageable quadrants. Those more astute will notice that this is what Rainman does when counting matchsticks. You then count through the blocks in your head and you will be at your total. The next step is to total the money instead of the sheer number of coins; you do that in the same way.

What this does is literally force your brain into honing in on details right from the get go and only in a very short space of time, whilst retaining the images and making sure that their integrity remain intact whilst you do what you need to do with them.

So it is with this in mind then that we look at the link system of memorizing. This is the first of many techniques in our quest to memory mastery.

You will see how applying a sense of logic to your memorization will aid in retention for longer without as much effort, which is something that is not found in many of the books. Remember at all times, with the construction of your images, that the crazier and more colorful they are, the longer they will be retained for. This is because we are designed to glaze over the benign and dull and more inclined to remember the weird and wonderful without much conscious effort at all. Let me put it this way. You are walking down the street and see a man with a briefcase and a blazer and seconds later a man who is on fire is walking behind him. He too is wearing the same blazer and is trying to put himself out with his briefcase. I guarantee that you will remember the second man for longer than the first. With all this in mind with these techniques you are involving more areas of the brain in your retention and, should you want to commit them to your true/long term memory, they will be there if you follow these techniques.

LINKING

It is a very powerful tool in memorizing and at first getting used to the ability to make quick associations between almost intangible pieces of information. It has benefits to all forms of memory work and if you wish to store a completely linked up system of information this would then move into what is known as the journey system of memory work. You will learn all about journeys and how to store them correctly and efficiently. Let's not get too far ahead of ourselves. The link system is basically exactly how it sounds. You are going to imagine one thing and link it to another thing in one picture. This technique works best for lists or pieces of information that are required to be regurgitated in sequence. The average person who has no experience of mnemonic technique can remember between 5-9 nonsensical items. By this I mean items that have no direct correlation or emotional attachment as these are considered the most difficult to remember. So just to prove the direct power of this method, you will now remember a list of 15 random items that may form part of the worst shopping list of all time:

- *Optimus prime (The leader of the transformers group The Autobots)*

- *A beach ball*

- *A post box*

- *A banana*

- *Barack Obama*

- *A steam train*

- *A magic wand*

- *A washing machine*

- *A monkey*

- *Bacteria*

- *Charlie Sheen*

- *Soap suds*

- *An owl*

- *A football boot*

- *Park Bench*

Now then, here is what you are going to do in a few minutes. You are going to remember that list and have the ability to recant it forwards and backwards all in under a minute. Now for the uninitiated to memory systems you are more than likely thinking to yourself something along the lines of '*Go forth into the world young man for I will never be able to do that*'......Which is the first port of call for me to be telling you that you can and will! You will also find this whole task so tediously simple after, that you will wonder why on earth you ever thought that in the first place. It is only that you have yet to be shown how to use your memories properly. At the minute you have taken a deck of cards and thrown them randomly onto the floor. There is no way you could find any card that was (go with me on the metaphor) named. What we are going to do is basically show you how to take information of any size and turn it the right way up. Now then onto the list. You are going to imagine a series of images that will link to the next item on your list and when you do this just make sure that you imagine each image as vividly as possible. Really make sure that you can smell what would be there and taste what might be there and feel the way you would feel about the things that are in this image.

Picture each one of these in turn:

- *Optimus prime, stood on a beach wearing speedos, and he is frolicking up and down with a beach ball, which he bursts.*

- *A Beach ball with arms and legs stood in front of a postbox,* crying because he can't fit his package inside which is also a little beach ball.

• A postbox with arms, legs and a mouth stood in a supermarket gorging itself on bananas, there are so many skins on the floor that it eventually trips and falls.

• A Whitehouse press conference and all the press are bananas. Barack Obama walks out eating a banana and greets everyone by saying " My fellow Bananas."

• Barack Obama running after a steam train at the train station screaming "I'm president, you forgot me." He eventually has to stop because there is so much steam he cannot see where he is going.

• The Hogwarts express (The steam train from Harry Potter) has been painted to look like a giant magic wand. White tips on either side and pitch black in the middle.

• A life size magic wand with arms and legs trying to fit as many smaller magic wands as he can into his washing machine and he is getting incredibly frustrated that his washing machine is not magic enough to take them all.

• A washing machine and all of his washing machine friends swinging through the trees making monkey noises whilst the silverbacks look on bewildered from below.

• A monkey with an incredibly camp voice says to his friend " Turn around and I'll pick all the bacteria off you as you're so dirty". The other monkey begins to cry because all he can see in the mirror is bacteria and feels dirty.

• A collection of bacteria is screaming on a piano "don't snort me!!!" as Charlie Sheen looms ever closer, giggling maniacally.

• *Charlie Sheen is sat in his bath surround by soapsuds. He is angry due to the fact that it isn't tiger blood. The angrier he gets the more soapsuds there appear to be.*

• *It is midnight and soap suds surround an owl family who are in their tree home worried that daddy owl won't be able to go out and make his twit-twoo noise tonight as he keeps coughing up soap suds and they are all over the house.*

• *In a shop filled, with football boots, they begin to make owl noises, which freaks out all of the workers and customers, who are all owls.*

• *A couple are walking through the park and they chat about how odd the choice of park benches are as they are giant football boots and are almost impossible to sit on.*

Now then go through the list once and do this genuinely now. Go through the list once and imagine everything as described as vividly as you possibly can. Then go and get a piece of paper and a pen and go through your images one by one, starting with Optimus, and write down the standout pieces from each image.

Go on....Optimus was at the beach running with a...... This thing was then stood in front of a ....getting angry that he couldn't fit his parcel inside.

How did you do? I will bet money that you got all of them after seeing the list only once. Now without looking at the list again, turn your piece of paper over and start with final image......These things cannot be sat on because they look like a giant.......which were the same things that were in the shop making.....noises. Work backwards through the list that way and really amaze yourself.

So now you have just proven that with the correct areas of the brain engaged you can defy the books that tell you only 5-9 items are possible. Not only that, you can do it forwards and backwards all in less than a minute and having looked at the list only once. So it is at this point you may wish to go back in time to slap the old you in the face forever thinking that you couldn't do this! This method is the same for 15 items as it is for 115 items. If you can make your images as vivid each and every time then no list of information will ever keep you down.

Then think of all the other possibilities with this method. Let's say, for example, you have some public speaking to do and it is the content which is important. Not so important that you stick to your notes word for word, but that the main points are gotten across. In this case the link system would be something that you would employ to eradicate the need for flash cards and the like. You bullet point the main ideas you want to come across in your speech in 1-3 words, come up with an image for each and then use the link system to make your speech seamless and more user friendly. To the people watching you, you are someone who knows and are passionate about your material because you can simply look them in the eye when giving your speech. If you are in school and need to remember the complete works of an author or the list of Prime ministers for the last century then get them into chronological order and come up with an image for each and then that huge bulk of information becomes so simple and easy to recall that you will ace any test on this material. Limited by your imagination only!

PEGS AND PHONETICS

This requires a different imagery but can do the added bonus of allowing you to pick off specific information from any given list. To demonstrate this point I pose this question to you. Everyone knows the alphabet, but could you name the 18th letter without counting? Chances are highly likely that you cannot.

With this system you would be able to do just that. This alphabet trick alone is worthy of demonstrating your extreme mental capability.

To begin pegging you must first become very comfortable with the Phonetic Alphabet. This will help you convert the seemingly intangible numbers into pictures which you can contort with your imagination.

THE ALPHABET

0 = S,Z	6 = J, SH, CH
1 = T,D	7 = Hard G, Hard C, K
2 = N	8 = PH, F, V
3 = M	9 = P, B
4 = R	
5 = L	

These equivalency letters are indicative of sounds. The ones that don't feature here are the vowels and W H Y. The easiest way to remember this is WHY aren't the VOWELS in the phonetic alphabet?

What this will help you to do is to encode numbers into pictures as well by combining the sounds and in order, to create images. For example let us think of a picture for number 81:

8 = Ph, F, V

1 = T, D

With this we can make the word FAT we can supplement letters from the ones that do not feature. FAT can conjure up all sorts of visceral imagery to play with in your head and this is how we begin to create what are known as peg words.

40

These will aid with the aforementioned ability to pick out say for example the 16th letter of the alphabet without counting and the ability to remember long lists of numbers with ease and perfection, basically anything with numbers. It is best that you formulate your own as the images will be idiosyncratic to your own personal way of thinking but I will give you the first 50 just to get you started.

PEG IMAGES/WORD

- 1=TIE

- 2=NOAH

- 3 = MA (MOTHER/MUM)

- 4 = RYE (KEY INGREDIENT IN WHISKEY)

- 5 = LAW (POLICEMAN)

- 6=SHOE

- 7=COW

- 8=IVY

- 9=BEE

- 10 = TOES

- 11 = TOT (SMALL CHILD)

- 12=TIN

- 13 = TOMB

- 14 = TYRE

- 15 = TOWEL

- 16 = DISH

- 17=DOG

- 18 = DOVE

- 19=TUB

- 20 = NOSE

- 21=NET

- 22=NUN

- 23 = NAME

- 24 = NERO

- 25 = NAIL

- 26 = NOTCH

- 27 = NECK

- 28 = KNIFE

- 29 = KNOB

- 30 = MOUSE

- 31=MAT

- 32 = MOON

- 33 = MUMMY

- 34 = MOWER

- 35 = MULE

- 36 = MATCH

- 37=MUG

- 38 = MOVIE

- 39=MOP

- 40 = ROSE

- 41 = ROD (ROD STEWART)

- 42 = RAIN

- 43=RAM

- 44 = ROWER

- 45 = ROLL

- 46 = ROACH

- 47 = ROCK

- 48 = ROOF

- 49 = ROPE

- 50 = LACE

So now you should fully understand how to create images based on the phonetic alphabet. Before memorizing anything using this my best piece of advice would be to become completely comfortable with all information on pegging imagery that has been presented thus far. Then, on to how to use them! Let us take the previous list from the linking section but number them each in turn.

1. Optimus Prime

2. A Beach ball

3. A Postbox

4. A Banana

5. Barack Obama

6. A Steam Train

7. A magic wand

Then you take each of the images and associate each to its item. Take the image for number 1 and Optimus Prime. You might picture him putting on a series of ties for a job interview. Take the image for two and associate that with a beach ball. You might picture Noah and all the animals on the Ark playing with numerous beach balls. You continue do this for your entire list.

Once you have done this, you now inadvertently know the list inside out and back to front. So then, prove it I hear you cry! Do not re-look at the list from here on out at all, do not cheat!

What is the 7th item on the list?

At what position on the list do Beach balls fall?

You know that the peg image for number 7 is Cow, so now remains only to ask yourself what you have associated with Cow and then you will have your answer.

You know that Beach balls were being played with on the Ark with Noah and that Noah is the peg image for number 2. This means that Beach balls falls in the second position on the list. This is the foundation for many memory feats. For example, this is the building blocks of memorizing your first deck of cards that have been randomly shuffled. There is another use here and that is combining 2 digit Peg images and linking them or using 3, 4 digit peg images to remember longer lists of numbers. For example, what if I told you that you could remember the number below for as long as you wanted to remember it and after only reading it once.

645753014102

You would know doubt tell me that it would be impossible, when quite the opposite is true. Using the phonetic alphabet you can turn the number into this

6457 530 14 102☐

Sh, R, L, K, L, M, S, D, R, T, S, N

Now we just sound that out and add the missing vowels....

SHeRLocK hoLMeS DR waTSoN

You will now be able to deduce how easily you can now memorize long, seemingly random numbers. When you have to memorize a number, no matter how long it is, you can now break it down into consonant sounds that then will suggest words to you. You get to choose your own words so have fun with it.... You are becoming a genius by the way!

You can take the words that your number suggests to you and turn them into a sentence, whether it is coherent or nonsensical. You will remember this phrase and be able to decode it back into the number when needed.

OR...

If you employ a Memory (Mind) Palace, you can skip making a sentence and attach each word to a peg in your memory palace. Just be sure to peg them in the order you walk through your palace or your number is not going to come out in order. That is rather obvious to those of you using a Memory Palace, but I will get to that more in depth a bit later on.

LET'S TAKE A JOURNEY

In very simplistic terms the journey or Loci method of memorization is the attachment of images to specific points on a very familiar journey you have taken in your life. This method will form part of the basis for building your memory palace so if this is your ultimate memory goal (and I think it is an invaluable one for the modern Deductionist) then you should master this technique in its intricacy. I will need you to think of a journey that you take; it could be the route you take to work, what you do in the morning when getting yourself ready, where you take your holidays. It can be literally anything, so long as you know it in complete detail.

To use this technique most effectively, it is often best to prepare the journey beforehand so that the landmarks are clear in your mind before you try to commit information to them. One-way of doing this is to write down all the landmarks that you can recall, in order, on a piece of paper. This allows you to fix these landmarks as the significant ones to be used in your mnemonic, separating them from others that you may notice as you get to know the route even better.

You can consider these landmarks as stops on the route. To remember a list of items, whether these are people, experiments, events or objects, all you need to do is associate these things, or representations of these things, with the stops on your journey.

You can use the journey technique to remember information both in the short term memory and long term memory. Where you need to use information only for a short time, keep a specific route (or routes) in your mind specifically for this purpose. When you use the route, overwrite the previous images with the new images that you want to remember. To symbolize that the list is complete, imagine that the route is blocked with cones, a 'road closed/road out' sign, or some such.

To retain information in long-term memory, reserve a journey for that specific information only. Occasionally travel down it in your mind, refreshing the images of the items on it.

One advantage of this technique is that you can use it to work both backwards and forwards, and start anywhere within the route to retrieve information.

For larger pieces of information, this method is quite invaluable as the journey can go on for as long as you want it to. You can of course use it in conjunction with other mnemonics to make your journeys shorter but you would need to create more detailed images.

These techniques all form fundamental parts of memory mastery and memory palace creation. I will cover many of the other techniques toward the end of the chapter covering such topics as how to remember the alphabet out of sync so as to be recited in whatever order is called and how to remember a shuffled deck of cards in less than a minute with practice.

MEMORY PALACE'S AND HOW TO BUILD THEM

Now then friends, this is the moment that many have been waiting for. How do I go about building a memory palace in my head and is it possible to get it as structured and as detailed as Sherlock's in the BBC show? We will build it together in foundations but, make no mistake, it is no overnight piece of mental calisthenics! You can and will get to one as detailed and with as much retention as you would like but you will have to work on it.

The **Method of Loci** (loci is the plural form of the Latin word —locus, meaning —place or —location) is a mnemonic device introduced in ancient Roman rhetorical treatises (as described in the anonymous Rhetorica ad Herennium, Cicero's De Oratore, and Quintilian's Institutio Oratoria). It relies on memorized spatial relationships to establish order and recollect memorial content. The term is most often found in specialized works on psychology, neurobiology and memory; though it was used in the same general way at least as early as the first half of the nineteenth century in works on rhetoric, logic and philosophy.

The Method of Loci is also commonly called the —mental walk. In basic terms, it is a method of memory enhancement, which uses visualization to organize and recall information. Many memory contest champions claim to use this technique in order to recall faces, digits, and lists of words. These champions' successes have little to do with brain structure or intelligence, but more to do with their technique of using regions of their brain that have to do with spatial learning. Those parts of the brain that contribute most significantly to this technique include the Medial Parietal Cortex, Retrosplenial Cortex, and the right posterior Hippocampus. In other words, the ability to do this does not lie in preexisting intelligence, but rather it is a learned tool.

Now then, this method is by no means new but what I have done here is to add some updated theories on how to cut down the need for tracking through your imagery whilst maintaining the high degree of accuracy. Memory palace's, the roman room method it all pretty much refers to the same principle and we are not here to quibble over the history of the techniques but to inform you how to create a monolithic memory mansion inside your head. So first of all, instead of calling each room you create a palace I am going to be referring to the entire place you use as the palace and each room within just as a set room. Employ a logical choice in your selection of palace, as this will help the recall of whatever information you need to be much easier. Let us take my palace for example which is both my high school and college combined. Now if I need a piece of information relating to history then I can just immediately be in the history room as that is a place that I immediately associate with history. The cognitive link will be much stronger and will cut down any chance of slip-ups in the retrieval process. So instead of going through the journey of imagery that you have placed in your palace to get to the history section you can just be in the necessary place.

This is where the employment of logical choice will come in very handy, you can of course do this with anywhere that you associate specific types of information with and then join them in the creation process. This is something that has not been touched on before when choosing your palace/rooms, but as we all know, rationality is key in thinking this way. You will need to spend some initial time travelling your chosen palace in complete detail so that you know it intimately and completely inside and out. The second step is to trace a clearly defined route through your memory palace and the rooms therein and visualize particular objects along the way. If you are considering your home for example, your route may start with your front door. You may enter into a hallway and notice a mirror hanging on the wall. Start with one object per room and follow an easy path (such as, left to right) until you are back at your starting point.

Practice following this route in your memory palace, making an effort to remember each specific object in order. This shouldn't be hard to do if you choose a place deeply embedded within your mind; consider the house you grew up in. Each object you see and encounter is known as a 'memory peg'. Start with one object, or 'memory peg', for every room in your palace, or every stop on your route. A simple example would be: you walk through the front door and see the coat rack, then you walk into the kitchen and notice the stove, then you walk into the garage and notice the ladder. Coat rack (front door), stove (kitchen), and ladder (garage): already, you have three 'memory pegs' in three different rooms in your Memory Palace. You can of course choose smaller places and locations to use as your ethereal building of memory if your chosen topic of information is smaller than creating an ongoing Holmesian one.

Now, think of something that you'd like to remember, such as a shopping list or your agenda for the week ahead. Place items in a particular order and integrate each with a memory peg (object) within your memory palace. It helps to conceptualize objects as being bizarre or perhaps cartoon-like at this stage.

Memory does, after all, perform best when operating in a strong, visual way. Since we created three pegs in the above example, the coat rack, the stove and the ladder; we can now utilize those pegs. If your grocery list only consisted of three items such as milk, bread and cheese you would then 'peg' them one at a time. Your first peg in the example is the coatrack; you walk through the front door and see the coatrack. So all you have to do is visually connect 'milk' and 'coatrack.' It is important to make your images as animated and bizarre as possible, so see the coatrack spewing milk from all its ends. At this point you would take a moment to really 'see' this image, and burn it into your mind. Now you would connect 'bread' to 'stove.' Keeping in mind that merely getting bread out of a stove isn't dramatic enough for memory. So I would see a man beating the stove to pieces with a gigantic loaf of bread. Done and done. Now just connect 'cheese' to 'ladder' i.e. A man is trying to climb the ladder and failing because it's made of cheese. Your simple list would now be committed to memory.

At the store, all you ever need to do is walk through your mental memory palace and your grocery list will fly right back at you. You will walk through the door and see milk spewing from the coatrack, then you would walk into the kitchen only to find a man beating the stove with a ridiculous loaf of bread, you then walk into the garage and see a man climbing the cheese ladder. Milk, bread and cheese is a pretty easy list to remember without a palace, yet you can begin see the power of the method.

The amazing thing is that your memory palace is EVERY bit as effective at storing enormous amounts of information as it is at storing very small pieces. Now that you have your own memory palace, expand it. Some people are fine with memorizing a grocery list but some of us like to take things deeper than that. Some of you only need to create more 'pegs' to objects within your current memory palace while some of you will be ready to develop new palaces and link them together to form this labyrinth of instant access to vast amounts of information. Whether you want to memorize vast amounts of information for school exams, figures and stats for your job, maps all the way to superhuman math systems; or just remember the playing cards that have been played in a game, at some point you're going to want to dive into your

51

memories and expand your palace and create new ones for specific purposes. Let us begin that process now.

Every new palace should have you taking notes. The written word seals the deal. Every single time you create a new Memory room the best thing to do is to write it down immediately. Even though we will almost always use a location we already have sealed in our memory, writing it down and mapping it out when you first decide to 'induct' it as a Memory room inside our palace, is an often overlooked step. If you can, draw it to the finest detail. Artistic or not, write down the name of each palace, and the rooms therein. Name/map every inch.

As some of you know by now, a Memory room is almost always a place you have literally lived in or been to frequently. Yet you can also easily include routes you know well, paths you've taken often, anything so long as you are intimately familiar with it. Having adapted the stories journey to the mental walk technique. The possibilities of places from which to create your first set of Memory Palaces are literally endless.

The first and foremost Memory room we all create is the home we know the best, or have lived at the longest. Secondary Memory Palaces can be created out of the school you remember/know so well, the layout of your current or most memorable job environment. Then, additionally, we tend to add all the routes, walks or drives to and from these places as separate Palaces/rooms themselves so long as the information you wish to commit can easily be related without conscious effort to the location used. That is why mine is 2 of my old schools, it requires no thought to be where I need to be, and each room remains unshakably accurate in my mind because I have used them so much.

These are the first and best choices mainly because they require so very little effort to picture them clearly in your mind.

While it may seem like these are the ones you don't need to write down, you will want to do this. It will prove extremely advantageous later to have a list and overview of your current palaces when you decide to combine many of them into attics of Sherlockian accuracy.

An alternative source for palaces, of whatever degree you wish, is to step outside the realm of reality. This includes: a home of a friend, which you can mentally walk through without issue: a video game that you once loved and can still walk through each level with your eyes closed.

Think of a photograph in your house. Just by creating a starting and ending point in the photo as well as defining a clear route to the next, you will have successfully turned an already known photo into a useful source to add to your ever growing palace. As such, it can be installed as the photo and take up very little room, yet encode a plethora of information.

Hopefully by now you can see that since the method of loci is literally a mental walk through a known place/route, you can start the building of this intricate building in your head and keep it going for as you long as you require.

Then next evolution in ANY memory palace is the adding of addition pegs. From five pegs per room all the way up to 50 pegs per room depending on how extensive those rooms are.
You must set this in stone and every time you close your eyes you must walk through your palace in the exact same footsteps. This is why keeping notes of your palaces is such a valuable thing to do. Once you have your path completely down, you then create 'pegs' out of every stationary object you pass along the way during your mental walk through the palace. Start one room at a time, step into the room and slowly scan the room with your eyes from left to right. Create five, ten or twenty pegs based on what you see. See this in as much detail as you can in your head and you will be on your way to

the foundation of an extremely strong Memory Palace. With anything and everything you need to memorize and wish to fix in a location in your palace you need to make it absurd, creative, vibrant as sensory as possible. Feel what you would feel there, smell what you would smell etc. and above all, the thing that I am my most proud of is a logical approach to storing the information used. So really think about where it is going and how it is going in, further highlighting the purpose of note taking.

Filling your Palace is one thing. However 'Sherlock' couldn't have sorted through every memory by using only a mere couple of Memory Palaces/routes/rooms. This is where I come in and combine the ideas of old to create a new supercharged and super easy and most of all, super detailed memory palace. Each one can be filled with rooms and each room with information that you can fill to the brim. As Bruce Lee used to say:

"In building a statue, a sculptor doesn't keep adding clay to his subject. Actually, he keeps chiseling away at the inessentials until the truth of its creation is revealed without obstructions. Thus, contrary to other styles, being wise in Jeet Kune-Do doesn't mean adding more; it means to minimize, in other words to hack away the unessential."

Now then, let me be clear. I am not saying that all I have taught you so far is nonessential. Quite the opposite in fact, all I have taught you so far has served the purpose of laying the essential groundwork to formulate your new palace. This will be a streamlined version which will check all the boxes of memorizing huge chunks of information without the need for journey upon journey. We are going to combine the benefits of all the systems of memory mastery. As previously stated, it is beneficial when choosing your rooms to have them logically associate to the information you are going to store therein. You have, then, only to carve out your journeys within each

54

place and the pegs within each room will be related to each individual piece of information in there, like subject headings of a book. What I am saying is that using this method you could ostensibly store an entire book worth of knowledge within one room.

To demonstrate the practical application of using my technique this way, I would like you to imagine the house you live in, in all its intricate detail. Take a mental walk through your house right now. Take in every detail in your mind, ask yourself which shelf of your bookcase would you go to for a certain book? Where did you put your keys when you came in? In your kitchen what is in the cupboard under the sink? How many tins of beans do you have in the pantry? Or even a really tasking question, how many knives do you have? Really take your time with this and imagine everything in as much detail as you possibly can, use your logical deductive powers to answer such questions as the tins of beans one. How many did you buy when you went shopping? When was the last time you used them?

Now then, you probably won't have answered everything perfectly, however if you did then kudos to you! If you didn't, then have no fear, because you probably got somewhere very close and either way you should be more than proud of yourself as you did this without much effort and no practice. What you have done is proven that your imagination is capable of great things and that you already have a lot of pictographic information stored in your head. You want the bleach? Then you know where you would go to in your house for that because it is in the room where it is supposed to be. Now then, if your house was your palace then all of the pictures and pieces you focused on along the way to answering our questions would have been your pegs that you could have then decoded to retrieve your information.

I then proceed with this technique in mind to create the

formidable memory palace. Let us carry on with my example from earlier in the chapter. Should I need to know anything relating to history, I need only wander through the history room, and the journey within, to retrieve whatever is necessary. I don't need to go through the journeys to get there. This is where the ability to store information efficiently will come in very handy. It is like wandering around your house and throwing one shoe off in one room and the other in another room, then dropping your car keys somewhere else. When it comes to the time that you need to retrieve them it will be very taxing as they have not been stored correctly and neatly. But also, as this room is imaginary (so long as it maintains its look and therefore link to a basis in your head) you can mess with it by whatever means you need. For example, my history room is about as tall as three regular classrooms, though it maintains the look of the history room that I know intimately. It can, therefore, store more information as its simply bigger. To continue this example, .When I committed the historical figures and information regarding their lives to that room, I used the bust of Einstein that was in the classroom already as a starting point. Then, every new person that is added gets a bust, until the shelf becomes full and then a new shelf can be added above it. This is when all the foundations of your memory work really start to come together particularly with information of this nature.

If someone were to you ask you if you have a certain DVD title in your collection, you would know without much thought whether you have it or not. Now how is this possible? Some people have quite considerable DVD collections and they have never stopped to commit to memory what they have in their collection and what they don't. True memory will get a look in here. You will have gone through the action of buying it, or receiving it as a gift, and experienced whatever feelings you felt because of it. And whatever feelings you felt when you watched it, they got stored away. So after you have committed your new bust to your history room, a couple of times of going over it and then you will know without having to go over the images in the room whether you have them stored or not. In doing things this way, more areas of the brain are involved in the course of memorization and therefore retention will be greatly improved. Something that has a logical basis as a starter can then be taken to new and unrealized heights. This conforms to the whole idea of memory mastery. What you would then do is store each piece of information on the bust itself as it saves a lot of unnecessary room that way.

As touched upon in a BBC show, and something that many people have scoffed at, is the idea of having things such as bookcases and filing cabinets full of information in your memory palace. I say it is very possible and incredibly useful to have them in your palace. They won't fit in everyone's palace but you will have to test them out in order to see whether or not they will.

To use yet another analogy, we all have a draw in our house or a cupboard or a shelf, that's sole purpose is used to collect junk. It contains all sorts of random things and objects but if a question were to arise over whether or not you could locate a given item, you would know if it would be in that drawer or not. The same can be said of using filing cabinets and other such items in your memory palace. As long as the information is stored appropriately and coded with care and order, you can use just about anything. Filing cabinets have a purpose of alphabetical order about them so as to locate needed files and paperwork when using them in real life. So, when using them in your memory palace, they will follow the same order. Just make sure you know what each cabinet contains. Paint it a certain colour, make it a model replica of something, set it on fire it doesn't really matter what you use so long as it relates to the subject matter inside. This way it will always remain a memory peg. You can store journeys that are specific bits of information as films in your geography class, you can store tattoo and work uniform symbology and meaning in the art room. It is really limited only by yourself.

With all that in mind you now have the capability to build and work on your own memory palace, I can only take you so far as it is down to your own idiosyncrasies to make things as weird and as logical as you can when committing them to memory. Be sure to take heed of everything I have detailed here for you!

SOME OTHER TRICKS OF THE MENTAL TRADE

First up as promised is the alphabet trick. Name any letter of the alphabet and then tell the person what position it falls in. It is an effect that strikes a chord with almost everyone and will aptly demonstrate your genius like capabilities in showing how you can manoeuver around information. To do it, is quite simple. You need to create an image for each of the letters of the alphabet and then attach that image to the peg image for the corresponding number

A = APE☐

B = BEAN☐

C = SEA☐

D = DEAN (AS IN DEAN OF A UNIVERSITY)

E = EEL☐

F = HALF☐

G = JEANS☐

H = AGE (CLOCKS/TIME)☐

I = EYE☐

J = JAY (BIRD)□

K = CAKE□

L = ELF□

M = EMPEROR□

N = HEN

O = EAU (FRENCH WORD FOR WATER)

P = PEA□

Q = CUE□

R = AIR/HOUR

S = ASS (DONKEY)□

T = TEA□

U = EWE (BABY SHEEP)□

V = VEAL□

W = WATERLOO (NAPOLEON/ABBA)

X = EGGS□

Y = WINE□

Z = ZEBRA

You may have already realized that you can disregard the first couple of letters from the beginning and the end of the alphabet as where they fall will be something that you will just know. You then have to associate each picture in as peculiar a way as possible. As in, an emperor pictured with a tomb, and a ewe with a net. Then you will be able to backtrack on what letter is called at what number and vice versa. That is pretty much it for that one.

THE INFAMOUS 52 DEMONSTRATION

Infamous? Yes! Difficult? Not at all. You can use the journey method or the peg approach to remember the shuffled pack but you must first know exactly how to code the cards. For this I will use card words as first given the idea by Harry Lorayne:

	Clubs	Hearts	Spades	Diamonds
Ace	Cat	Hat	Sid	Date
2	Can	Hen	Sign	Dane
3	Comb	Ham	Sum	Dome
4	Car	Hare	Saw	Door
5	Coal	Hell	Seal	Doll

60

6	**Cash**	Hedge	**Sash**	Dish
7	**Cake**	Hag	**Sock**	Duck
8	**Cuff**	Hive	**Safe**	Dove
9	**Cup**	Hoop	**Soap**	Dope
10	**Case**	Hose	**Suds**	Dice
Jack	**Club**	Heart	**Spade**	Diamond
Queen	**Cream**	Queen	**Steam**	Dream
King	**King**	Hinge	**Sing**	Drink

You will see that each picture of each suit begins with the letter of that suit i.e. for the 3 of hearts = Ham, Ham starts with the letter H and so does hearts. This is true of every picture except for the queen of hearts. The jacks of each suit are just the name of the suit. The numbers from 1(ace) - 10 follow the coding of the phonetic alphabet. For the other queens and kings, their images are forged from work words that sound like their affiliated playing card i.e. Queen of clubs = Cream, Cream and clubs start with the letter C and cream sounds like queen. As you shuffle up a pack you attach each card picture to its peg or point on the journey you are using. See, it's very simple. It just takes practice to be done with ease and speed.

There is a very nice twist on this technique that you can use to know what cards are left to be taken from the stack in a card game. It again is also very simple. As you see each card that is dealt or played, in whatever game you are playing, you then completely destroy the image. For example if you see the 5 of spades has been dealt then you would have to destroy a seal in your mind. Graphic we know but you won't forget it. Then, in order to find out what cards are still left in play, you go through the images in your mind of the cards and see which ones are alive and untouched. Go ahead and try it now. Go grab a deck of cards and remove 1 suit just as starter. Shuffle up the suit and take out 2 cards sight unseen. Then deal the remaining cards face up and destroy each image as it goes by. After you have completed them all, go through the list of images in your head for that suit and see which ones are unharmed. Those will be the cards that are still left face down or in game terms the cards left to play.

There is much food for thought here within the pages of this chapter and I encourage you to go through it at least a few times to digest its detail in full! With that I say, have fun stocking your attic!

FACING THE FACTS

EVEN WHEN THE MOUTH LIES, THE WAY IT LOOKS STILL TELLS THE TRUTH - Nietzsche

When you want to know what someone is thinking and how they are feeling about it. Whether they are lying, or simply trying to conceal their emotions about something then it is the face that will let you know. You have only to learn how to read what you see. We humans do this all the time and often on an unconscious level. I am sure we have all been privy to the storyteller in your social circle who begins to spin another yarn about some glorified escapade he has embarked upon, or some illustrious liaison he had with an impossible female. Now this could, for all intents and purposes, be an absolute gold star truth! But you don't buy a word of it. What is it then that tips you off as to the prevarication contained within his story if you have had no specific training? Our internal process of the proverbial b.s can feel at times quite reliable but, for what we are doing here, it would certainly be of considerably more benefit to have the science behind you.

There is a great myth surrounding the face and that it is the clearest way to garner accurate reliable information from, every time. This is simply not so. The face is in use all the time in public interaction and as such we have gotten used to displaying rules and social encounters and concealing what we want. Fake smiling (Duchenne) etc. The face remains closest to motor and cognitive control and therefore will display what is required to get the individual through their day as desired. However there are a great many ways with which we can read and deduce a hell of a lot of information from the face and be able to do it as accurately as possible. This is through reading micro expressions, pupillary movements, deception detection, concealment, emotional spikes and the rest of the list that we will shortly get into.

In the days of the genius detective, which governs the work of this book, I would like to draw attention to the way he is able to control his face so successfully by the characters he is able to slip in and out of with the greatest of ease in his unique knowledge of disguise. Whether it is down to the inherent sociopathy is something I will not get into here but to inhibit his own natural expressions to represent the countenance of others so remarkably, and so often as he does, shows a very singular command of the face and knowledge over what it should and should not do. Holmes was also extremely adept at the task of spotting liars in the room. This is a skill which is shown throughout the many adaptations he has seen throughout the years. These are all skills that you will walk with away from this chapter.

The limbic system (or the paleomammalian brain) is a complex structure that lies on both sides of the Thalamus and just below the cerebrum. These structures contain the hypothalamus, the amygdala and the hippocampus. These are involved in motivation and emotion, learning and memory. It is the amygdala that I am particularly concerned with here as it is concerned with emotion which is revealed in the face. The limbic system also governs our fight or flight response. Though modern behaviorists now consider it to be the freeze, fight or flight response. We all have a different reaction which is again something that can be seen in the face.

So even though the face can be greatly controlled, there are a great wealth of techniques that can aid you in your deductions of what is real and what is not. The simple fact is, that there is a great deal of information that can be viewed here, the more that you practice the more you will instantly be able to recognize what people are thinking, feeling and more importantly, why.

EXPRESSING YOURSELF

As soon as anyone begins to discuss the idea of reading faces as a matter for deduction, mentalism or otherwise, there is one name that continually pops up more than any other. This name is Dr.Paul Ekman. Here is a man who took it upon himself, in his research, to set about proving the universality of emotional expression in the face. This was a theory that was first purported by the great legend of science, Charles Darwin. Rather than this chapter turn into a treatise on his work I shall keep the explanation as brief as possible but it will serve the purposes in showing you the reliability of the expressions of emotion you spot leaking in your subjects.

The theory was that expressions of emotion were largely down to the way society had engineered them. That when we as kids looked at Sesame and saw people talking about being happy and happiness whilst smiling we made the connection. The theory had the same explanation for all emotions. Step in Dr.Ekman. He had travelled to see tribes in some very secluded parts of the world, most notably Papua New Guinea. These are areas of the world that are so remote that they are surrounded by jungle and have never even heard of a TV or magazine before. With his team, Dr.Ekman conducted a series of experiments through the showing of pictures or an interpreter who could ask them questions to find out how they would feel in response to certain situations. For example, how would they feel if one of their goats was killed or if they had recently become a father? They would describe how they would feel and then be asked to show their emotions in their faces. These types of experiments were repeated again and again, always conforming to some new query or specificity regarding the proof. The results proved the universality of 7 basic emotional expressions, these are:

- Happiness
- Disgust

- Fear
- Anger

- Contempt
- Surprise☐
- Sadness

Findings on Contempt aren't as clear as the rest though it is enough for it to be universally recognized. In the early 90's Dr.Ekman expanded the list of basic emotions to include a range of positive and negative emotions which aren't necessarily encoded in the face. These are: -

- Shame
- Sensory pleasure
- Satisfaction
- Relief
- Pride
- Amusement
- Contentment
- Embarrassment
- Excitement
- Guilt

What does that mean for us here? These expressions of emotion leak in the form of micro expressions. These are little fleeting moments where the expressions flash on the face for less than a second and are a way to glean a person's true feelings at that moment. Which is a remarkably great way for immediately (and often within a few seconds) getting to know someone's mind and the way they think. For example, were you to go into a situation of deducing a murder suspect, there are three possibilities in one room and you know beyond all measurable doubt that one of them is the culprit. You begin to question one and fire them home, you then accuse this person who protests his innocence admirably. The other two flash relief and contempt. You know the feelings at that time of all three people, but the one who flashed contempt which is the emotion akin to narcissism and believing yourself to be better than someone, in this case the questioner. This would alert you to the real culprit in the room.

For now though let us look at each of the 7 main emotions one at a time in depth, which we can only recognize thanks solely to Dr.Paul Ekman's work.

HAPPINESS

The happiness expression is characterized in the following way, and as an added bonus you may enjoy these terribly embarrassing pictures of me performing the expressions for you.

- Natural 'crows feet' wrinkling in the corners of the eyes

- Pushed up cheek muscles

- Movement in the muscles around the eye (Orbicularis Occuli)

- Action in the corners of the mouth, though they don't always reveal the ☐teeth (Orbicularis Oris)

- Pupil Dilation is akin to a leak of happiness.

Don't take the smile to mean that someone is happy as there are many different smiles that appear on the face in many completely different emotions. When you see this expression on the face of someone you are now clued in to their true sentiment at the time.

ANGER

Characterization of Anger

• **Eyebrows** lowered and drawn together, which gives a vertical line toward the middle of the brow ridge. The lower lid of the eyes is also tensed, when seen in combination with tension of the upper lid, this is indicative of significant anger with the whites of the eye on display.

• In the lower region of the face, the lips can become narrowed or even squashed together when trying to mute anger. Often the lower jaw moves forward slightly and is tense as well. This is known as a chin jut.

FEAR

Facial characterization of Fear

• Wrinkles can appear on the forehead due to the eyebrows being raised and pulled together. This can give a peak or a triangle effect in the middle of the brow ridge.

• The upper eyelid is also tensed and the whites of the eyes are shown. Strong fear is usually only shown in the eyes.

• The mouth is stretched back horizontally to the ears. When the lower lip is pulled out it is a sign of the attempted containment of the emotion.

SURPRISE

Facial characterizations of surprise:

● The eyebrows, only, are raised this time and the raise is centralized, whereas with fear they are raised and pulled together in the middle. The eyes are wide open with the whites clearly visible all around the iris.

   ● The mouth is open and relaxed.

● Something of note about the emotion surprise. It is a very fleeting emotion that often flashes on and off. So if you see the emotion for an extended period of time, it is almost certainly false or embellished.

SADNESS

Facial Characterization of sadness:

● The inner corners of the eyebrows are drawn up as well as the entirety of the brow being slightly raised. There is also a loss of focus in the eyes as well.

● Lip corners can become drawn downward toward the chin. The bottom lip can be pushed upward while tensing the corners of the mouth. Sadness can also be muted in the lips if the bottom lip protrudes forward. It is often akin to sulking.

CONTEMPT

Facial characterization of contempt :

 lip corner tightened and raised on only one side of the face

Contempt is known as a neighbour of anger, but in this instance, it is the type of scorn that is directed at an individual who is deemed lower in status in the mind of the person that is flashing contempt on their face. That feeling that they are superior to the other person.

DISGUST
Facial characterization of disgust:

- Wrinkling in the nose, nostrils partially flared

- Upper lip raised. The more severe the disgust the more of the teeth will be shown.

These are the emotions that everyone expresses in the same way, the exact same way. The only difference in their display would be the degree to which they experience them. So to give context from an example of my life of performance, when the reading of these micro-expressions has benefitted me greatly:

' I have a routine in my repertoire of performance which involves me demonstrating the ability to somehow divine a random persons memories. This is accomplished through the reading of these basic emotions on their face. When someone's baseline facial behaviour doesn't change dramatically and it has taken them maybe 1-2 seconds to come up with a memory, I know that it doesn't cause them any great discomfort to think about it as their face has not displayed any change and they were in a comfortable happy state before the effect began. Based on the deductions I have made about the person from the other fields, I can further narrow down the possibilities of the memory. So, if I see a smile that is suppressed, the head lowering associated with embarrassment and dilated pupils, I know it is a happy emotion that is concerning some stunt that made them feel special. This could be both kinds of special, positive or negative. Now then, being able to tell someone about their memories in distinct and accurate detail is something that only Psychics purport to be able to do. I count my successes in this area down to the ability to read the emotions and experiences that flash on their face at any given time'

There are then, of course, a plethora of other expressions that can be seen on the face at any given time but these are displayed differently in different people. The muscles in the face can react in a multitude of different ways to create in excess of 10,000 different expressions. Now there is no real need to learn all them, even the great 'Human lie detector' Paul Ekman himself hasn't done that. You are wise to make yourself aware of them though. They are there for all to see in the Facial Action Coding System (FACS). I would also highly recommend making yourself aware of the muscles in the face and how they move and why. This can also help you to make some very cool deductions. Once you know the natural movement of the muscles you will be able to know things like if any plastic surgery work has been done, any other form of treatments, and the inferences from these two simple remarks alone can run quite deep.

THE FACIAL MUSCLES

EXTRAOCULAR MUSCLE - These govern the movement in the eye. There are 6 involved. 4 control the movements involved in up, down, left and right. The remaining two are involved in the adjustment of counteracting head movement.

MASTICATION MUSCLES - There are 4 muscles of mastication, 3 are involved in adduction (pulling the jaw in to the midline) and 1 involved in abduction which is the moving of the jaw forward. All four engage in lateral movement. The sternohyomastoid, hyoid and the lateral pterygoid are involved in the smooth opening and closing of the jaw.

EYELID MUSCLE - The primary function for this muscle is to ensure the blinking of the eye so that it can remain moist and safe. This is called the Levator Palpebrae superioris muscle.

NOSE MUSCLE - Primarily made up of 4 muscles. Procerus, which is situated between the eyebrows on either side of the midline. It helps to pull the skin between the eyebrows downwards, which can also assist in the flaring of the nostrils. Its use, which is worthy of note in this chapter, is that it is a contributor to the anger expression. Nasalis, which compress the nasal cartilages to further aid nostril flaring. The depressor septi nasi, is the direct antagonist of the other muscles in the nose. It is situated below the nose and in the middle of the top lip. The Levator labia superioris alaeque nasi muscle is involved in the disgust expression. It allows the nostrils to flare and the top lip to rise, giving you the snarling look.

MOUTH - Most often misrepresented as a sphincter muscle, the orbicularis Oris is a small group of muscles that encircle the mouth. This aids in smiling and the successful blowing of brass and woodwind instruments. The risorius though, is the most prominent muscle involved in smiling. The Buccinator muscle is involved in the contempt expression of drawing the cheek back and tight. It also helps to keep food in the mouth when chewing. The depressor anguli oris muscle is another muscle of facial expression much like the risorius. This muscle depresses the corners of the mouth which is involved in frowning and sadness. The depressor labii inferioris is involved in the expression of the same emotions only this muscle depresses the lower lip completely. The mentalis is involved in the middle of the chin to aid in wrinkling, mostly akin to emotions of displeasure.

There are other muscles in the face and head but I have given you the list of the ones most highly featured in facial expression, the most frequently used throughout. The other muscle groups for the sake of posterity are: -

● Scalp ● Ear ● Pallet ● Tongue

So what can you deduce through your new knowledge of facial muscles. Well now you know what they do normally, any abnormal movement will stand out to you. Take for example asymmetrical movement in the upper eyelids i.e. one side moves slower than the other. This could infer to their medical history and that maybe they once had Ptosis. Inactive Procerus and Frontalis Muscles will point to Botox or even plastic surgery. This has inferences to be drawn in their personality and their personal lives as well. Also you will have more clues as to which emotions are fake or not due to being able to see which muscles are involved and which are not.

So, beginning to practice the safe reading of faces allows you the necessary time to build your confidence, as that will be one of the main things that will hold your success back. First of all, begin by learning the facial characterizations of each expression and to the point that you know them backwards

I would suggest one of two tests to begin your training with these expressions. The first would be to design, for yourself, a series of photo flash cards of a variety of different versions of the aforementioned expressions and to write on the back the names of the expression shown. If you can't or don't want to create your own cards, they are available for purchase from Dr.Paul Ekman's website.

You are then to shuffle them up and quickly flash them in front of your eyes and try to tell what expression you have just seen. It is best to check your answers as you go. Your alternative would be to create a different group of photos designed to create a different emotional reaction. These would be photos of things like cute puppies playing in a field, an abrasive argument, a still of a murder scene from a movie. These would provoke instant reactions to all who viewed them. You then need to engage the use of a partner to help your training. Hand them the group of photos and ask them to select one and describe it to you. They can either tell the truth or lie about what they see. You will be able to tell by the emotions they leak and the micro expressions you see what is really going on. If you see a disgust flash in the nose, followed quickly by a smile coming across the face and they feign an ease in their description of the puppies running, you can bet that it is more than likely the murder scene which is true to their nature. Their first initial reaction will be the honest one that you can successfully glean. This will develop your confidence to take it out onto the road, to the public.

SQUELCHED AND CONTROLLED EXPRESSIONS

These types of expressions can be micro but are, more often than not, macro in their length. They are also a conscious expression unlike the micro expression flash which leaks out. These squelched expressions are shown on purpose and are often a mix of emotions. They are direct signs of deception from the wearer of the expression. They are shown at the time when the owner can feel an emotion building inside them that they do not wish to leak out. For example, keeping yourself from yelling at the idiot at your office, who keeps screwing everything up but does try ever so hard. You feel like you want to strangle them but that wouldn't be the best way to deal with it and s, you, in essence, squelch your emotion as small as possible and the expression that is revealed will show this as well. The most seen social squelched expression is the smile with anger eyebrows, or the smile with the disgust wrinkling in the nose. The smile, being the most notably easy to fake, it is the other emotions that can be seen that will be the true way that the person is feeling at that time.

A controlled expression would be that of the fake smile. Studies have shown that children have learned fake smiles, from as early as 10 months old, when they are paraded in front of the gaggle of strangers for the obligatory cheek pulling and making of daft noises. The most likely cause is that evolution has taught us to make people believe that we are happy when we aren't and then people will stay out of our business. The fake smile is a very easy tell, once you know it. It is because there is no movement in the Orbicularis Oculi muscle which causes the wrinkling around the eye. Most people will be completely inactive around the top half of the face. Another tell is visible bottom teeth. During a genuine smile, the zygomatic major muscle is in use and pulls the lips upward which will hide the bottom teeth. Last, but by no means least, even if the most successful of fake smile's gets by you then there is a final tell that will allow you to see whether their smile is genuine or not. This is the amount of time it takes for the smile to dissipate. Real happy emotion fades from the face over approximately one second. If the smile and subsequent happiness is as quick to fade as its onset, then it is most likely a big fat fake.

EYE THINK THEREFORE EYE DEDUCE

For those who do not know what eye accessing clues are, chances are you don't watch a lot of cop shows on the television. This is a theory based on what the eyes do when accessing certain parts of your brain for information. This was a theory originally developed by Dr. Richard Bandler and Dr. John Grinder. Based on questions that were asked, the eyes would apparently look in a variety ways dependent upon which sensory system was being employed at the time.

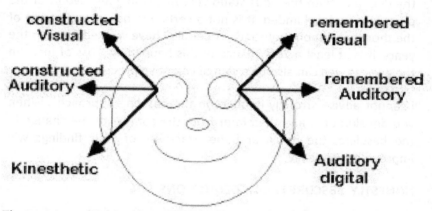

The top 4 are fairly self- explanatory given their title but the bottom two are explained as follows:

● AUDITORY DIGITAL - A person accessing their internal dialogue, that little voice in your head that is akin to cognitive processing.

● KINESTHETIC - Is a person accessing emotive ground. The myths surrounding this were that you could use it to help discover whether culprits were lying or not. Eventually it was believed that it would then help you to be able to know what any person was thinking about at any given time. This is simply not true. Even the hemispherical split in the brains functions between the right hemisphere controlling the creative side of thoughts and the left side controlling the logical and analytical thoughts is not true. The simple fact of the matter is that the brain has many different areas that relate to many different sensory parts. So what you do here is to check for a baseline, as you should do with normal reading of people, regarding the rest of the body. You can ask questions directed at each sensory part of the standard six directions and then make a mental note of whatever direction their eyes dart off to. One thing that I have noticed whilst doing this is; were you to note that they are the complete opposite to the standard 6, as noted in the diagram, then the odds stand very highly in your favour, of the person being left handed. It is not a certainty, however, but out of the thousands upon thousands of people I have worked for over the years, it is at least a 70% chance of this happening. Loss of focus in the eyes as well can also be a sign of cognitive processing.

I cannot advise strongly enough on the baseline approach. When you develop one, and then infer from the context of the change in the baseline, the detail and the exactness of your findings will improve dramatically.

HONESTLY OBSCURE FACIAL DEDUCTIONS

Now then I have discussed what the face does and what it can do, and what this means by way of the expressions they show. Let us now discuss the other rather obscure deductions you can make via the face. The first thing we can touch on is that of the facial piercing, now unlike most children's schoolyard banter they do not possess any particular meaning per se. With facial piercings in particular, they suggest many things, but mostly in terms of personality. In this instance I am referring to everything but the ears. This shows a person so comfortable in their own skin and who they are that they can show the world in the same way a tattoo might but definitely far less visceral. It speaks to the bohemian sensibility, and the creative nature within the person. Tongue piercings are usually indicative of the more excitable and cheeky types. With men, they are more often seen in the more amorous of individuals. This could also bear some inference on the type of job which the owner of the piercing does as facial piercings, of this nature, are thought of as highly in the business world as visible tattoos. If they can wear this piercing as part of the job that they do, then this narrows the field massively. But, on the other side of this coin, if they take out their piercing to do the job and then put it back in when they have finished their shift, then this also tells you many things about the kind of person they are, what job they might do and how they feel about their job at that time.

With ear piercings they are considered to be an extension of a woman's beauty, as a way for them to accent their facial features with whatever sparkly delight takes their fancy. These earrings, which are chosen, are also a visual link to their styles and personal preferences. For example (pertaining only to women here):

• Stud earrings - most often seen on women with piercings in the business world. Demonstrative of confidence and taking pride in your appearance. Probably   worn by the woman who has the dominant position or strives to obtain it.

• Dangly earrings - This pertains to any earring in this field that dangles. These earrings can contain fancy jewels and are thus indicative of economic status. They can contain charms showing the outgoing nature of the wearer. These are most often luxury items to be worn on a night out or a party event of some kind. Hoops are the earrings most often seen on women going out to a few bars, as they are considered to accent the romantic and the vivacious side of the wearer and the bigger the hoop the bigger these feelings and personality.

On men, these can show an entirely different ideal. Historically speaking they were worn by men as a symbol of rank in places like

Babylonia. They were largely considered an art form. Nowadays, however, it has simply become a part of mass culture and fashion that men wear them. It does not suggest any kind of sexual preference. It suggests someone who has a very strong and independent idea of who they are. One thing, you can be sure of, is you will not find a devout Christian male with his ear(s) pierced.

'Do not let your adorning be external—the braiding of hair and the putting on of gold jewelry, or the clothing you wear'

Peter 3:3

Now we shift to an idea which only concerns men and that is the shaving of our face. We all know it. We all most likely hate it. There are many styles and forms and consequently deductions we can make because of it. Let us not forget Sherlock Holmes' deduction on Dr.Watson in *'The Boscombe Valley Mystery'*:

"You shave every morning, and in this season you shave by the sunlight; but since your shaving is less and less complete as we get farther back on the left side, until it becomes positively slovenly as we get round the angle of the jaw, it is surely very clear that that side is less illuminated than the other. I could not imagine a man of your habits looking at himself in an equal light and being satisfied with such a result."

Yes we could pick a part that a man of Watsons nature would have checked by running a hand over his face to confirm the neatness and not left it as Holmes puts it 'Slovenly' but the point to be taken here is that we can make deductions about the man before you, based on the way that he shaves. It, is a possibility.

So then, to start with, how do you tell the different shaving styles apart by sight only? There are many points to make yourself aware of:

• Electric razors are useful for providing speed in a shave and ease with respect to being able to shave anywhere. They do not require the use of any soaps or gels either. They are an expensive item and are useful for those men who want to shave a goatee or any other beard pattern on to their face because of the added attachments that come with it to aid in this ability. Electric shavers do not shave as closely as a manual blade due to the way they roll up the skin on the way past and trim the hair. So these will give the appearance of a close shave but will sound rough when the man touches it and will induce the inevitable '5 o clock shadow much quicker than shaving with other blades.

• A wet shave provides the closest shave possible. Also, this is how 99% of men learn to shave so even if they don't use it currently they will at least own one. Though electric shavers are very expensive, manual razors only expense adds up over time. They are comparatively cheap to buy in bulk; this also includes the extra creams that one needs to purchase as well. With manual razors providing a very close shave this also increases the risk of getting cuts and nicks to the skin aplenty.

So then, the visual test of spotting the difference:

Which blade does this guy shave with? The only thing I will tell you is that it was taken 3 days after he shaved.

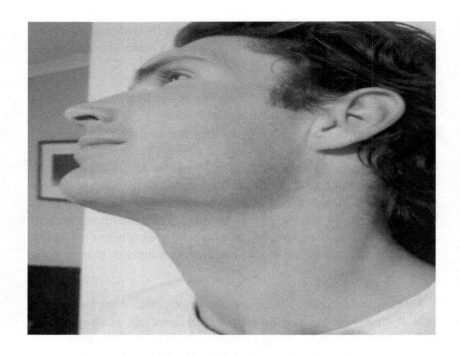

Answer: Manual shave, known because of the very slight reddening around the Adam's apple and the growth is all of even length. The line by the side burns is almost ruler straight.

What about this guy? Don't just say electric because the first was manual!

It is an electric shave: Patterning, slightly uneven hair length on the chin.

Now then so what? Is a question that might be on your lips at this point. I now know how to tell what style of shave a man has had. What do I do with that? The answer is there are many things that you can do with this.

• Manual shave is indicative of time and patience. Someone who has taken the time has to have the time to do it or may need to make the time to do for their job. Many food preparation jobs do not allow facial hair of any kind due to its unhygienic nature and as such will demand a manual shave be taken. Obviously the more cuts and nicks you see are indicative of an either or situation. That is either the person's patience is waning or they are simply not well practiced at shaving yet.

• Electric shave. The styles are indicative of someone who is more than likely a creative person by nature and is showing off their flare and personality through the hair on their face. Usually a luxury item of sorts, and so the owner will be financially stable, and in an economically generous job. A person with a very strong idea of themselves.

There are also a few anomalies to consider. Professional shaves can offer the closeness of a manual shave with the facial hair style of choice. They use the old- fashioned 'Sweeney Todd' style blades and you have someone to do it for you. The skin is taken care of as well to a much higher standard, which you may have already guessed with it being a professional shave. An application of a hot towel is applied to the face to open the pores and to make the shaving as comfortable as possible. An anomaly. Yes, but remarkably easy to spot. Smooth all over skin, no blemishes or reddening anywhere and at least one other luxury item on the person at that time. For example, look at the many changing beards of Derren Brown.

Don't just believe that when you see a beard pattern it must immediately be an electric shave. Treat it more like the reading of body language in this sense, that the cluster of tells is a more reliable clue than a single tell alone. So, if you see the smooth even shave associated with a manual but with a clearly defined beard pattern, then this will most likely be a professional shave. There are, however, a couple such as the goatee, Balbo or soul patch that can be shaved in successfully with a manual blade. So look for uneven lines in the design and any blemishes to the skin. This is a person with a clearly defined image of themselves but without the capital or patience to get it going.

So then, let us test your newfound knowledge of the face and what you can see in it:

What can you tell me about what job this man might do? And why?

Answer – Appearances are clearly quite important here. This person is a creative person judging by the neatness, style and patience that has gone into the craft of his facial hair. Clearly this person is comfortable enough in front of a camera to show their frustration so he would be extremely confident by nature. Most likely then this person would work in customer service in some fashion. The most popular choice in this section for men of this approximate age is tele-sales.

When this photo came through, these are the exact same deductions that I made and, as it happens, he worked on the phones in sales for a major mobile phone company in the UK called VODAFONE.

Tell me as much as possible about this man and why you think what you do?

Propping up or rather framing the face like this is an inherently feminine pose, combined with the highly stylized hair and vacant expression. This speaks to a highly narcissistic trait that will no doubt spill over into a regimented gym routine and personal hygiene. Perhaps even a chest shave to further develop the narcissism within. At the time is currently single, is low in confidence and the fingerless gloves and piercings suggest someone who has a non-generic personal preference list that often verges on highly eclectic most likely with music. Shaves with a manual razor which could have inferences to his job with respect to hygiene, as we mentioned earlier. But also could reflect his feelings toward his appearance and body hair. In whatever respect the job will be something physical.

As before these were the deductions I made and it was proven that he is highly narcissistic and because of his low confidence this often over compensates. He does regularly visit the gym to maintain his look and does in fact shave his chest. He works as a janitor for McDonald's and counts his musical tastes as Britney Spears and Dubstep dance music.

There you have it friends! A lot of knowledge to take in and practice! The face can tell you a whole lot but make sure you remain keenly aware of the 'tells' that hide true feelings and mask sentiment! You can now read make many facial deductions, take the leap and change perceptions!

OBVIOUSLY DECEPTIVE FACTS (THE DEDUCTIVE TRUTH ABOUT LYING)

What you do in this world is a matter of no consequence. The question is what can you make people believe you have done –

Sherlock Holmes, A Study in Scarlet

When it comes to the ability to spot liars and detecting deception and even half- truths, the television and media would have us believe that it is a very simple matter to do and once you have learnt the skills you will essentially become a human lie detector. This is simply not the case but we shall get into this shortly. I feel it best to first discuss why this is such an important skill to have in your arsenal. To the modern Deductionist, being able to spot liars in a regular everyday setting is such an invaluable skill and there aren't many skills that will help you get to know a person better and faster than being able to sift your way through the vast amounts of rubbish that falls from people's faces on a daily basis. On average, people tell between 6-10 lies of the white or huge variety per every 10 minutes of conversation, which is a startling amount when you think about it. So being able to decipher what is fact and what is fiction will be able to tell you their true feelings about the subject matter. What they are choosing to lie about (if there are any hot topics that they feel especially uncomfortable with). This will tell you why they felt the need to lie, how they think and you can then draw inferences about their confidence levels and the kind of personality they possess. I mean the list does just go on and on.

From a performance aspect it is just as interesting to be able to demonstrate what so many of the lay public wish they could do. A skill where you encourage people to try and be deceptive is a very exciting premise not only for the subjects, who are asked to misbehave but for you as the Deductionist. Natural lies, which flow in normal conversation, are tough to get to grips with but giving people time to think about what they are doing and then to plan out what they are going to say, and act accordingly, is a difficult challenge to see through. When you do, your deductive capabilities will improve dramatically. It is a topic that you should endeavor to continually improve upon. Even with Mr. Average, who doesn't know anything about the topics and merely guesses, it is clearly possible that they could achieve a 50% hit rate. So, with the proper training, you will take your hit rate up considerably.

I feel it very pertinent to the clear up some of the myths regarding lies and lie catching that popular media would have you believe to be true. First up:

THE LIE DETECTOR POLYGRAPH MYTH

The simple fact here is that, thanks to talk shows and improper use in legal settings, due to incorrect settings and questions, the polygraph has developed into what popular culture believe to be a fool proof method for catching liars. This is not the case. It's a detector of autonomic arousal, not of lies. As a consequence, people who become highly aroused in response to the relevant questions, but not in response to the other questions, will tend to fail the test. Then the dullards reading the test see the emotional arousal and perceive it to be an emission of guilt. The developer for the polygraph test was also the original pioneer for the character of wonder woman and her individual lasso of truth. This was William Moulton Marston and since there is no specific behavioural or physiological response to lying, the polygraph continues to be prone to many 'false positives'. This is the polygraph reacting to the emotional spike from the sitter, which in truth, could be caused by anything, from nerves over failing the test, even when you are of the most innocent possible, to a story that is particular to the investigative field and the legend of the polygraph. A woman, who was interrogated for a crime, was deemed to look guilty and suspicious and was pursued as such during questioning. Failing the polygraph was the final clue they thought they needed. However, she rightly continued to protest her innocence and in the end, it transpired that, during the time of her interrogation, she was so worried about where she had parked her car and whether or not she needed to put more money in the meter to prevent a fine, that her emotional spike registered on the machines and signaled her as guilty; Even though it was an entirely unrelated topic. A polygraph does not detect lies; it detects an autonomous emotional spike response to a stimulus/question. It's the machine's interpreter who deems whether you pass or fail the test. The machine doesn't detect lies, it can't! So then, it is for this reason, that the test is subject to a considerable amount of human error, that its evidence has become inadmissible in the courts. This is why psychologists, behavioural scientists, body language experts and the like have been cataloguing and developing a series of other attributes to make the detection of deception a more correct procedure.

It is in this field of lie detection that Sherlock Holmes again gives us a brilliant insight into the way to get the correct mindset to allow you to do this with more successful results:

'The Emotional Qualities are Antagonistic to clear Reasoning'

Sherlock Holmes - The Sign Of Four

It is not to be cold or heartless but as in lie detection, with all deduction the emotions will cloud the mind, and consequently affect your diagnosis of certain situations. Let us take an example as a demonstration of this point.

You have become quite adept at detecting deception in others. Now, the person sitting in front of you, whose guilt or innocence you have to decide, is the very embodiment of some moral outrage within you. It could be that they are a suspected wife beater or a proven paedophile. The way you feel about them and their acts (if you let your emotions get the better of you) will taint how you are able to perceive the situation. It then becomes in essence down to confirmation bias. In the sense that your feelings are telling you things about this person and the kind of human they must be to do what they have or are suspected to have done. This then means you will only look for ideas that support that hypothesis. You will achieve the greatest success here if you can quiet that part of your mind, to stop any grit from being in your lens as it were.

As previously stated, anyone could have a 50% success rate at determining the liar in the room, but it is only through training that people, as legendary in the field as Dr.Paul Ekman, believe you can take your success rate up to as high as 90%. Take for example his most notable skill of spotting micro-expressions on face. It is a skill that can be learnt and applied in a very short space of time and will tell you anyone's true feelings on any topics they are trying to conceal information about. It is like having a facial anomaly highlighted for you because we all see them, we just don't register its meaning. However, when that meaning is learnt and fully understood and appreciated it is hard not to see them.

Humans with the acquired skill of quieting the emotional voice within and detecting deception through body language, facial expressions, gestural timing and emblems, as well as language slips and the skills that are about to be laid out in front of you right now, will always be much more reliable than any machine!

THE BASELINE APPROACH

It is first advisable to get an idea for the baseline behaviour of the person you are talking to. This baseline, basically means, to know how they move and talk and react when not stimulated emotionally, when not lying essentially. This way the emotional spikes in behaviour will stand out against their baseline behaviour. First of all the baselines will change depending upon the situations you are in. For example the stress levels will inevitably be much higher in an interrogation situation than in a performance setting and the reason is simple. The stakes are much higher, in the sense that there is more to lose in one situation than in the other.

So in the higher stress situation, the body language will reflect this as part of the baseline. Some nervous behavior, such as pacifying gestures or manipulators, are to be expected due to the very nature of the situation and this is irrespective of their true guilt level. The next step is to relax them as much as possible in order to gain rapport. This will make any stress related body language stand out like the proverbial sore thumb. It is then that you will need to make conscious note of the mannerisms and movements they make at rest as well as any pacifying behaviour that is used. As the questions continue you can make note of distancing behaviours in response to any stimulus, as well as an increase in pacifying behaviours and manipulators. This will clue you in to the areas, in particular, that for want of a better phrase, stress them out. There are two times during these moments when you can expect to see this stress related behavior. Once, when the particular topic is brought up and once when the pacifying behaviour is needed to calm them. So, after the rapport is flowing and the baseline is developed, then you begin your line of questioning. Feel free at any time to check your work. For example, when your interviewee is asked about the possibility of stolen funds, they go from leaning forward on the table with their hands flat down, thumbs just slightly rubbing together, to leaning back in their chair, hands clasped over the crotch area and thumbs still rubbing. Then they rub the back of their neck as well, this is a pretty positive indicator of an emotional spike. As you continue on with your questions about other aspects of the case at hand, such as other employees that may be involved or what they did on their last shift at work, you see that they begin to sit back forward in their chair and place their hands back on the table. Not in the exact same manner as before but strikingly similar. You then bring up the topic of the stolen money and again they sit back in their chair and cover their crotch again. You are then pretty much as certain as you possibly can be of their guilt or at the very least at their guilt over withholding knowledge on the topic.

Now then, with respect to the lower stress situation i.e. performance of lie detector tests most popularly seen by mentalists. This is most often referred to as the 3 truths and a lie game.

So in your mentalist act, set one of your audience aside in your head, that you are going to play this game with and observe their behaviour. So that when you come to play, you can go right in to it. I will explain the test question phase in a while when I get into the eye accessing cues. The things you want to watch out for in their baseline are:

VERBAL CONTENT: By this I mean how they talk. Do they speak as though they are from a middle class background or with quite a colloquial twang? Do they speak quite offensively and stern or tame and meek. What kind of tone is there to their voice? Do they have a sore throat? Etc. All these are major verbal points that when differentiated from become 'bat in the face' kind of apparent and would probably point the arrow toward deception.

NON-VERBAL CONTENT: This basically refers to whether or not they are an animated person when they are speaking. For example, if someone who talks and explains things with their hands suddenly stops or their movement with them decreases and there is an increase of pacifying behaviours on statement number 4, then you can bet that this one will be the lie. Also you can be animated with your feet during your daily life. Do they stand still or bounce wildly? Do they kick out every now and again as though an electric current has just passed through them? Again when any of this is differentiated from it does stick out like a sore thumb.

VOICE BEHAVIOURS

There is only one behavior that I have noticed as a sure sign of deception in this game, with the voice and that is, the tone of the voice. When we panic or become nervous, our throat goes dry and begins to close. This causes several things to happen. We swallow harder, and during the hard swallow the chin will dip slightly. Licking the lips and clamping the mouth shut after saying something, is subconsciously trying not to say things or regretting saying it after and trying to keep the questions at bay. These behaviours do often combine with the hands and they tend to creep up to the mouth area and may mask as an itch or a comfortable stance but they hang there for an unnecessarily long period of time. In some cases the finger may even come across the lips as a kind of self-hush emblem. Like we were told to do as children in school by a teacher when we couldn't control our conversation, we were told to put our fingers on our lips.

The most notable thing in this situation is at the end of the statement the tone of voice goes up. Much the same as the stereotypical cheerleader in America sounds like. Like when the statement is made it sounds not so much like a statement more of a question.

Before I begin this game I will usually ask a couple of test questions, so to speak, in order to see if people are going to adhere to the previously discussed NLP formula. Those questions are:

- Do you have a good imagination?

- What would you look like with pink hair?

- Do you have children?

- What would your kids look like with pink hair?

I ask these questions in this order because I want to know from the first question if they are going to see the images I ask them in my next questions in their head; The 2nd question because I want to see if their eyes do in fact go up and to the left; The 3rd question sets up for the 4th really. If they don't have children then just go for pets or parents. This 4th question is so I can really make sure that if they do look up and to the left on the second question that it wasn't just a one hit wonder. Now logically in answering the 4th question they will have to see their kid's faces in their mind and then change their hair colour. What this means in terms of the eye accessing cues is you will see almost a roll from top left to right. If you get this far then these cues will be of reliable note in the game and if not then feel free to ignore them.

STACKING THE ODDS IN YOUR FAVOUR

Before you even begin your game there are a couple of things you can do to stack the odds of success in your favour. Emotion is such a major part of this game so when you ask them to make 4 statements get them to make them about something they can connect to. Like their daily routine, or their children, who their favourite musicians are, whatever they are trying to sell to you. Make it something that will speak to their emotions. It doesn't matter how powerful it is, just so long as they do.

Pressure! Taking into account that the average Joe is not completely comfortable with the ability to prevaricate, turn up the pressure and it will be easier to spot. This is to do with the aspect of the stakes of the situation again, that there are none. So it becomes up to you to increase the tension, which will increase the guilt/pressure and consequently the non-verbals when the lie happens. This comes in the form of your own body language. During your spectator management you should be comfortable enough to get them standing, square onto you, hips directly facing one another, and maintain your eye contact as much as possible, which are 2 pieces of slightly aggressive behaviour but eased in with a polite gentle tone of voice. So you achieve the pressure thing and not just 2 stags butting antlers.

LET'S PUT IT ALL TOGETHER NOW

Well what do you do with all of this information I have given you"? No one piece of behaviour is an indication of a lie. What you are looking for is a cluster of behaviours that differentiate from your baseline; these are your most reliable assets when trying to detect the liars. Clusters are 3 or 4 deceptive movements that occur within the timeframe of the statement. So don't immediately jump at a possible lie just because you see someone covering his or her hands. Wait until you have seen and heard everything and then make your decision.

It's tough to do what I am about to try in a book but I'll give it a shot anyway. I am going to write out statements, from a recorded game of this, that I have played and these statements are written verbatim, and give you notes about what I was thinking at the time. Then you see if you can guess which one is the lie! This would work so much better if I could show you the actual video, but alas I cannot.

After the test questions: It seems that the lady in question conforms to all the eye accessing cues. She speaks with a very colloquial tongue, lots of slang phrases. She does use illustrators but only with her left hand, her right seems to rest naturally on the table. She is leaning her weight on her right leg.

Statement 1: *'I drove here today in my dad's car'*

Just before she spoke her eyes moved up and to the left. She stood exactly how she was stood. She seemed quite relaxed and gestured with her hand and her head toward where the car park was. Both palms were facing me in a very open manner.

Statement 2: *'I actually forgot to brush my teeth this morning, feel like a right minger' (Common British colloquialism, referring to feeling disgusting)*

She looked straight at me. She smiled a genuine smile which you could see because the muscles in the corners of her eyes were activated. You cannot activate these when faking a smile. She brought her hand to her mouth as she said 'Minger'. Nothing else changed.

Statement 3: *'I dropped both of my children off at school this morning'*

She shifted her weight on to her left leg, so not so much her hips but both of her feet were pointing away from me. Her left hand went down to her side after she said it. Her eyes did a roll from left to right and then down to the left. She rubbed her index and middle fingers together slightly on her right hand. She said children instead of kids

Statement 4: *'I had to borrow this dress from my sister'*

Her weight shifted back to her right side. She smoothed down the front of her dress as she said it and gestured toward her sister with her left hand. Her sister also smiled.

What did you think the answer was? Yes my friends that's right the lie was statement number 3. If that seemed obvious that's what it will be like playing the game after you have played it for a while. Not all the time granted. It does take a while to build up your peripheral vision and observation skills so you can still comfortably watch and take in everything that they are doing whilst looking them in the eye.

How do you apply the thinking of Occam's razor here? Well the one anomaly from the actual lie was the roll around the top section of the eye which would suggest that she saw an image from her statement. So what part of it was true? The fact that I was performing on a school night suggested to me that she has only one child and not more than one. Her age aided me in guessing that she had a toddler and that she did actually take her child to school, which was right. I asked this question 'What are they like in the mornings' She tutted; so immediately I told her that she had a boy, which was correct. Stereotypically boy's mess around more than girls so during the morning rush to get your child to school this can cause frustration, which was released by her tutting.

So to add insult to her injury not only was I able to spot her lie, well really an embellishment of the truth, but I was able to tell her what specifically she was lying about and the sex of her only child without her really saying anything.

This is a very useful practice game for the study of perception detection. It is much more difficult to play with those closest to you, when practicing, as you will have emotional blind spots where they are concerned and it will take time to learn to get it under control. So for the baseline analysis of your 'sitter' it is all driven by context. The situation, the stakes, the potential loss or gain of the situation will also have an effect on the way they behave as part of their baseline. Thus concludes the exponential importance of establishing baselines in the correct reading of non-verbal communication, especially when trying to decipher when someone is lying and when they are not. The rest of chapter will be dedicated to the other specific skills involved in the detection of deception.

Just remember to be concerted in your observation.

STRESS BEHAVIOURS

Let's take a little more in depth look at the tell- tale giveaways regarding stress behaviour in all its forms. The behavior, we subconsciously revert to, in order to try and calm ourselves down in times of great stress and panic, both immediate and slow building.

PACIFYING BEHAVIOURS

Joe Navarro is the man who first popularized this term in respect to body language definition and it refers to a link back to our childhood and what our parents would do to aid in the calming down of us when we were feeling a little fractious. This is merely the title that Joe Navarro has used. They have also been referred to as manipulators in other forms of body language definition but it all means the same thing.

As a child you would likely see this in the form of thumb sucking or a light caress of the nose in order to calm down. When we grow, these gestures change and adapt. It might be that the thumb sucking is scaled down to a mere rubbing of the thumbs together. Though technically not the same movement it will have the same desired effect through years of subconscious behavioural encoding. These are emitted in times of great stress, so if they are not observed in the baseline analysis of your sitter then you will understand their significance and importance right away. The following is a list of the most frequent pacifying behaviours you will see:

• **LEG CLEANSING** – This is when the palms of the hands

are run down the middle of thighs, as if straightening out the creases in the trousers

• **RUBBING THE NECK/FOREHEAD** - This is again derived from the rubbing and patting and soothing that one receives as a child. This could also be the rubbing of any other area. It is just that the neck and forehead are the most frequently pacified.

• **NECK VENTILATION** - This is profoundly a male trait for the simple fact that more men than women wear suits and shirts with a tie to work. The ventilation comes from the loosening of the collar around the neckline. It is most popularly associated with the phrase, feeling hot under the collar. There is an inherently feminine version of this involving the touching of the suprasternal notch, which is on the neck just in between the collarbone and below where the Adams apple would be or, playing with jewelry around their necks at this point.

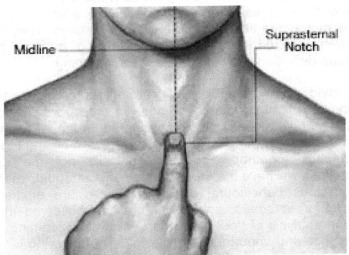

• **PULLING OF THE EARS/TWISTING OF THE HAIR** - This is most often seen in the times when the brain is off searching for an answer to any questions that cannot be found. An attempt to assuage the onset of fear and panic ensues and this manipulator is born.

Aside from an obvious emotional spike as a sign of guilt or stress it can also be a low confidence response to a stimulus, which has the same effect as giving away prevarication but means an entirely different thing in this situation. For example, you see a high police chief official giving a press conference regarding their apparent imminent capture of a malicious perpetrator. As part of the stress cluster of behaviours you see, one of the previous pacifying gestures appear. It can mean that they have no confidence in what they just said and so they are consciously trying to convey the right image, or they aren't adept at public speaking. CONTEXT.

NUMBER OF BEHAVIOURS

This doesn't mean that you have to continually count every movement that is made in order to make this reliable and workable for you. What it means is, as part of your baseline development you are to make note of the frequency that movements are made and the animation involved in their natural speech pattern.

For example, Illustrators are the arms natural way of punctuating the conversation. Though this is only one of the 5 parts of the kinesics of body language, we are just looking at this first. For example, we nod our head when we say yes, shake our head when we say no, stroke our stomach when we are hungry, and shake our fists when we are angry. These are all illustrators. Illustrators tend to be more universal than other kinds of body movement. However, they can also be misinterpreted. Even men and women regard the simple nod differently. Many women may think a man is agreeing when he nods his head as she speaks, but actually all he is saying is "I hear you." When they get into a meeting together and she finds him speaking out against her idea, she may be surprised and angry, because she thought she had his support.

Now then during times of lies when the subject is aware that they are about to lie soon, the natural flow and number of their illustrators will decrease and the number of manipulators will increase. A clear emotional spike then, that wildly differentiates from the normal standard set down by the baseline of their behaviour. This is just one example of the technique but it can be anything that aids in the differentiating from the norm. Breathing patterns: Normal conversation means 90% of people talk and breathe through their nose so to literally take a deep breath and exhale from the mouth puffing the cheeks out would be different behaviour both in number and style and conform to a stress peak.

The unconscious reaction to stress can pour out in many different ways and it takes the concerted observer to be keenly aware of them. Breathing can be held, literally and released when the perceived stress is passed. This only happens when the sitter is either watching the conversation or simply not talking. Nostrils can flare as a sharp intake of breath is taken. This can be a way of trying to inhibit an angry reaction, which isn't technically a lie but is someone controlling their own behaviour.

RHYTHM OF MOVEMENT

The body will always betray the true meaning of the person, irrespective of the words that come out of their mouth. So what you are about to learn about is the concept of gestural timing. This is when the illustrators of the situation are designed to be in line with the main points of the speech that is being spoken and to highlight the necessary points. The best and indeed the most popular example I can give you of this is the infamous quote from ex-president Bill Clinton.

'I did not have sexual relations with that woman Ms. Lewinsky'

He does fall foul of concealment gestures and asymmetric expression as well but that will come later on in the chapter. He begins quite well, bringing his index finger to a point and slamming it down on the '**Not**' and then the '**Have**' in perfect timing with the apparent sentiment of his words but the speeding up toward the end with the words mean that his behaviour was out of time and gave the false impression. Were he truly ready to get hold of America's tension and make them listen to the truth of his words if they were true, then it would have held its tempo, the hand would have been dropped down on every word that it was designed to accent. A good example of when gestural timing is completely congruous and truthful is when all parents at one time or another are forced into a conversation with their children. This doesn't necessarily have to be shouting but very often deteriorates into, regarding their recent bad behaviour. Accentuated in their own idiosyncratic way but each point they want the child to take notice of will be highlighted. The timing of the spoken word as well, in this instance, is worth highlighting as it can betray in the same way gestural timing can. Let us return now to the exploits of Mr. Clinton. He begins well with the points he is trying desperately to make America understand. "I did not have sexual." Timed well and sounds to the point but he speeds through the latter half of the sentence as though the words don't taste right which of course being a lie, they won't. It is completely incongruous with the beginning of the sentence and therefore falls foul of the gestural timing tell, in lies. These are not quite as clear in prepared lies like this one but in unprepared lies, in that of regular conversation they become even clearer.

Asymmetric expression and concealment

Each person has their own personal beliefs on the definition regarding lies and the lies that are told so we are going to go over items from each type. Concealment and asymmetry are essentially the same thing. They are expressions that are always seen in symmetry, in both halves of the body, so when someone wishes to convey the meaning behind these gestures but isn't entirely feeling them, or isn't feeling them at all, then their asymmetry will give it away. For example, take the classic please believe me stance, both arms out and palms are up facing the person begging for their belief. Now picture this with only one arm in the gesture and the other one inactive. Insincere is it not?

This is basically the way that the low confidence in the words will have an effect on the way it is shown in the body. The following are two of the most popular concealment gestures:

- **One-sided shoulder shrug** - The classic movement symbolizing 'I don't know' or words of that sentiment. When they do know, or even if they are just trying to conceal some information inside their own head, then this is a very likely gesture that you will see.

- **Asymmetrical smiles** - Not to be confused with the smile in relation to the contempt expression but this is a smile that has nearly all the markers of a normal genuine smile just on one side. The same meaning as a false smile and is often blended with the expression that is the truth of the matter.

These are used in a variety of situations from flat out lies to trying to be nice in a situation where all you want to do is to throw caution to the wind and scream your head off at some unfortunate person.

Asymmetry works through the rest of the body and it's natural language as well. Take Bill Clinton (I should point out that I aren't picking on anyone here just that this is a very famous lie with a lot of footage for you to source and see in action on the internet) and his pointing. The natural position of the body in this situation would be to the press and the people at home who are sat before him. Instead he is pointing one way, looking another way and his hips are facing somewhere else entirely. This gestural confliction is clearly indicative of a panicked mind over their impending lies and this is one more way that the body has been kind enough to show it. When there is one truthful point to get across then the body aligns and demonstrates it perfectly!

An exquisitely apparent concealment gesture is found in the eyes and it is that of eye blocking methods. This is one behaviour which is ingrained into our personalities in some fashion from a very young age. When our parents castigate us for our recent spate of naughtiness we avert our gaze, when we see something that we don't like we avert our gaze. Eye blocking behaviour is so reliable in this sense that there have even been studies done into children who are born blind and it has been discovered that even they will cover their eyes when they hear something they do not like. Simply put, this is a highly used stress management, non-verbal, but pours out in such ways as covering the eyes, shielding the eyes, rapid eyelid fluttering and lowering the eyelids for a prolonged period and delays in opening of the eyes. Popular English actor Hugh Grant has popularized this behaviour when he comes across so delightfully befuddled in his films.

It most often occurs when we are troubled or frustrated or indeed struggling with some kind of emotional turmoil. Research also shows that when we are nervous or troubled our blink rate increases; A phenomenon which is often seen with liars but also frequently seen with people under stress. You could not call a person a liar simply because their blink rate has gone up but it is a clear indicator of stress and when seen as anomaly during a baseline analysis of someone's behaviour it can point in that direction. I give you Joe Navarro's blink rate figures from Bill Clinton's speech and from Richard Nixon during the infamous Watergate scandal.

• When struggling with the facts Richard Nixon went from about 12 per minute to 68 times per minute.

• Bill Clinton, during his deposition, showed a high blink rate at times in excess of 92 per minute.

The etymology of this behaviour is that, whenever there is something that we don't want to acknowledge or that we need to get through, then we try our best not to face it.

GRAPHOLOGICAL TRAITS

Before you snort derisively allow me to explain. You can still develop a baseline in the same way as you can a person's body language baseline; you need only to have a sample of the handwriting, beforehand, during the normal writing style

at rest. However I would like to point out a few reliable traits, which on their own, can indicate prevarication.

To demonstrate this point I designed a game to play with a couple of friends, in which I gave them a ring that I was wearing. I told them both that they were to decide who was to keep hold of the ring and who wasn't and then afterwards they were to both write on a single business card each, the words 'I have the ring'.

The method for this part is purely and simply through using almost nothing but Graphology. Graphologically speaking 'I' is the written link to the ego, and most of us by our nature do not like to be dishonest or at the very least don't enter into it wholeheartedly when we are asked to do it. As Derren Brown kindly points out, lying has some very horrible stigma attached. Funny and very, very, true. Using the word I or letter rather, presents a very useful de- personalization technique. Using I or your signature when writing, is a subconscious link to the self, so if you imagine it like this. Were you to actually, physically be the letter I on the card then you would want to be as far away from the actual lie as you can, because as we have just mentioned, the everyday person displays a certain amount of discomfort when lying. So subconsciously we distance ourselves from lies and deception when verbally lying and, when writing them down. The first aspect that will clue you in to the liar then is the 'I' will be further away from the 'have the ring' part of what is written down than the person who is telling the truth. The second major clue is how neat the writing is. I don't mean whether it looks like Victorian cursive or perfect print. I mean whether it is in a straight line or it waves somewhat, in particular if it waves upwards, as you don't provide any lines on which to write on your business card. The person with some discomfort in their minds will usually reflect this in waves in their handwriting. Graphologists have studies to prove that when the handwriting wanders into the upper zone, it is a link to a thought process. The mind, so to speak. This is usually only apparent in the liars as there are a lot of thoughts wandering around in their heads. (I won't bother with the jargon like form level score and trizonal dynamics, as I am just giving you what you need for the ability to spot the lies in the handwriting).

What follows is some examples that I have collected from real people when performing this almost routinely, at the end of this part I will explain my thoughts, then leave you to guess whether or not they are liars or truth tellers.

Now I don't consider myself an expert but these are things that I have noticed that actually work and I have tested. I also found scientific studies that support this as well. They are all written proven techniques from other sources that are adapted to this game/routine. I should point out that clues to deception are not singular, as in no one thing from a person's body language or handwriting, or any other source will tell you who the liar is. Clusters of traits are the best of deception clues that will give you a greater chance of spotting liars. Now in case you are unaware at this point spotting liars is not a foolproof method.

- Could have been written on a line if there was one there.

- Attempts to be individual with the 'a' in the word have: not being written how we are usually taught.

- I is relatively close to the have

- I is further away than the I in the previous photo, with smaller cross bars too.
- Gentle increase to the line of the handwriting
- The E in 'the, has been written over twice, which demonstrates a degree of uncertainty.

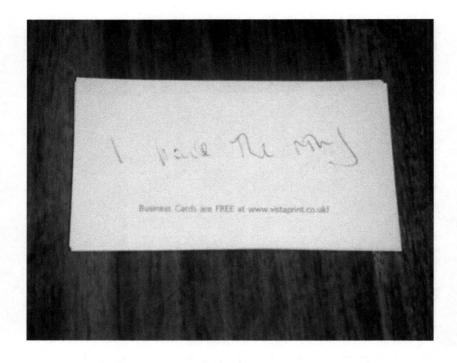

- This was from a right-hander, as such it demonstrates a pessimistic tendency
- The I is quite a distance away from the have.
- Gentle increase to the line of the handwriting.

88

114

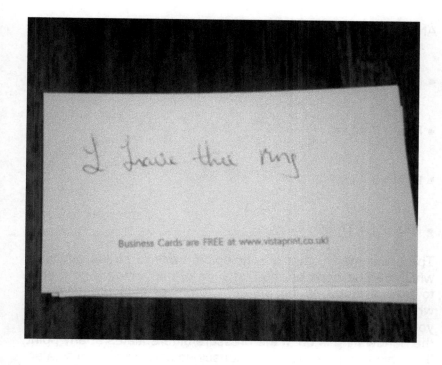

Business Cards are FREE at www.vistaprint.co.uk!

• Quite A posh style of writing, as such it demonstrates a controlled nature, which could mean that she is a good liar, but compared to the next points I believe it to mean she's an obvious one. As she was of an elderly generation (50+ at a guess) it would mean to me that if she was lying it would be very obvious.

• I is closest in this picture.

• The sentence is very straight

ANSWERS

- Photo 1 = Truth

- Photo 2 = Liar

- Photo 3 = Liar

- Photo 4 = Truth

There are many other graphological traits to stress analysis, which can be done on the first sight of the writing. And that is to take a study of the different forms of pressure used on whatever piece is in question. You can study this in running your fingers over the other side of the sheet of paper to that the handwriting is on. If the pressure differentiates at any point then this is a sure sign of unconscious stress being alleviated through ones handwriting. As well as a varying incline to the writing and if it changes throughout the piece. These are all sure signs of an emotional stress peak.

In conclusion, the salient point that I wish you to take away from this chapter is, that in lie detection, you develop a baseline based on as many factors as you can muster. Learn the techniques specific to deception detection, and apply them. Above all practice, practice, practice! It is the only way to beat the dreaded guessing percentage mark. Become concerted in the observation of whatever differentiates from the baseline of the behaviour that you observed in your subject.

Occupational Observations

"By a man's finger-nails, by his coat-sleeve, by his boots, by his trouser-knees, by the callosities of his forefinger and thumb, by his expression, by his shirt-cuff — By each of these things a man's calling is plainly revealed. That all united should fail to enlighten the competent inquirer in any case is almost inconceivable."

Sherlock Holmes - A Study In Scarlet - 1887

In the modern world of today, in which the Deductionist roams, it seems to be a bit of a Holy Grail almost, to be able to accurately deduce what someone does for a living. The quest for the Holy Grail was a long and arduous trek that (depending upon which belief you ascribe to) has not yet finished. The semantics of the quest are simple; you go out with your map and tools and retrieve the Holy Grail. The same can be said with regard to deducing someone's job role. The semantics of the task are decidedly simple. You merely have to be familiar with a lot of different job roles and their signs. The reality of it is a little harder, though not a lot, and it is only to file and catalogue as much information as you need to, in your respective memory palaces.

Throughout the course of other chapters in this book I have and will give you a heavy amount of information pertaining to the deduction of job roles. The chapter you see before you will consist largely of testing your knowledge already and putting your observations and reasoning skills to good use. However, toward the end of the chapter we shall examine the prospect of finding a psychopath in your workplace, how to find them, what jobs you are statistically most likely to find them in and what to do when you find them.

Now with the tests that follow, what it will be is a picture of a person or persons unknown to you. There will be the observations possible to make, listed underneath and from this you will deduce their job role. If you are a complete newbie to deduction and reading this monolithic bible is your first excursion in to this wonderfully accurate field of work then you should be happy with a near guess. As an added test, do yourself the courtesy of covering the observations I have made for you underneath with your hand or a slip of paper. Then test yourself on these as well. So get a pen and some paper and set your phasers to observe. Here we go.

TEST 1

- Job where no uniform is required

- Based in a house

118

- Though it is based in a house there is still filing and therefore paperwork to consider

- Clothing suggests it isn't based inside though. Shown in the warm jacket.

- The phone can be taken two ways. Either a lot of different people need to be reached at any one time or the job is relaxed enough that casually using one's phone is un-noticed.

- There is a landline as well, which confirms its residential basis.

TEST 2

• Lots of people and smiles, is clearly a commemoration photo

  • Stylized clothing, hair and make-up.

  • There are mirrors at a seated height and a full length one.

  • Female dominated area.

  • All of a similar age group.

  • Few empty coat hangers.

120

TEST 3

- Short smart hair

- Authoritative ventral fronting pose

- Clearly visible fingers on some kind of reflective material

- Big Built

- Clean and pressed uniform

TEST 4

- High class establishment

• Group of close friends, with whoever was in the empty chair taking the □picture.

- Long term inferred by age of the women.

- Not family.

- Not a wedding reception

THE BRICKS COMPLETE

Test 1 - Due to the relaxed nature of the clothing and the fact that it is in a residential set up whilst also requiring some formal paperwork is suggestive of someone who needs to come into someone else's home to complete their work. Multiple phones being used suggests there is only so much knowledge this person has and combined with the position taken on the sofa is clearly comfortable in the house and the people that live in the house. So this is a job she has done for a while. The paperwork must be varied due to the need to wear glasses as well.

So no uniform + house/homely environment + multiple people involved + varied and plentiful paperwork = Residential care service/Support worker.

Test 2 - Initially it is the fact that it is a female dominated area combined with the environment in terms of the mirrors and the coat hangers. All are very close and suggested by the comfort in their body language is that they spend a lot of time together. Clothes share a colour scheme and style, as well as hair sharing a similar look.

People of the same young age who spend a lot of time together + mirrors and coat hangers + clothes are maybe a costume = Students at university who are studying the performing arts in the theatre.

Test 3 - Clearly people who visit the gym and, thanks to their pose, haircut and ventrally fronted body language, have the narcissism to go with it. Clearly visible is someone taking a photo, the fingers can be seen in the reflection as well as a badge. The badge is the same badge that one of the men has on. Large men with short hair + muscle bound + suits + photo taken by someone else = two men who have recently started their job as security workers for a local supermarket. The photo is a commemoration.

Test 4 - High class establishment suggests how much money is at play to be able to book such a location. As is the norm with these outings, one of the party will take the picture and then someone else will get up so the previous person can be in one. We just have one of the shots here. Close knit friends suggested by the proxemics of the situation, the length of the relationship further suggested by the age of the women. Clearly not a family due to all the different genetic features, clearly not a wedding reception as there would be name cards, favours on the table and a lot more lights.

Close friends + not a wedding + group shot commemoration + high class establishment = Works outing for a milestone. Bank or healthcare professionals.

You can now further understand that with a combination of reasoning, observation and a healthy bank of knowledge in your head you can accurately target the job roles of almost anyone when the clues are there to observe. It is an ongoing practice and nobody will ever be perfect but your accuracy can and will be razor sharp the more you do it, much like anything. Observe carefully and deduce shrewdly friends.

PSYCHOPATHS IN THE WORKPLACE

I am going to take a brief moment here to discuss the idea of deducing and recognizing psychopathic traits and elements when at work. It can, in the right circumstance, be very useful for the modern Deductionist to be able to recognize them.

These are the people who quietly work in the background or their high ranking narcissism works for them to be able to manipulate and lie and bend people to their will, all without the slightest human compunction. They are most prevalent in some jobs more than others due to the circumstances with which a psychopath needs to thrive. What follows is a combination of the work from your humble author and leading author Dr. John Clarke.

There are several markers of the workplace psychopath:

- Absolutely no guilt/conscience. No sense of culpability

- Grandiose behaviour. This can be in the form of anything from lies to stories about what they have accomplished. They are seen to be the best at everything.

- Shallow and quick emotions. Often false in their appearance. They can go from happy to sad to angry and back to sad again with some speed. This can be quite intimidating to witness.

- They are good judges of human character. If someone opens up to them, they will use it against them. This should be enough information to put you on to the possible scent of the office psychopath. Combined with the following list should be enough to make it a near certainty that you can spot the psychopath at your workplace.

  - Superficial charm

  - High sense of self worth. To the point of Megalomania.

  - Pathological liar

  - Cunning.

  - Zero empathy

  - Heightened promiscuity.

  - No long term goals

- Impulsive

- Irresponsible.

Dr. Clarke has coined an interesting life mantra that the psychopath at work could live by: *'It's not what you know, it's who you know and how you play them against each other'.* Power and control is the reward for the office-based psycho, they enjoy seeing people suffer at their hands and get a big kick out of it. The following is a list of jobs that are most commonly associated with finding psychopaths in the workplace. They allow the standards that they need to flourish which is labelled as being a + (positive) psychopath job, the ones that are labelled - (negative) psychopath jobs are the roles which conform to the literal opposite of the spectrum when allowing psychopaths chance to flourish:

+ PSYCHOPATHY	− PSYCHOPATHY
1. CEO	1. Care Aide
2. Lawyer	2. Nurse
3. Media (TV/Radio)	3. Therapist
4. Salesperson	4. Craftsperson
5. Surgeon	5. Beautician/Stylist
6. Journalist	6. Charity Worker
7. Police Officer	7. Teacher
8. Clergyperson	8. Creative Artist
9. Chef	9. Doctor
10. Civil Servant	10. Accountant

[via *The Wisdom of Psychopaths: What Saints, Spies, and Serial Killers Can Teach Us About Success*]

So, why? is a question that will come up and, in the simplest terms, it's as previously stated. The jobs on the right in the negative side require the presence of humanity, compassion caring, nurturing and all the things that a psychopath does not have and that will allow them success in their job. The same is said of the positive side, they are all the jobs that require some or all of the psychopathy traits in order to become successful. There you have it friends. What you have encountered and will encounter over the pages in this book should allow you complete mastery of the deduction of a person's job role to near perfect accuracy. As well being able to read your fellow.

Workmates already. Take heed of the nuggets of information
laid out before you,

The Hounds

"There emerges a young fellow under thirty, amiable, unambitious, absent- minded, and the possessor of a favourite dog, which I should describe roughly as being larger than a terrier and smaller than a mastiff." *The Hound Of The Baskervilles 1902*

A Study In Pets

A potently useful tool for the 21st century Deductionist as the inferences one can draw about the subject based on pets alone are vast and can be very detailed. A pet is no doubt in some way reflective of parts and at times, all of the owners personality, and in the times when it is not completely reflective of the owners personality it will give you details about the life they lead.

Deduction regarding pets in all its forms has been featured regularly throughout all Sherlock Holmes tales, films and adaptations. Everything from the hair to the observations about what the owner has, to the personality of the pets themselves. Lest we forget -

"'Is there any point to which you would wish to draw my attention?' 'To the curious incident of the dog in the nighttime. 'The dog did nothing in the nighttime. 'That was the curious incident,' remarked Sherlock Holmes.'"

Taken from Silver Blaze.

Aside from being part of a particularly awesome tale, it is suggestive of what we can take from how a person's pets can shine a light on to the details of their lives. Let me paint you quite a vivid picture and you will see how much a
Person's pet alone can tell you a great deal.

'Lestrade brings a dog into your living room at Baker Street. He tells you that he has a list of suspects as long as his arm and the dog is all they have to go on at the minute. You look him over and notice that he is a big Alsatian dog, typical guard dog, however he flinches when you go to stroke him. His fur is matted and smells like mud and only half of him is dry. He is missing a nail on his right paw. You'd look for a violent person with the a history that reflects as such, lives in the suburbs and has a garden or at least a moist wasteland with plenty of trash and junk outside, a fence or a wall around the outside and a shoddily constructed "kennel" for the dog itself. Lestrade is clearly overjoyed as this narrows his field from thousands to a mere few'

That is just the basic people reading skills applied to pets. Not to be trivial over the way someone should or should not treat a pet but if something is kept around an individual for so long then it will impress parts of the owners personality on to them, in the same way we can make deductions about a person based on the objects that they have on them or in their house. There have been many studies recently done into the personality of dogs and how they can perceive body language and emotion which gives them an emotional capability of the average 3-5 year old child but, more on that later.

PET PERSONALITY

We can begin our inferences immediately and confirm them as we go with deductive reasoning. When we know what pet they have we may already draw inferences based on this alone and what we know about it, What it would take to successfully nurture and take care of the animal. I will get into the traits of those mistreated and malnourished of animals later on in this chapter. This is a particularly good place to start.

DOG: A caring and compassionate person, that would be able to regularly walk and clean their dog as well as feed them and keep them warm. You will be able to tell by a clean coat and friendly demeanor, its own bed and place for food. This denotes the dogs belonging in the house. Dogs represent the sociable side that is within us.

CAT: A person with an incredible sense of self and who they are, much like their cats who can clean themselves and go wandering the streets at times making their own fun. The more toys you see around the house the more dependent upon the pet for affection the person is. Yes the cat gets the enjoyment of playing with them, but by default, the pet is also in the house a lot more.

RABBITS/GUINEA PIGS ETC - Typically the pets of children, these are usually owned by people that spend a lot of time at home and have no problem with long periods on the floor. This is due to the fact that these are small flexible creatures that can get themselves stuck in all manner of places so in order to care for them properly you will need to be a person of patience and understanding and capable of sustaining routine.

FISH - A lone goldfish bowl with a couple of small fish in are typically owned by children but the personality traits can be extrapolated again for the owners of aquariums and koi carp ponds. For children it is to ingrain the qualities needed to look after something successfully and show responsibility, which is part of growing up. For the elder among them they show people who aren't particularly emotionally stable. Pets are meant to be shown affection and not watched. The exception to this rule is allergies. Fish are however known as the best pet for stress relief; college students in America often keep fish for just such a reason.

SPIDERS/SNAKES ETC : Requiring specialist set up and equipment to ensure that they stay safe and warm in the houses they live in, so the number of them would give you an idea of the size of the house in which they live given that each cage needs lighting and heating and easy accessibility. They have special diets of, well nothing that you could get from the local shop. So these are the types of pets that reside with niche market personalities and tastes. They are commonly associated with unconventional proclivities such as motorbikes and rock and rollers. This is mere stereotype and nothing to form a basis on. Think niche in the terms of artistic, creative, quiet.

Now there is always the off chance that the person you are deducing owns a far more illustrious pet than the typical run of the mill variety. These are pets such as tigers, alligators, bears and the like and are only allowed to be kept as such, within certain areas of the globe. The bigger the animal the more details you will be able to tell about the person just from knowing the animal they keep. For example you learn that someone keeps a tiger at their house. These are the thoughts that should immediately pop into your head:

• Tigers are a large carnivorous animal and will require a lot of food to keep them healthy, which means correct storage

• they need room to move and exercise to be as healthy as possible.

• As they are so large they will require a lot more care and time than the average household pet.

Which creates the image of a person with a job that pays well enough to facilitate a tiger at their home, so you would be able to have some idea of where they live, made more apparent that there are only certain parts of the world you can keep tigers. If they take care of the animal themselves then this will tell you more about their job, as they will need to spend a lot of time at home with the animal. This cuts down the list of job possibilities immensely. Then the person themselves will be flashy and extravagant by nature but with a caring side, if it is them who is taking care of the animal. If they have hired a team to do it for them then you can forget the caring side as it then becomes all about status and a symbol from then on.

HOW TO TELL CAT AND DOG PEOPLE APART

I made myself aware of a variety of tests and surveys and then put the information presented, into practice. These are not results from a study in personality profiling but more my findings using these as a basis and having gone out into the world and tried and tested my thoughts thousands and thousands of times.

From a sample of just under 5000 people these results were recovered from press-petside.com to understand people's preferences on the two animals. 74% like dogs a lot and 41% favour cats. Conversely it's easier to hate cats over dogs, even if you have no particular preference over the two. Only 2% hated dogs the most, possibly due to the nature of the animal in relation to care and relationship.

There is a belief that people's choice of cats or dogs relates to the behaviour of the animal before domestication and these have a reflection in personality traits. For example, dogs have a strong sense of relationships, they are usually sociable pack animals I mean think about the phrase man's best friend, there isn't one for cats. Dogs are mostly active between dawn and dusk, whereas cats are usually solitary hunters, who groom themselves and are active mostly at night. Domestic dogs have an even greater need for social interaction. Without people surrounding them they often look sad/bored, which is when they will begin to intrude on activity to try and obtain company or play.

Cats are often not seen during the day and are somewhere doing their own thing, only seeming to appear in the evening when it is feeding time. Cats will occasionally engage in social play but rarely for long periods of time. Attention will wane and after a few minutes they wander away. With dogs it's often the reverse. If you have ever seen someone playing fetch with their dog it is often the human who will quit first.

There are many universities in America that have investigated this and many psychological studies that have been done and each has determined that there are majorly different personality traits in dog and cat people.

DOG PEOPLE:

- Higher Sociability

- Are generally more extroverted and agreeable

- Slightly more conscientious in the sense of more self discipline

- When needed to complete tasks and goals

- Often have more conventional hobbies/interests

- Sounds cliché to say but dog people are often the ones who go for the house, marriage, kids...e.t.c.

CAT PEOPLE:

Slightly more neurotic, however are slightly more open than dog people. Introverted

- If they do have an openness it is toward and for the appreciation of art, emotion, unusual ideas, and curiosity.

- Can be cold at times

- Hold unconventional beliefs and hobbies/interests

• Low dominance- timid, bashful. A few things that I would like to mention in particular that I have discovered from reading these documents and going out and testing the theories, are that if a dog owner had found a kitten or had been asked to keep a kitten they would do so whereas cat owners would not do the same for a small puppy. People who own both cats and dogs tended to reflect similar personality traits to that of purely dog owners. People who currently have no pets but grew up with cats will often adopt the cat people personality traits and the same for those that have no pets but grew up with dogs or both cats and dogs will often take on the personality traits of dog people. So as a matter of mere context then I will describe a number of people here as a miniature test almost, make sure you don't cheat and look for the answers at the end of the chapter.

• A woman running alone on a crowded footpath, listening to alternative rock on their headphones with a tattoo on her forearm of her favourite line from her favourite poem.

• A man who stands at a staggered angle to you when talking, but can look straight into your eyes and uses his hands to gesture. He is talking to you about his son's latest win at their football match and refers to his wife as 'the mrs'.

• A woman who refers to herself in conversation with her friends and the local Nail Salon as a 'WAG'. Tells her friends that she is on her way to meet her husband after he has finished training.

• A woman who teaches a fine art course at university, who continually brings her walking boots work to change into after she has completed her day.

These are the most prolific of the household pet you will come across when out on your day at work in whatever form this may be, everything from performance to detection.

I will get into the deduction of other animals later in the chapter but other areas will need to be covered first. So watch out for that a bit later.

Spotting hair by sight alone

Now there are some that would say that the only way to tell the difference in pet hair by sight, would be to take your sample under a microscope and to analyze it thoroughly. To those people I say, have you actually studied and practiced doing it by sight in normal conversation? Most likely there answer will be no because it is absolutely possible. Don't get me wrong, it does take a keen and observant eye and training, but it will come with time. It is a difficult skill to master and should be continually practiced.

As this isn't a book on forensic analysis I won't go into too much detail, more bullet point the worthier things to note. Chemical testing and micro-analysis will help you gain certainties in this area but you can't very well do that when out in the general public as it will somewhat detract from your normal interaction. As such, this section will be purposely brief and keeps in mind the idea of how to get this far on sight alone.

Most hair can be divided into three parts, the bulb, which is the root, the shaft which is the middle part and the tip which is self explanatory and where the hair thins. Then from the inside to the outside of the hair goes the Medulla, the cortex and then outermost which is the cuticle. We won't concern ourselves with vellus hair as this is extremely fine and nigh on impossible to see apart from straining under the correct lighting conditions.

Human hair has blunt ends and as such, haircuts and shaving will be very easy to spot when on clothes as they will only stick to the places where sweat and moisture builds, which could be on the clothes or the body, whereas the hair from cats and dogs come to a tip. Dog hair tends to be straighter and shorter than cat hair, which often tends to be the opposite. If the cat hair is short then is often still wavier. In my opinion this is due to the serrated cuticle structure of cat hair. An anomaly that I have noticed in making these deductions when out performing is this. You have come across what you believe to be dog hair, it is straight and uniformed and then begins to curl and wave at the end. This is a sign of old hair or a new coat that is coming in, or recent brushing. Faded colour is also a sign of a new coat that is coming in and you will have a better chance of guessing correctly dependent upon when during the year it is you are working your deductive skill. The straightness of dog hair can still have a curl to it however, with cat hair the waves will go the whole way down and be more obvious than that of the dog hair. Human hair often has the same texture and feel to it throughout the hair itself, whereas animal hair can often have a double texture to it.

The length would then denote the species, once you have narrowed it down to whether or not they own a pet with hair or not. So this then presents options for you, if you want to ascertain whether or not the person owns a pet with hair or not then you can use the deductive methods laid out at the beginning of the chapter and toward the end of the chapter. This way, any hair you see after this moment will denote the breed of the species. However if the person doesn't own any pets, least of all animals with fur/hair then you are left to make your deductions by sight alone.

The following list is an example of the most popular household animals with fur. The first in the list is statistically most likely to be the longest hair down to the end of the list which is most likely to be the shortest.

- DOG • CAT • GUINEA PIG • GERBIL/MOUSE

In some breed of guinea pigs the length of the fur can get up to around the same length as cats but you can differentiate based on what you can deduce about the person (cat like personality/family). Also, guinea pig hair is marginally coarser. All it will take is practice! It will seem difficult at first but it is completely achievable as I do it on an almost daily basis.

We can assume then that at this point the hair recognition technique is a work in progress with your success growing with every moment you can continue to practice. The next step is being able to ascertain the breed of the animal that you see based on the hair that you discover. Again, this sounds like a ridiculous skill to be able to try and learn but I can assure you again that it is completely achievable. It just can, and will, take time. The method is fairly simple but to employ with any degree of accuracy will take time to be able to do.

The method is to simply store as many breeds in your palace as you can, as well as their most common colours. Be aware of the placement i.e. where it is, as this will also give you an extra hint as to the breed of dog. Certain dogs and cats grow to certain heights. Volume of hair, and the colour of it. For example, the colour of the hairs you see are black with a brown tip and are just above the knee height on one leg, combine this with the reasoning that you have come to, that they are a dog person. This would suggest a Rottweiler; longer hairs of this style and the reversed colour scheme would suggest Alsatians. White hair around the knee/shin area for dog people would suggest Westies and for cat people possibly a Blue Somali.

As a lot of the time you may want to 'perform' this kind of stuff as it were, at a party/function, the guests there will have gone through some personal hygiene routine before leaving which means they should have cleaned themselves of a lot of these signs but if they don't and you still see them then that also tells you things. For example they may have had to leave in a hurry, which if they are both drinking at the party you can blame on a late taxi/lift. If the hair you spot is collected around the wrist area then, and this may seem like a long shot, ask if they have recently had a new pet. This often happens, the most in new couples between the ages of 20-30 but what may have been the last thing they do is to say goodbye to their new addition, much in the same way they would if it were a child. I don't see this a lot which is why I mention it as a long shot but it hits more often than it misses.

I won't be going into what types of people are more likely to have what breed of animal and the colours of the hair as well for you to store as that would take a whole other book. However what will follow is an invaluable place to begin your palace storage.

TOP 10 MOST POPULAR SMALL DOGS (Also most likely to be in a house with children)

- Maltese

- Pug

- Yorkshire terrier

- Miniature Schnauzer

- Beagle

- Brussels Griffon Terrier

- French Bulldog

- Cavalier King Charles Spaniel

- Havanese

TOP 10 MOST POPULAR MEDIUM SIZE DOGS

- Poodle
- Airedale Terrier
- Basset Hound
  - Australian Shepherd dog
  - Border Collie
  - Boxer
  - Brittany
  - English Bulldog
  - Golden Retriever
  - Labrador retriever

TOP 10 MOST POPULAR BIG DOGS

- Bernese Mountain Dog
- Collie
- Mastiff
- German Shepherd
- Newfoundland
- Australian Shepherd
- Great Dane

- Rottweiler

- St Bernard

  - Irish wolfhound ☐

TOP 10 MOST POPULAR CAT BREEDS☐

This takes into account the personalities that they most often cling to and the fact that they would be easy household cats to successfully manage, as such we are excluding Bengal cats and Siamese cats.

- Known as the people pleasing cats. The Persian breed.

- The Maine coon breed. Known as the gentle giant.

- The Persian's cousin, The Exotic Shorthair.

- Lively, active and inquisitive, The Abyssinian.

- The truer craver of affection, The Ragdoll.

- The versatile personality of The Birman is a favourite of their owners.

  - Not too active or placid is The American Shorthair.

  - The loyalty of The Oriental Shorthair is famous

  - The even intelligent and friendly Sphinx is very popular

- Now, not to put too fine a point on it, but the eternally popular mixed breed or affectionately entitled household cat, is often chosen for its individual personality or looks and appeal. There are of course crossovers for every domain. Take, for example, the common household dog the Pug, or the

Chihuahua. It's statistical commonality is that it would reside in a family household however they are also quite popular among the W.A.G type of personality and for those that are unfamiliar with the term this is the cliché footballers wife/trophy wife type. A pretty status symbol as opposed to a pet that shares companionship with the other. So what you now need to do is to familiarize yourselves with these breeds, intimately and then store them away in your palace for use every time you come across such an applicable subject. The more you use this knowledge the easier it will become. It only serves to be able to continue on by yourself and add to your pet database more and more!

A guide to the detection of other household pets

Here I offer the formula for being able to deduce what other pets if any are in the house in which they reside. Use the differentiating between cat and dog people, as a basis for your initial thoughts and then your deductions will allow you to take it further, particularly relying, then on the ambiguous questions that you ask. So what follows is how I deduce pets and their names completely cold when out performing my close up act. Showing how I practice and hone my skill as a Deductionist when out working in the world of mentalism.

Upon ingratiating yourself to a group of people you have a choice as to how you want to begin. Do you want to deduce who has pets in their house or do you simply wish to ask? Either method gets you to the same outcome. To sort out who would have pets and who wouldn't, you are merely to employ a few commonalities of sociology. That is, a few normal sounding introductory questions for brand new people such as where are you from? What do you do? You can then know a little information about their home life already, which can give you a clue as to what pets they may or may not own. Basic people reading skills will tell you what kind of personality they have as well. You have only to sit back and observe what it is that you see.

Dependent upon the size of the group of people you are working for, depends on the number of people you read. Groups of 4 or less would be 1 person at a time and any more than that would be 2 people at a time. So you begin with an opening question, or an opening deductive thought regarding what I have affectionately entitled a base pet. This will be whether or not they are cat people, dog people or cat/dog people.

Either way, how you begin will tell you what they will or will not have in their house. Now I will say this though, that dependent upon the situation in which you are reading these people, it will determine whether or not the tells that you are reading will be easy to spot or difficult. As I have previously stated, during times of performance as the entertainer of the reader of minds persuasion, your audience will have gone through their own personal hygiene regime before leaving the house which in turn will wash a lot of the clues away and your reading people attributes will have to take the forefront. However should you be out and about at the shops or even working a case then these clues will be there for you to see.

So what will follow is a breakdown of the method a piece at a time so you can gauge a full example of what is needed to do this. It is also an incredibly fun way to practice and become better at this kind of critical thinking approach in the real world, especially for family and friends. Let us say you come across this person (the one in the photo on the next page) when you are out performing at a club

What do you know already? Even just from the picture -

• Clearly a sociable person with close friends, embodies confidence and comfort in front of a crowd.

• Has 1 very close friend for sure judging by how close their faces are in the picture and the expressions that are shown. A reasonable inference then is that there are several other friends close by as it is an extreme rarity to see only two women out on their own in a club.

So what pet does that point to already? You could test yourself and go back to the differences between cat and dog people part or you could carry on, as the answer will follow. I hope you choose the former as opposed to the latter.

This points to a Dog person

So what I did here was to ask how long she has had her lovely dog?' Now if she corrects here, and says dogs, then you still have a hit, or you could merely say 'I see that but I meant the smallest'. Either way you still have a successful hit. Now as you continue on you are wise to ascertain details of her family life at home. In this case I was presented with a new wedding ring, which was recognized as such because of its cleanliness and upkeep. There was also a picture attached to the key rings hanging from her handbag of her family at her wedding. This was also a new photo and in it, it depicted the woman above, her new husband and their daughter.

So I went over the small dogs section of my palace and, as this wasn't a person so fashion obsessed as a celebrity and who didn't take herself too seriously due to the nature of the photo and her personality in person, this would therefore cut out the status symbol animals, pugs, bulldogs, beagles and Chihuahua's etc. and go for a playful and friendly animal; Something that reflected her personality; Something like a Jack Russell or a Terrier. Which sounds like a direct assessment of what she keeps in her house but this covers all affiliated breeds as well as cross breeds too. As it happened she had a Jack Russell and Border terrier cross, which is an exact deduction of the pets in her house. You have the opportunity of carrying on here, which would open with a question.

' Any other pets? ' You had already covered the chance for

multiple dogs earlier by giving your subject the opportunity to mention this possibility. This will drive them into thinking of the other animals in their house. If they say no then you have thus performed a miracle of deductive prowess. However if they say yes, then you are to compare what else you know about them at this point and what they show in their expressions. For example:

• A man says yes and flashes a contempt grin. He is heavily tattooed with a baldhead and a huge beard. The grin tells you something about his personality and the animal he has in mind. He is confident that you will never get it, meaning it is a rare and uncommon household pet.

• An artist woman, who you have established owns a dog. However she is very comfortable in a group and enjoys making herself the centre of her own social group. Most likely option then at this point is that she has a cat or was raised in a house with cats. If it is the latter then, the most statistically popular next choice is fish due to their calming effect. Context will drive home the answer to the final part but after having completed the first round including species, breed and name to continue on and repeat the same effect would be a poor choice so cement your skill at this by naming the species that they have left. So what follows are a few lists of popular pet names for you to store in your palace to be used when you need them, I will illuminate the fact that cartoon names (as we call them) such as Mr. Fuzzywhiskers or Sir Humps-a-leg are few and far between, though they do exist. These are the names for pets whose owners verge on the obsessive and are often quite cartoonish in their personalities as well. Think along the lines of Mary's roommate from the Film 'There's Something About Mary'.

https://www.dropbox.com/sh/gr54lf9qc3t4g8o/AADwaCEDYR0CK _2qnFAPVi02a?dl=0

The above is a link to a folder containing the most popular pet names for cats and dogs that have been alphabetized for the years 2014-2015.

That is just Cats and Dogs so at the risk of explaining and detailing just name upon name, there is a guided formula for other pet names for example Birds. Dependent upon the breed, they get named in relation to their colour or their personality and even metaphors of such as well. For example Sunshine is a popular cockatiel name, or Merlin, which is a popular name for a Parrot. Fish tend to be the household pets that have the more common of household names. For the Deductionist the names won't precisely be a point of concern but for the mentalists using deduction this will be a fun topic and something that will take a different approach with each and every time you do it.

So what you will follow here will be an example script to give you a better and clearer idea of how this works in performance, so to speak. This was a woman, in a local supermarket.

Deductionist: *So how long have you had your cats then?* **(Starting with the base animal here, a pass or fail statement. There are more ambiguous ways to begin with but the confidence will come with practice)**

Subject: *We've had them...how did you know? But, well a couple of years now.*

Deductionist: *You have 1 of each sex though yeah?* **(The 'Cats' remark wasn't questioned and the most likely choice here is that there is 1 of each sex in the house. This adds to the possibility of breeding also)**

Subject: *That's right yeah.*

Deductionist: *Any other animals? And which one is the Blue Somali, the boy or the girl?* **(Noticing grey cat hair gives the most popular pet choice. The way it is phrased makes it sound so direct though but finishes with a question)**

Subject: *To be honest I don't actually know.* **(It is rare that a pet owner will not know the breed of their pets. So the next most likely inference is they belong to the roommate/boyfriend as she used the term 'we' when referring to how long they have had them)**

Deductionist: *Did you have a dog in your house when you were a child?* **(She is fine with cats in her house but doesn't know much about them. This points to the person having had a dog in her life and if she doesn't have at this moment in time then the next most likely inference is that it was from childhood)**

Subject: *Who are you?! Yes I did!*

Deductionist: *About this sort of size wasn't he?* **(Use the hand to gesture to the most suitable size you believe your deductions fit. In this instance I kept it to around the medium dog build. Also the statement presumes a boy but as it isn't the main point of the question this will often slide by unnoticed. If you notice the stir of someone about to correct you, you should jump in and change your origin inference of the sex)**

Subject: *Well...*

Deductionist: *No don't say anything...* **(Seeing the squint tell)**...*most likely a collie, jack russell, terrier. Do you remember his name?* **(This will be where they correct the sex if needs be)**

Subject: *I do*

148

Deductionist: *Okay well just scream the first letter in your mind for me, over and over. It was your parents that named him right?* **(She confirms)** *and now scream the last letter in your head, just open your mouth slightly, and the first letter again. Is the dogs name Cooper or something close to that?*

Subject: *Holy shit! That's very close, his name was Copper. My dad was a policeman.*

That is essentially how it works. This script was derived from an actual moment during the filming of my web series. I hope that gives you greater detail and understanding in how to approach these methods. It is quite difficult to detail this on paper for you. The names of the pets when learnt by themselves can be indicative of personality traits with which to deduce from as well.

There was survey carried out in the U.S regarding the relationship between pet ownership and job title/salary. The survey was carried out by Harris Interactive and questioned over 2,400 people. These were the findings:

• Employees in top level positions were primarily dog owners

• Snake and other Reptile owners are among the highest paid workers. Often encroaching on the 6 figure boundary.

• Bird owners are most likely to be satisfied with their jobs.

• Entertainers, IT professionals, those in the military, nurses, and professors are more often than not dog owners.

• Doctors, Lab Techs, machine operators, personal caretakers and realtors are more often than not Cat owners.

• People working in the financial field, hotel and leisure industry, in farming/fishing/forestry careers, human resources

149

and transportation are more likely to own fish.

● Editors and writers, engineers, marketing and PR professionals, law enforcement officers and social workers prefer reptiles as pets

● Bird owners are found in administrative jobs, advertising, construction and sales. To conclude, this will take continual practice in order to master and make the techniques work for you. Remember to store them well in your palace and continually update as you go. Happy inferring :)

ANSWERS TO THE EARLIER TEST

● A woman running alone on a crowded footpath, listening to alternative rock on her headphones with a tattoo on her forearm of her favourite line from her favourite poem. (**CAT**)

● A man who stands at a staggered angle to you when talking but can look straight into your eyes when talking and uses his hands to gesture. He is talking to you about his son's latest win at their football match and refers to his wife as 'the mrs'. (**DOG**)

● A woman who refers to herself in conversation with her friends and the local Nail Salon as a 'WAG'. Tells her friends that she is on her way to meet her husband after he has finished training. (**DOG**)

● A woman who teaches a fine art course at university, who continually brings her walking boots work to change into after she has completed her day. (**BOTH CATS AND DOG**)

PERSONAL-ITY

"I have heard you say it is difficult for a man to have any object in daily use without leaving the impress of his individuality upon it in such a way that a trained observer might read it. Now, I have here a watch which has recently come into my possession. Would you have the kindness to let me have an opinion upon the character or habits of the late owner?"

Watson - The Sign of Four 1890

The great charlatans that are the psychic community may have not been too far wrong when they said that 'objects that have been in someone's personal possession for so long will often give off personal psychic vibrations about the owner'. This sentence is often uttered during a performance of psychometry and is in essence utter crap but the underlying principle is sound. That someone can keep something on them for so long and it will leave a mark of their character on it in someway. Be it an emblem of some sort or a stain or scratch, a list, anything could potentially be telltale. This relates closely to the work that a lot of forensic psychologists and criminal profilers do when faced with the task of getting to know a suspect without actually having the person there to talk to.

Wandering through their home looking at the setup and the objects contained therein. They will have transferable qualities; take for example someone with O.C.D. They are not just obsessive at home, they take it everywhere with them. In some form or another so does everyone else too. This chapter will take a magnifying glass to the objects that people carry around with them and the deductions that are possible to make from them. As with everything, you need to be confirming your work and your thoughts as you go and look for clusters of traits that support your thoughts in order to move forward with confidence. You can (and I do) move forward on

3 or less traits but there is a higher chance of a miss in these instances unless, the single trait is huge.

Home of the money

Given that so much of today's civilization relies on the social construct of money it is inevitable that wallets and purses are something that are used incredibly frequently through day to day life. So, if you approach the wallets in terms of the contents being a metaphor for this person's life and livelihood, you will be on your way to making speedy and accurate deductions about the person to whom it belongs. So let us begin at the outset, style of wallet. This will give way to ownership. The models, as it were and there are varying different styles for obviously different purposes.

These are just a mere pittance of the sample of wallet styles that are out there on the market. The larger type of wallets, like the chequebook style wallets (seen at the bottom of the above collection) are a popular wallet of choice for the elder businessman, given that cheques are a thing of the 20th century business minded person and yet all are made of the finest leather and are hand stitched so they are quite expensive to buy and use. Due to the nature of their size they are stored in inside jacket pockets of blazers or in briefcases. As they are made from leather they will deftly point to how long the owner has had it due to its wear and tear. Corners of the wallet are the first things to begin to soften and in essence flatten down. That is a sign of constant use.

153

The more modern billfold wallets that can fit in everything from side jacket pockets on suits to a front trouser pocket are the most popular wallet of choice for almost all people of all backgrounds. The one main tell that tips a person's stature is in the style of the design on the wallet. Businessmen and people of a more grandiose position in life will have the plain black leather wallets. Whereas something like the photo below shows a style that would be found in the possession of someone younger (obvious hobby/passion no doubt) as it accurately demonstrates the younger sensibility. Due to the sad nature of our society we are taught to grow up and look professional and get a safe job etc. etc. Therefore the sleek cool black leather tries to send out this image to the world. This is only indicative of people that care enough about this world to try and maintain the image; there are of course exceptions. Artists, athletes, performers are the breed of people that are the exception to this rule. As they live in a world of colour and tone and this is reflected in their objects and personal possessions.

Women's purses are an entirely different ball game. The professionalism will be reflected in cultural attitudes toward design and fashion as opposed to the slightly more obvious men's wallets.

These two wallets accurately demonstrate what a professional woman may carry with her. Sleek and expensive, and with just a hint of colour, to show their femininity. This is a quality that isn't said out loud in the business world but is surely sought after. It is mostly a male driven society so women will do this to help them get ahead of the pack. You will notice though that they still keep their essence of dark colours.

Whereas the women who frequent the job spots of local business such as the local shop, pharmacists, beauty shops, pubs and bars can let their stylish flare go a little more as theirs are adorned with studs and brightly coloured designs, all in a wondrous array of difference.

The innards to the wallet can also tell a tale of sorts. Some wallets come with compartments for photos and if they are full or used then this shows someone who is close to their family by keeping their pictures close to them. This also affords the opportunity to get a sense for the make-up of the family. By this, I mean, the people who are in the pictures. It could just be that they are of a partner or of their children, family outings and get- togethers. These all tell a tale of the make-up of the family. The one characteristic that does stand out in this instance, is when there are photos in a man's wallet. The more photos there are, the more chance of the job the person does keeping them away from their family for longer. Often times younger women will put photos of best friends in their wallets or group shots from nights on the town. If a picture is in the wallet and it doesn't have a specific photo spot to be in, then this is indicative of something that is of extreme importance to the owner. Shown in the fact that they keep it with them at all times irrespective of the fact that there is no set space for it, they have made specific room for it in essence. Photos can give you an idea of where they are from, where they have been, where their most recent holiday was, where they most like to eat out. Photos can really speak volumes if you only observe closely what they show.

In 90% of examples the coin compartments are only found on female wallets/purses. Men will keep their change loose in their pockets. The more cards that are in the wallet the more dealings with money this person has. Multiple credit cards suggest someone who is not too good at dealing with money, possibly even in debt to some degree. This is shown by the very sight of more than one credit card. People will often take out another credit card to subsidize the debt that has been incurred on the other. More than one bank card (debit card if you are from the U.K) in the same name can be a sign of business accounts and personal accounts so this might be someone who runs their own small business. Membership cards to different societies are also found in wallets but these will obviously tell you details about the person just from looking at them. It is up to you to make yourself aware of the local terminology of societies, of everything from library cards to aquarium memberships. Something that does pop up quite a lot is the length of time that the person has been a member for. The longer the membership the more passionately this person feels about the society.

To follow on from this, a person's handbag or briefcase is a further extension of himself or herself that follows on from the make-up of the wallets/purses. Within these you will find further aspects of the person's life. In a woman's bag you will find everything from make-up to medicine and everything in between. In a man's briefcase/work bag you will find items that pertain mostly to work and anything they plan to do directly after work. Due to the fact that men, generally, don't carry around make-up, and if they need any medicine through the day they will go to the chemists for it. It is a stereotypical belief that many decades of societal engineering has made true in probably 95% of cases. So a knowledge of over the counter medicine (which will be different from country to country), the difference in cheap make-up to high end make-up, aware of sports specific clothing, hand sanitizer, local bar signs (receipts are something that often get mixed in with the junk of a bag, irrespective of the owners gender).

A more prevalent 'tell' with briefcases (and this is just due to the malleability of the bag itself) is the order to which the items within, are stored. If there is a place for everything and everything in its place, then this will point to highly organized and intelligent worker bee who leads a hectic work role and therefore needs to keep everything in its place in order to find it and make use of it with efficiency and ease. People who suffer from O.C.D can be caught here as items can be organized by colour, size, weight, texture. Any of these traits will allow you to spot the compulsion in their obsession.

Watch the watches

These are one of those items that have their parallel from the heyday of the era of Sherlock Holmes, the humble pocket watch. First and foremost with today's many, many varying different styles of watches, they can initially be considered as a status symbol of sorts. This would obviously depend on the brand that you have noticed on the watch, because there is a considerable difference from the price tag of a digital Casio watch to the price tag of a gold Rolex. This would therefore denote the amount of money that the person can access and in turn what kind of lifestyle they lead. Look for the watches that stand out on a person, if they don't go with the general aesthetic that the person is giving off. For example if you came across a skateboarder who was wearing a new Tag Heuer model this would stand out. This would mean that the watch is either a gift or an heirloom of sorts.

Watches, sometimes, come with a specific purpose in that they are water submersible to a few different depths and still work or they have several other watch faces within the actual main watch face itself. These will have other times on throughout the world. The water submersible watches are bought with scuba divers/free divers in mind hence their ability to work underwater. The watches with multiple time zones on are usually seen on the wrists of highflying businessman who do their work with people all over the world. They will therefore need to keep track of the time. In general, the rule of thumb is to think about what the ulterior functions of the watch can be used for and then apply them. This is applying the theory of reasoning backwards which, when done correctly will get you to the right answer every time.

A side note on time zones throughout the world, as when people return from their holidays they can often forget to set their watches back to the same time. So it would pay to know a little about the varying time zones throughout the globe or at

158

the very least how to successfully estimate, as nowadays most mobile phones will update themselves. So for example, it is 19:26 pm where you are (uk) and the watch you are deducing says the time is 11:26. Then the statistics say that, that watch has spent some time in America and has only recently come back. It will most likely be from Los Angeles or somewhere on the east coast as they will share time zones. For the watches that keep track of the date, these change when they pass the midnight boundary. This can help you again keep track of the travel, as some times it may have been quicker to take the time back to the correct time, by not crossing the dateline again. Which can, in turn point, you in the direction of where the watch has been, based on the time zones and what time it is where you are.

When examining watches the rule when looking at the size of the buckle is, the thicker the span of the wrist, the bigger the person is that owns it. With the buckle style watches (buckle as in the types of clasps that are found on Rolex's), once you have clipped them together you will be able to see how large the persons wrist is. This will, in turn, give an idea for the size of the person as a physical whole. The same can be said of the leather band buckle watches. You've only to look at the most weathered hole on the band and you can make the same inference about the size. Once in a while you will come across a tell on these kinds of watches that is quite unique. That is when there are 2 distinctly weathered holes at different places on the strap. This will point to either rapid weight loss or further proof of an heirloom of sorts. Rapid weight loss can be down to illness or a great change in their life.

To make oneself aware of the more expensive watch brands and makes will give you an idea of a replica versus the real cost. Brands such as Rolex, Breitling, Omega, Sekonda, Tag Heuer and many more. You see one of these on the wrist of someone then you will able to begin your deductions on a few things.

- They are economically well off

- It is a luxury/status item

- Their job must pay well ☐

The reason for the first one is fairly obvious as they cost a lot more than the average watch that does precisely the same thing. The second is that everyone has the time on another item that they all carry with them as well so it becomes about status then. Particularly in the business world, as sometimes it is often considered a poor non-verbal sign to be constantly getting your phone out to check the time, much more professional to merely turn the wrist to check the time. So then, as it is essentially a single serving item, that is that expensive, becomes about the message that you wish to send to the people around you. I am successful, I am confident (Particularly if it fits well. If it is loose fitting it creates the wrong image, much like a child wearing their parent's things). So it is therefore about the status of the wearer and the luxury of having that much disposable income to put down on a watch. Therefore whatever job they do must pay well.

There is the flip side of this, that they could be overcompensating for something or doing it to fit in but there will be other clues to this and all will not be derived from just the watch alone. For example in the BBC Sherlock Season 1 Episode 3. There was a deduction surrounding the life of the recently deceased Adam Woodbridge. It resulted in the conclusion that he worked as a night watchman for an art gallery. Now here the watch did set Sherlock on the right path but the conclusion was down to a plethora of other observations from the missing logo on his shirt that had been ripped off to the walkie talkie holster on his belt. This does however lead nicely into a solid observation surrounding digital watches. Button stiffness can be a clue to the most used button on the watch and depending upon what button it is, it

160

will tell you stories about the owner. Taking into account the watch itself you can tell a lot from its upkeep. A luxury Rolex style watch that has several scratch marks and scuffs, or general wear and tear upon it, would tell stories about the drama that is going on in their lives at that moment. Granted you will not get that just from the watch alone, but any casual treatment of an expensive item like that indicates that the owner is going through some kind of melancholy.

Style of watches will stay to certain personality types. For example, the leather band style of watches, in particular brown leather will belong to the people who enjoy refined and relaxing experiences, whereas the flashier silver watches belong to the people who enjoy the opposite side of that preference. This is made even more obvious when the gaudier gold and silver appear on the watch. The only exception to the leather band rule is when the leather is black. This is a very modern choice of watch and will most often be accompanied by a larger than normal watch face and is indicative of someone who likes to ingratiate themselves into today's urban culture.

Something that isn't very widely known is that leather can also absorb smells quite easily and retain them for quite some time. So never be afraid to smell the leather.

FAKES

There are certain steps to take in order to identify fakes but largely these will be down to your own research as there will be far too many to enumerate in one chapter. I shall divulge a fair few to get you going but the steps will be the same for all models.

• STEP 1 - **Familiarize yourself with the various collections of the watch brand you wish to purchase**. Every nice watch has at least one signature element to it that can't be replicated; if you can identify that element, you'll always be able to tell when you're buying a knockoff watch.

• STEP 2 - **As you're browsing, thoroughly inspect the watch you wish to buy**. Pay attention to the inscriptions and engravings on the face and back of the watch. The original watch will never have a smeared inscription or an unclear engraving. Typos and letter substitutions in brand names and inscriptions are also warning signs.

• STEP 3 - **Pay attention to the functions of the watch and its chronograph**. Most Rolex watches have a sweep second hand, while many fakes will have a tick style hand; however, some real Rolex watches have a tick style hand, so know your model. A replica watch that has a magnifying glass (called a Cyclops) may also have a weak level of magnification in comparison to the genuine item.

• STEP 4 - **Note the precise movement of the watch**. If you intend to buy a mechanical timepiece, you should try to take a look under the case back. Fake watches sometimes do have a mechanical movement, but it is typically of lower quality than the movement of a genuine watch.

There are maybe a few hundred different styles of Rolex, each one with its idiosyncrasies. There firstly is a myth that the Rolex has a sweeping movement and thus no ticking sound but this is not the case as most counterfeiters have gotten wise to this and even a couple of the Rolex models that are genuine now have a quartz movement.

Tell-tale watch signs:

Rolex Datejust - 5 piece links, oyster architecture, a Cyclops window on the date to allow you to view it better as the actual size of it on a real Rolex watch is quite small.

162

Rolex Submariner - No numbers on the actual watch face, they will be on the bezel mechanism on the outside and on a real submariner it will only turn anti/counter clockwise. It should take 120 clicks on a real mariner; anything more or less means a fake. Anything more or less than 25 jewels inside means a fake. The submariner still has a Cyclops window on the real model.

Rolex Daytona - Rolex crown design will be partially 3 dimensional. Smooth pinhole cut outs on the back of the watch. The numbers on the chronographs are specific to the model and the arrow hand on the face of it will be slightly raised on a real Daytona. Spherical ballpoints on the top of the Rolex crown are a dead give-away of a real Daytona and any flat ones are considered shoddy and would not be used by a genuine Rolex company.

Breitlings:

Navitimer - A very heavy watch by comparison to others and 220 grams at times. On the logo the b's anchors should be pointing upward. Smooth second hand as in no tick tock action. This Breitling model is subject to the most frequent spelling errors in fakes as well.

Bentley - On the clasp of the watch that has the logo on, if you flip it over to look at the other side then you will see the emblem through it and on the real watches you will not. Clean pin hole cut outs again. The bezel on the real models moves the inner and the outer ring whereas on the fakes it only moves the outer ring.

TAG HEUER -

Formula 1 - You'll see chrome buttons and screw down on the fakes as the real models have black ones. The back of the watch on a fake is flat whereas the real models are full and big. If you think of this in terms of a woman then the real models will have a fuller figure. The large date window, large enough to cut in to the second markers will appear on a real model and on a fake one the window will be small. Also on a real model it will have tag Heuer stamped on the side of the watch, replicas never do.

Aquaracers - Smooth movement to the winder, any tension is a sign of a fake. The window over the date will have circular edges. If it does not then it's fake, and clean the face, if there are fingerprints on the inside then, fake. Markings on the band mark a real model.

UP IN SMOKE

Now smokers come with a vast abundance of interesting paraphernalia, all of which can be found on the person. The simple fact is that it costs more to smoke proper cigarettes as opposed to roll ups. Smokers of roll ups will often incur tobacco stains on their fingertips, the longer the nails the more chance of staining and fragility within them. Staining to the fingertips will often be of a more jaundice yellow tinge and is seen on normal cigarette smokers and excessive roll up smokers. There is a dryness to the skin in the hands and excessive wrinkling (when cross referenced with the persons age) and dryness of the forehead. This is due to the fact that the smoke rises from the hand and over the face through the course of smoking. The chemicals within essentially suck out the moisture and leave its wrinkled, coarseness behind.

Tobacco traces can be differentiated. The roll up tobacco is more flakey and flowery than that of the tobacco that can come from normal cigarettes. Zippo vs normal Bic lighters will often tell a tale of status. Zippo's are seen in the hands of people attempting to give off that 'cool' vibe through the media. They gained their popularity in use by the U.S military and therefore made their way into the subculture of bikers and the professional smokers, (an affectionate term for someone who is an excessive smoker). This is believed to have helped to gain their popularity as windproof lighters, lighters that will keep their flames on

They have nowadays become insanely popular with backpackers, and hikers. Zippos can also be engraved as they are an expensive purchase and therefore can, and often are, given as gifts. So remember, context in deductive accuracy will be key!

Roll ups are a cigarette that is quicker to smoke than a normal cigarette due to the ingredients that are in cigarettes. Therefore people who use these will very often have to smoke them quickly during the day which is suggestive of the time frame they get on breaks at their job. Smokers are also habitual by the mere fact that they smoke which induces the nature of the pseudo craving which again gives further insight into their personality. The hand someone uses to control the cigarette they are smoking is 90% of the time the dominant hand. This is a subconscious response to holding the cigarette with more control.

FOB OFF

Keys can be quite an intriguing bunch once you get hold of them. You will find initially the more keys that are on the keychain the more this person has going on in their life. First of all, they style of keys that are on their ring will tell you something about the age of the doors they go into.

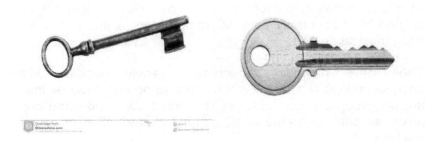

As seen above in the older key that is on the left and the newer, modern house key that is on the right. They each open a specific type of door. The key on the left will open doors on houses like older cottages, or old rustic Victorian housing, seen in castles and the like but also in smaller form of this style of key can be found on older British council and suburban working class family houses. The key on the right is the standard for all doors of the 21st century. The more house keys that are on there then inevitably the more doors this person uses. You can use this information in context with your ongoing deductions about the physical person as in; do they look the kind of person who has a huge house or an important job? The keys, which are the size of coins and have the teeth on either side, are used for opening things like windows and money boxes. Many windows means a larger house, and if it was for their place of work then the window keys would remain there. Very few people have widow monitor as their job description you see! The car key can and will appear on there. This will tell you about the car that they drive, not the exact model but the age of the car and the make. Now dependent upon how well you know your car fobs then you can have some idea as to whether person owns a brand new Vauxhall or is driving a really old ford. Then you put this into context with the other information you have derived from the keys and you will have made some deductions on the success of this person's job, whether they have endured any economic

166

trouble during their time there and this will all be down to the keys. Van keys in some instances are styled different to car keys, and some key fobs now are so technologically equipped that they only have to be inside the car to allow the car to start. All this knowledge can add to the information you get from the keys. Key rings and pictures are something that also appears on keys. The more key rings this person has then the more artistic and creative this person is as their flare is literally leaking over into their keys. If you are holding the keys you are deducing the information from then take as much time as you can to look at any photos that appear on there. If observed in passing then you will have to make sure that your eyes and memory are both razor sharp, as the photo will only be small.

In some instances you will find there is an attachment to the keys to help them to be clipped on to something or someone. This shows that these keys are needed at any moment throughout the day, and will therefore be used for work.

HOME SWEET HOME

This part of the course on the Feng Shui of things will look at the personal zone of someone's house and car. This is where we go to relax, this is where we take personal time and do the things that make us happy. The first thing that may stand out when entering someone's house is the upkeep of it. Mess can tell you whether or not someone has left the house in a hurry or if they are going through a decidedly rough time in their life and everything in between. If someone has merely only done something in a hurry they may have only 1 or two items left out of place or lying around in the house. It might be that they have left their dishes from Breakfast on the kitchen counter and not had chance to clean them, or it might be that they had left their coat on the side of the sofa because they forgot to take it with them. Minimal items that are clearly not where they are supposed to be is indicative of hurried motion. Someone who is running late for a date might not have put their toothbrush back in the holder or left the iron and ironing board out. However when you come to a home that has many things out and lying around, paperwork strewn across table tops, many dirty dishes, coats on the back of every chair with the coat pegs virtually empty this is a sign of someone who is stuck in a rut in their life and can find no way of getting out of it at the moment. Someone who maybe hates their job or is having excessive money troubles and it is getting them down. The way you decipher between these is in the items that are most prevalent. In the previously cited examples it might be that the paperwork that is strewn about the house are bills and payment requests, or that the only thing that's messy in a house full of neatness is the person's job related materials (briefcase, suit, key cards etc.). It is this that helps me slide neatly on to the next point and that is, that the items that usually stand out in the house are for a reason, be they objects that provide pleasure in some form or related to their hobby. It could be that there is an ironing pile on the floor and yet the person's tennis uniform is neatly ironed and hung up next to his racket. This would therefore stand out and show the importance of tennis to this hypothetical person. In short, mess does not have to be messy, it can be eloquent! It can show you everything from how recently someone has cleaned, to any objects that have been moved, to whether they are lazy or just plain slobs or even the creative and artistic types. The creative person doesn't tend to take the formal approach of sitting at a table to eat or wash the clothes in a machine that is at their house. These people are also toiling in dead end jobs or flowering in their own art and creativity. The details of the mess will point you in the direction of whether or not they have any dietary conditions, any problems they are going through, the list is quite honestly potentially endless. You have merely to observe them to know what the details are. Similar things can be said about any mess that is found in cars, numerous energy drinks bottles and sandwich wrappers suggests someone who spends a lot of time on the road for work and such. Receipts of familiar shops they visit, could be that they have been to the mechanics recently and you see receipts or paperwork in there telling the tale of what has happened or been attended to.

Conversely, neatness is quite indicative as well. Indicative of someone who is attentive, slightly obsessive and someone who is extremely self-critical. All of these traits can have good and bad sides in the sense that someone can be attentive, obsessive and self-critical where they create a warm, clean and friendly home where their decor is nice and matches everything. The fridge is nicely stocked, its warm in the winter and cool in the summer. The other side of this is that they can be obsessive to the point of making other people very uncomfortable in their home, items are scrubbed within an inch of their life, unconventional items are spotless such as the inside of the bread bin, the cutlery holder is sparkling. Yes it will be clean, warm in the winter and all the rest of the list however it won't create the same warm feeling environment. In the same way that viewing a set up kitchen in a store doesn't feel like an actual kitchen until it is in your house. If it gets to the point where all the ornaments are the same distance apart from each other and facing the same way, then this verges on obsessive compulsion to the point of bubbling psychopathy. Ornaments and paintings can give you subtle clues as to the likes and tastes of a person.

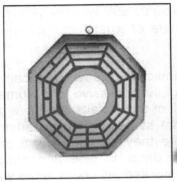

For example if there were a few of these lined up on the mantelpiece then the person's proclivities and tastes are quite obvious, and if there are this many in the house then it is a reasonable inference to draw that the person may have holidayed in the orient at least once. So keep your eyes open for themes and motifs that run through the house. Paintings can be anything from store bought works to popular artists, look for signatures and make yourself aware of the names of the popular artists at the time. This will again put you in touch with the person's bank account balance and therefore their tastes as they choose to spend their money on fine works of art. Photos are something popular so take a look at how many there are and who is in them. For example, if you see a lot of photos around the house, people are hugging and smiling, the mother appears a lot of the time but there is no sign of the father figure anywhere. Deadbeat? Unfortunate passing? In a family house full of possessions and expensive toys, gadgets and equipment there are a lot of photos but only of the father, always in a suit, always smiling and shaking the hands of different people. This indicates a father, invested in his job, who cares about the family by buying items to demonstrate affection as opposed to being there to do it himself.

House/homes are the base of operations for the owner's hobbies and how they prepare and indeed practice them. These can leak over into their car. Whether it's the yoga mat that is rolling around on the backseat, or guitar strings in the driver's side doorwell, if they are found in the car then this is suggestive of the person's busy job, so they will have to keep the things that they need for the hobby close to them and ready to go. They may have to go for the lessons or meetings straight after work. If the items are in the house then look for their placement. If they are found in the person's bedroom then this is more of a personal hobby, something that they like to keep for themselves and not share. If it is in a communal room then it is seen as the opposite. When it is a serious hobby there will be a set up involved, a small corner of the house dedicated to it. It could be the new gym lifestyle that they have and in the corner is a brand new treadmill with a water bottle and the trainers laid neatly next to it. It therefore has its position carved out in their lives, which is their own little place to leave the world and do what they love. It could be the weights bench in the corner, the running shoes and sweatbands. That is also indicative of it being a serious and important part of their life.

Items such as clothes can follow along the lines of metaphorical placements. A mix of clothes is generally seen as 'normal' with the separation of the man's clothes on one side and the women's on the other (as is the sociological standard). What will reflect someone who is particular and obsessive is when they have their work clothes, their going out tops, trousers, shirts, everything separate.

Homes are where morning routines take place; teatime routines take place and other family specific routines. What you will find is objects that betray a person's dominant hand (As in whether they are right or left handed). The fact that this is a person's dominant hand means the actions that they do around the house in their routine are habitual. When a plug is used in a two-plug socket the dominant side will be used, cutlery is suggestive when right-handed people use the knife in their right hand and the fork in the left. Left-handed people are vice versa. Right-handed people spread butter on a different side of the knife to left- handed people. When a bowl and a spoon have been used, the spoon goes back into the empty bowl on the right hand side for the righties and on the left hand side for lefties. Look at the direction a cup handle is pointing when it is set down on a table as it will be in the direction of the dominant hand. Frequently used objects will be on the more dominant side. The tells will be there, you have, simply, to observe them.

Homes are a personal sanctuary for all sides of the people that reside within them, keep your eyes peeled and deduce shrewdly.

Often times, depending on someone's job, they may have to bring their work home with them. Whether it is in the form of any swipe cards and keys to allow access to buildings, insignia of the company they work for, or some materials in use there, textbooks if they are still studying, electrical equipment or even tools from a job they have done. It can be a highly useful observation to make when attempting to ascertain someone's job title. These would be items that conform to the ideas of standing out in the room, and be there in abundance. Let us say, for example, that in your investigations you are walking through a house where there is a missing person and you need to track down his potential whereabouts. It's a semi-detached house, as you go in there are several t-shirts and polo shirts with the badge of a local gym on. (Okay but anyone can buy them if they are a member), there is also a kit bag and water bottle with the badge emblazoned on as well, there are a large set of keys hooked on to the side of the bag, and you can see a folder inside. There are also several pieces of gym equipment in the house as well. This person is a member of the gym no doubt about that but he/she is also a personal trainer who works there as well. All this is then confirmed thanks to your astute observations of the house. The idea here is that the materials that give rise to your deductive observations regarding their job could potentially be a list of almost anything, it is therefore vital to begin to catalogue all the information and pieces you see on the way through the house.

It is with all these ideas in mind that I close the chapter on the observation of objects that are in a person's possession. At all times keep in mind that you should never twist facts to suit theories only let the theories support the facts that you have in front of you. Keep in mind the importance of clusters of tells as a clean guitar stood up in the corner, with new strings that have yet to be cut at the end could be something someone uses for their hobby, it could be part of a memorial they keep in their room to a partner they had who played the guitar or it could be the start of a turning point in their life after some recent turmoil. You will only be able to deduce which it is after collecting all the relevant data.

THE FIRST, SECOND AND SOMETIMES THE THIRD STAIN

'by his coat-sleeve, by his boots, by his trouser-knees, by the callosities of his forefinger and thumb, by his expression, by his shirt-cuff — By each of these things a man's calling is plainly revealed. That all united should fail to enlighten the competent inquirer in any case is almost inconceivable.'

SHERLOCK HOLMES - A STUDY IN SCARLET 1887

Much in the same vein as shoes, phones and any jewellery, it is our clothes that go with us everywhere. That is of course until nudism becomes a little more socially acceptable. It is with these in mind that each item has the prospect of telling its own unique story of the wearer of the clothes. Everything from the

Styles of clothes that someone can wear and what they mean, to the wear and tear, crease marks and their meaning, the ability to tell the difference between high-end expensive clothing and the other end of the spectrum.

With all this information to be deduced from, you will be able to understand what social group someone is a part of, and therefore, what their likes and dislikes are, where they have come from and what they have been up to that day. All this and much more!

Let us begin with the recognition of what it means to belong to certain social groups. The more familiar you are with each group the more you will understand the person. Granted that each person will add their own little character nuances but the general ideals and tastes will remain the same and is a fine way to get to know someone immediately.

A GENTLEMAN AND A SCHOLAR

Now there are many different meanings of a gentleman that have occurred throughout time but the general term I am using to cover this group is the higher class yuppy group and though the subheading had the word gentleman in, this also applies to the ladies as well.

First and foremost then, the fascia of this look is anything that aids in the exuding of suave confidence. Very much in the way James Bond is written. Someone of this nature will wear clothes that are not necessarily of a preppy nature but are highly maintained, and are not scuffed, nicked or ill-fitting in any way. For someone of this nature, to step outside in something that has a stain on, or is last season, or ill-fitting in the shoulders would suggest money troubles and things going against the norm in their life. Outfits, largely consisting of a vast array of formal wear and a vast array of differing suits. House suits, business suits, formal afternoon dress are popular here and when out in the country there is varying degree of tweed related outfits and leather, so long as it is 100% real. Women share similar attire here, business suits and pencil skirts, evening gowns and when out in the country tweed isn't as popular. Think more browns and beige colours, leggings and high tipped leather boots. Think horse riding.

These types of people are courteous (sometimes overly so), the gentleman's handshake will be firm and practiced so it is comfortable, no sign of any foul language and will annunciate. They avoid conversational unpleasantries; they will have firm and exquisite posture. Personal possessions will always be well maintained. Common courtesy such as manners, helping out when required in other peoples establishments. It is plain and apparent when it is faked and will look unnatural and uncomfortable. This is faked most times by men in order to gain things in their life. Now then, there is an anomaly within this category here and that is the socialite group. These are the people that are the shells of what the label suggest and don't keep any of the particulars as part of who they really are: The fine diners, the well-spoken nature, the travelers, but with a healthy dose of narcissism. Characters that would frequent the Hilton residence, the hills and Made in Chelsea.

GOTHIC AND LOVING IT

This is without a doubt a complete way of life that cannot be done by halves. It is necessary for someone new to the game to not dive in completely feet first as that could have the effect of putting you off. There are many different styles of the gothic look to make you aware of. Some like the tailored velvet jackets and others like the studded collars and hair extensions. There are huge boots decorated in metal. The aesthetic look will give you an idea as to the kind of character the person has. The rule being the more abrasive and attention the outfit gets, then, the more heavily ridden with the angst, outgoing, and over compensating for their low self-esteem.

You rarely find any labels in the wardrobe of a true 'Goth' so low end high street shops or even thrift stores are raided, all for the various pinstriped trousers and bright buckled and tailored jackets. A lot of the time it is original clothing that is tampered with and cut up, sewn and had bits of lace added to it, all in the manner of style and creativity. Band t-shirts and tight clothing, even on the men are a particularly prevalent part of the clothing look. Always boots and never shoes. Now the Goth folk come with more stereotypes than most social groups but the facts about the group's way of thinking remain quite small. There members of this community that are doing it for the attention or to belong to some bigger group that they have no particular affinity for. These will be the people that are unaware of the music by the band on the top that they have on, who look uncomfortable in the makeup they have on, the excessively long coat. And, in that vein, they are quite anti-goth as the whole idea with this social group is embracing one's own uniqueness and diversity. Not all Goths are suicidal and do drugs and listen to heavy metal and dress all in black. In fact there are quite a large number that enjoy vivid and lucid colours and cabaret outfits and corsets, listen to music other than Goth rock.

The idea behind meeting someone or deducing things about someone from this social group is that they will be artistic which can come in many forms, have a strong and independent sense of their self, which is statistically most popular within the arts of music, writing, reading or drawing. The things they invest time in will be alternative and against the mainstream.

EMO-TIONAL

Now for the most part this appears to be more of a personality fad than anything worth committing any psychological principle or ideas to, I only mention this briefly and for the point of clarity. Skinny jeans, retro or oversized sunglasses, clothes with retro cartoon/TV show characters on them. Hair is a hot topic but more often than not neon highlights are visible. These items of clothes can appear in such a wide array that this is the only real description of such you will need. The likes and interests do often blur into the realm of Goth-hood. The general aesthetic and look here is a lot more versatile and the attitudes tend to reflect that of the Goth approach just with a heavy fixation on the angst, misery and attention. So you can expect any flash in the pan Emo approach to fully reflect this profile.

SKATER-Z

The look and approach to dressing for someone of this

178

proclivity is as follows. Flexible and flat soled shoes, like vans or converse, Visible brands on the clothing or apparel that relate to the sports (baker, billabong, quicksilver), flannel shirts on top of t-shirts, often no jewelry is worn but on odd occasions a sweatband will be sported. These are the members of society that do what they do because they love it, are generally unphased by most aspects of life that are not to do with skating and are a largely non-committal group. This helps to easily spot the fakers and the posers, as these are the skateboarders that are looking for attention when skating and have cheap boards, and carry their boards in places where it is possible to skate. Or at the very least, ask them if they ride regular or goofy. With this culture as in the Goth culture and Emo, and any other for that matter where the person is a faker or doesn't really want to belong for whatever reason, examine the larger qualities of what the breed of person would represent. In that there would be some definite identity issues, unmet need for attention stemming from childhood concerns and a heavy lack of direction, drive and isolation.

There are many other groups that I could go into but then this chapter would look more like a social treatise than anything else. Let me be perfectly clear when I say though that is not my intention to pigeonhole anyone's creativity or personality. I am merely making everyone aware of the mass social groups that do exist and the personality dynamic therein as these will each provide information much to be deduced about their personality. It is therefore the clothes that will clue you in to the group.

WEAR AND TEAR

The wear and tear on clothes comes in many wondrous and diverse ways. Though there are all these different ways for them to appear, the simple approach of noting on what item they appear and few simple deductions about the person they are on, will clue you in every time to its origin. Another potent principal about clothes (and one that isn't often spoken about) is the crease marks that are prevalent and what they mean.

Now then, there is no particular stand out approach or tell tale signs that allow you to predict the identity of stains as they can come from anywhere. So with stains in mind (by this I mean anything that falls on to the clothes and marks it in any way) the way to ascertain its provenance is to look at the placement of the mark itself. For example, a mustard stain on the shoulder of a polo shirt is simply that. Until you look at the fact that mustard can only get onto the shoulder in a small number of ways, which would in essence come down to either falling from a higher level or placed there by someone else. Now as this hypothetical stain is quite small and collected only around the shoulder, this rules out the possibility of it coming from a higher shelf/location. Polo shirts are a popular work shirt of choice for fast food industries so the most likely outcome of a friendly altercation with food at their place of work.

Stains by themselves are not the tell tale sign but in conjunction with the clothes and then cross referenced with the placement add up to what has happened. White liquid stains that are dripped down the back of the shoulders of most clothes, is suggestive of new parents attempting to 'burp' their child. Mud stains on the boots are a normal sign for boots, but when they appear on the cuffs of shirts and knees they tell an entirely different tale of falls and trouble. Make yourself aware of uniforms and their details, and the amount and placement of the stain that appears as well. Bleach marks always appear in a contradictory colour to the clothing and frequently are a shade of orange. Dependent upon the style of clothing you will see them on, it will point you in the direction of cleaning clothes, sweats/house clothes or unknown accidents that have happened.

This forms part of the foundation of sound analytical reasoning and using the excessive knowledge base that you have built up in the recesses of your memory palace.

"Data! Data! Data!" he cried impatiently. "I can't make bricks without clay."

Sherlock Holmes - The Adventure of the Copper Beeches 1892

The clay being the placement, amount and clothing, and the bricks being the end result. Now, wear and tear in the form of scratches, rips and other such holes follow the same approach. Pockets and misplaced buttons are always the first thing to go. Pockets get caught in desks and on tabletops, buttons fall off after excessive use and stress to the threads. The first real tell here is the ferocity with which the hole has appeared. The threads that hold the material together will either fray or come apart naturally. The fraying of the thread implies force, which will suggest accidents and mistakes, linking to stressful days or scuffles. Naturally, this implies things like weak thread and cheaply made clothes and excessive use. So let me cite a few examples here to further prove that with the right clay you too can make bricks.

Example 1: Man in a suit but no blazer. You see in his car he is looking off into the distance with suffused lacrament glands. Slight tear to the left shirt pocket and the shirt is slightly untucked on one side.

The Brick: Suggestive of a man who comes from money, vacant stares are indicative of an emotional response to stress and fear with a hint of a sadness. Add the visible tears to the clothing and the disheveled look suggests domestic scuffle. Most likely cause is a spousal affair.

Example 2: Man who has a button down collar but the buttons are different, his tie doesn't match his shirt. There is also a long streak of blank ink on the cuff of his shirt on the right hand side.

The Brick: A right-handed writer who hasn't experienced a lot of success, is old fashioned and set in his ways, and who also currently lives alone. As is shown in the cheap clothes and mismatched buttons, the dominant hand is shown in the ink smudge, which would come from pen hitting paper. This also shows the old fashioned nature of writing as nowadays most is done on the computer.

You can therefore see the way in which putting the whole setup together adds up to the solution when thought about and deduced in the proper way. I could continue to cite example after example to demonstrate this point but here I give you a tale from my deductive repertoire involving a shopping trip and coco pops!

' *It was early on a Saturday morning around 8:00am and I was in the local supermarket doing my food shop for the week. I had noticed a young woman, coming up the aisle toward me with her child in the trolley seat. I had noticed that crushed up on the knees of the child was the resemblance of coco pops (chocolate cereal for those who don't know what they are). The woman also visibly tired had missed buttonholes on her shirt and was looking for something that she couldn't find which was stressing her out more than it should. I spoke to her to try and help her to de-stress. Now then the deductions from the clothes and the marks on them had led me to the information that she had left the house in a hurry that she had only recently moved into due to becoming a single parent quite recently as well, the child had been sat in the living room most likely on a games console or watching TV whilst the mum was doing other things. I did continue on and go into much more detail with her but the aforementioned information was all obtained thanks to the clothes of both parties and the marks and looks of them as well. Coco pops on the knees of a child signified attention being elsewhere which for a child of the 21st century the most likely cause is TV or computer games, leaving the house in a hurry was shown in the misplaced button holes and the marks of cereal on the knees of the child as well. My mother would never let me leave the house with dirty marks on clothes least of all on her own clothes, this further emphasizes her lack of attention, stress and speed with which she left the house. When small items stress a person out too much it is down to a build-up and in this case just getting into the swing of being a sole carer for their child. The cumulative result of all these observations is a recent break up and the new house was merely an inference that followed on logically from these observations. All of which was confirmed to be dead on the money and all of which began with the marks on her child's knees.'*

You can now see the difficulty with which describing every possible mark and wear on clothes would present. It would be far too varied and become a series of books all by itself. Better to teach you all how to take in everything you see and reason backwards from it to find its solution and cause. Add up all the results and then go from there and you will figure it out in no time at all!

CREASED UP

Creases in clothes are a delightfully eloquent piece with which to gain insight and information. Clothes wrinkle due to heat built up in the fabric which breaks bonds that hold the polymers in place. With these broken, the fibres become less rigid and can easily shift into new positions and stay there when they have cooled. Nylon, wool and polyester are the fabrics that don't wrinkle as much as say cotton or linens. It can only take a couple of minutes for wrinkles and creases to appear which is why they can provide such a unique insight into the person. Much in the same way as the fabric tears of clothes, wrinkles/crease marks can tell the same tale based on their visible appearance. Single uniform lines on the clothes are indicative of time spent with precision to fold the clothes in the needed manner. It is therefore done with purpose and poise. The more haphazard and infrequent the lines on the clothes are, it can show carelessness or time spent in a certain seated/leaning position. Now then, much in the same way as stains and tears, crease marks will shine a more effective light on their origin once you combine them with placement, amount and on what clothes they appear. For example if you take the same collection of crease marks that are found on the lower back and buttocks region of a person will point to different things depending upon what kind of clothes they are found on. Let us say for example that they are found on someone wearing a shirt and trousers, they have endured a commute in a vehicle of sorts to get to wherever it is that they are going. If found on someone wearing overalls, then it is more likely that they have been working in some manual labour task.

Just like before then, let me give you some clay and then the bricks afterwards, but as ever, see if you can come to the bricks first.

Example 1: Crease marks collected on the forearms of a long sleeve shirt. There are a few and varied in place and length. The cuffs are also folded. Clearly a work shirt.

The Brick: Someone who has literally had to roll their sleeves up at work and for a long period of time. The time is shown in the fact that the cuffs are creased too. This could be for any numerous reasons the most likely solution is due to cleaning or a rise in temperature.

Example 2: Single straight-line crease marks on a polo shirt, 2 down the back of the shirt and one in each arm. They are crisp folds.

184

The Brick: This is a new shirt, straight out of the package. Not ironed. The crease marks follow the exact folds of how it goes into the package. People do this when caught in a blind and they need a new shirt and haven't time to iron it first.

Think in terms of the ingredients for creases, which are basically time spent in a position and warmth. One creates the other. So then, combining it with the placement of the marks you can successfully back track the observation. Like following breadcrumbs back to a source. So after you have observed the position of them, think in terms of what would the person be doing when they are in that position for so long. That gives the action/intent, then put that into context with the clothes that they have on. This will give you the exact meaning. So the more you make yourself aware of the different clothes then the greater chance you have of successfully deducing what has happened.

They also offer a chance for insight into a person's psychological makeup and routines they may have. This is in combination with the observation of someone's baseline of behaviour though. If you spy a man of age, who religiously folds his clothes in the exact same way everyday this speaks to a man who has had this indoctrinated into him for some time. This type of behaviour is reinforced in the services as well, things like cleaning and care of ones boots and a presentable clean shaven appearance. Now dependent upon the age of the person this could be someone who has been in the services for a long while, or someone who has recently been dismissed. Conversely then, continual crease marks on clothes, which are sporadic and never in the same place. Not with any clear-cut definition either. This is suggestive of a lazy single person who has self-esteem issues as seen in the fact that they have no real reason to make themselves look presentable. There is a very close neighbour to crease marks and that is imprints. Whether it is a beaded seat cover mark on their backs from the taxi ride to work or the imprint of a cufflink

185

from where they were leaning on a wall.

You can see the circle imprint that has been made on these obvious pyjama bottoms, even if the glaringly clear arrow weren't guiding your way. Due to the nature of creases being created by warmth and then cooling on pyjamas, this most likely the ring mark from a coffee/tea mug.

Crease marks can and will present job inferences, single or partner inferences, scuffles, home life, attitude. I know, because I use them on a daily basis so consider this my way of attesting their reliability when approached in the correct

Manner.

Cheap gold vs expensive tat

Being able to spot the difference between expensive clothing and the cheap clothing can be an invaluable skill when out working in the real world. It is the difference between certain job titles, money troubles, backgrounds work ethics and the list does genuinely keep going. The reason it can prove to be somewhat problematic to begin with, is because cheap clothes are designed to look like the expensive ones. As most parts of the world are in some kind of economic recession right now, one of the ways that high street shops stay in business is to market similar (sometimes remarkably similar) looking clothes to expensive designer labels.

This is aside from obviously being aware of the different labels and their locations on the price ladder. For example, you see a group of Wall Street bankers out to lunch and there is only one wearing a store bought suit. You will know then that he is the person who doesn't come from money, hasn't been in the job for as long as the others and is also keen, and very good at what he does; All this information, stemming from an ability to tell the difference in expense of the suit. Aside that is, from the label that is on the item of clothing. The rule is to look at the quality of the stitching in the clothing, the thread used and the fabric it is made from. The higher the standard and technical approach, the more expensively made (and therefore expensive to buy) the item of clothing is. Straight and/or zig zag stitching is a common stitch in machine based sewing and as a result, mass t-shirt production. Usually done in white thread or whichever colour matches the item of clothing. The monofilament thread used in invisible stitching is when the more technical abilities are needed, as it is known to be quite difficult to work with. This is where the charges begin to incur. Also the strength and thus the quality of the thread used in coloured stitching can be seen in how well it holds together from the inside of the item of clothing. The better it holds then the more care has gone into its creation.

This will start you on your way to being able to detect clothes that are bought in either end of the market. The labels can be sourced at your own discretion due to the differing volume and number of outlets in different areas of the globe. In today's modern day business world, being able to recognize the difference between a single breasted suit and a double breasted suit as a deduction can be vital in deducing a person's measurements, their economic standing, where they shop and therefore live/work.

The biggest difference between the single-breasted suit and the double- breasted suit is the way the jacket looks. A single-breasted jacket will have two halves that button together. The material in a double-breasted jacket, on the other hand, overlaps and gives the suit a wrap-around look. Another difference between the two styles of suit is the lapels. Single-breasted suit jackets often have notched lapels. Double-breasted suits typically have peak lapels although some jackets will have notch lapels instead. Peak lapels help to accentuate the shoulders.

A typical double-breasted suit jacket will also feature six buttons on the front. This number can vary based on how large or small the neck opening is or where the lapels are on the jacket. Jackets that feature lapels that are higher up on the jacket and that feature a smaller neck opening will likely have more than six buttons on the front. The single breasted suits come in 1-4 button styles and double breasted suits can be used for everyday use but are largely considered to be conservative in nature and are mostly seen at business events, work or weddings. Single-breasted suits are largely considered to be all year round acceptable clothing, whereas the double-breasted suits come in and out of fashion. Therefore, in the terms of practice (hypothetical scenario coming at you), if we saw a fashionista, someone whose life revolved around clothing to some description wearing a double-breasted suit when they weren't in style may be saying one of two things. I am experiencing economic distress or I am rebelling in some ulterior manner. The quality and expense of the clothing (which you will now be able to easily deduce) will inform you of which it is.

So what we can we take away from our ability to tell the difference between these 2 suit styles. Say, if I saw a large, stocky gentleman in a single-breasted suit. I would know that it would have had to have been tailor made for that person due to his size and the way single breasted suits fit a person. Therefore a person of money, where you see them will tip you as to its purpose and further the story of their day. Much like everything else in this chapter, context is key as to developing the accuracy of your deductions regarding clothes.

The spotting of fakes is also a useful task to take up and that will come from being as intimately familiar with the creation of the sewn in labels from each individual brand. The more familiar you are with what should be there on a real label, will help easily spot when something is missing or there when it shouldn't be on a suit that is fake.

ITS JUST A FLOPPY EAR HAT

We have spent many moments in these pages concerning ourselves with the clothes of the body but what about the clothes that go elsewhere on our person. This humble part of the chapter will concern the other pieces of clothing that one can see when out and about in the general public and this is the hat and the socks.

Hats first and foremost are a fashion accessory these days and secondly, are protection from any kind of weather. For these reasons the style has only a bearing on their tastes and preferences. If any are used for a specific job then they are emblazoned with the logo of the company, thus making the ability to infer a job role decidedly simpler. With these items you are able to decipher the size of the person, the last time they were wearing it, recent haircuts and very possibly where about they were when they had it on. Though the last one is an infrequent occurrence it can still happen.

'"Then, pray tell me what it is that you can infer from this hat?"

He picked it up and gazed at it in the peculiar introspective fashion which was characteristic of him. "It is perhaps less suggestive than it might have been," he remarked, "and yet there are a few inferences which are very distinct, and a few others which represent at least a strong balance of probability. That the man was highly intellectual is of course obvious upon the face of it, and also that he was fairly well-to-do within the last three years, although he has now fallen upon evil days. He had foresight, but has less now than formerly, pointing to a moral retrogression, which, when taken with the decline of his fortunes, seems to indicate some evil influence, probably drink, at work upon him. This may account also for the obvious fact that his wife has ceased to love him."

Sherlock Holmes explaining his deductions from a hat to Dr.Watson in The Adventure of The Blue Carbuncle 1892

The first and most obvious method for ascertaining the build and therefore height of the owner of the hat is to simply place it on your own head. The larger the head consequently means the larger the person and you can therefore narrow down to a certain degree the height and build of the owner. Though some hats, such as the Beanie and the ever-popular sock hat, are made from a more stretchy material so they can lose their elasticity over time. This can be easily recognized though thanks to feeling the lax nature of the outer rim of the hat.

This is a photo of a sock hat for those who are currently unaware of the difference between socks and beanie hats.

If it has no buoyancy or no spring about it then the hat is of age and worn and slightly stretched and if it has still maintained its elasticity then the size of the person can still be deduced with ease.

Now then, when a person begins to perspire, one of the first places to begin to grow in moisture levels other than under the arms is on the head. This is made even warmer when wearing a hat. This is how you can ascertain when the person last had the hat on and how recently it was removed. It may sound obvious to say but if the inner rim of the hat is still moist then the hat was only recently removed and given whatever the weather is of that day it could be as little as under an hour. If it has begun to smell of that familiar sweaty smell then it is somewhat longer. If the weather is cold outside and the hat is still warm and smells a little of sweat then this points to someone of an unhealthy constitution due to the fact that it is highly unlikely to break into a sweat when not doing anything strenuous on a cold day. This leads consequently on to haircuts and the simple fact that hairs will adhere to warmth and moisture. So after a recent haircut, the strands that have not been brushed away, that have then been covered with the hat can and do adhere to the inside. Particularly in the places where there is the highest amount of perspiration. The statistically most probable way to then gain the sex of the owner from here, if the style of the hat doesn't do it for you, is the length of the hair. Women's hair is more often than not a lot longer than a man's.

Now in the infrequent occurrence that you can deduce where the person was wearing the hat last, it is the smells from inside that will help you on the way. Foreign smells to a hat, so anything other than sweat we mean. Stale smoke, herbs and spices, aftershave on a woman's hat and vice versa, fresh bread, flowers, anything. This is why I say it is only an infrequent occurrence that it happens because the only real time you will get chance to smell the hat is when they aren't wearing it. This largely relies then on the information you have stored in the old factory regions of your memory palace. To demonstrate this point though here is another familiar hypothetical game.

Example 1: A baseball cap with an oil smell and a black smudge on the beck.

Where is the most likely place that this person wears the hat?

The Brick: A mechanics garage. The oil would come from being around the stuff all day most days and the smudge is from the fingers as he adjusts the hat on his head due to wearing it for great lengths of time.

Socks are for the most believed to be hidden by trousers and sometimes by shoes, but when they are glimpsed they reveal things like their tastes and therefore personality insights, home life and possibly where they shop. It is because the wearer of the socks believes them to be hidden and thus invisible that they attest to your amazing ability to gauge aspects of their life with such accuracy.

It is a short and quite simple explanation and that is socks, can have all manner of things stitched into and on to them. They come in thousands of patterns and contain even more characters and sayings from popular media. It is still firmly driven by context though. A child wearing batman socks speaks to their love of superheroes (maybe even who their favourite is) and the games they play, the toys they have at home but to see a man wearing batman socks speaks to their playful personality and tastes. They may still be young at heart, in a job and a world that is trying to force them not to be. Batman may still be their favourite superhero but they would have a favourite actor who plays the role, whereas a child would not because all they would see is batman. An elder gentleman, say in his early 60's, wearing Homer Simpson socks with a picture of the famed yellow man in a trance like state drooling on his sofa, will have been bought these as a gift by his family as a gag. This allows us to determine parts of his personality and the things that he does in the house. A young adult wearing argyle socks pulled up straight will speak to his aspirations of intelligence and a culture he enjoys living in. If jeans and trainers mask them then this may be a part of himself that he doesn't want to share with the rest of the world and if they fit with the rest of his attire then it shows that he lives in this culture already. You can see how it is the context that drives the meaning to be deduced here. Of course certain shops will only sell certain styles of clothing, so the more familiar you are with the commerce that surrounds the city you live and/or work in, the greater chance you have of knowing where it is that they shop, which can allow us to draw inferences about where they may live as well. If you see that they aren't wearing a matching pair of socks, then this points in a small number of directions. They may be colour blind, this is one of those deductions where the socks would not be reason enough to be certain so you would need to observe other mismatched colours on the person to be sure of this. They may live on their own and have left the house in a hurry that morning, eventually not having time to find that matching sock. The reason we can infer that this person may live on their own is that they are not on top of their washing load or arranged correctly, this is down to not having enough time to do everything that would need to be done in the cleaning regime. Look for signs of stress and/or sleep deprivation to support the observation. It may simply be that they are the rebellious creative type of person who believes that a pair of socks is simply 2 socks and does not necessarily mean a matching pair. In conclusion, context and reasoning backwards from the source and available observations will help drive you to a deductive answer. There is plenty of information here with which to go on, so store it well and use it wisely!

The Game Is A-foot

"Come Watson, come! The game is afoot! Not a word! Into your clothes and come!" The Adventure of the Abbey Grange

A Study in Shoes

The game is indeed a foot and in this instance what goes on to the feet. For our course into deduction we look at many things with which the owner can impress upon to them a part of their lives, character, personality. These are items which are frequently used by the owner, taken care of by the owner and kept for a considerable length of time. There are few items that travel with somebody as often as their shoes, so knowing the signs of what they can tell you without seeing the owner themselves can tell you much about them.

After all 'those boots were made for walking' figuratively speaking of course, but it is shoes that go with the owner on a night out, when they are off to complete a shift at work and when we like to go out and enjoy our hobbies. We buy our shoes because we like the way they look and fit in with our 'style'. They do indeed have stories to tell and when you have discovered what they are, they can tell you a great deal about the owner and the lives which they lead.

There is a very popular tale that is told of the man Sherlock Holmes was based upon, Dr Joseph Bell. A man who could deduce information about the clients sat in his waiting room and possible illnesses before they had even stepped into his office to tell him what ailed them. In one famous instance he could tell in what parts of the local city a man had been walking because of the mud that had attached itself to his boot; A case from reality here that proves the reliability of such a deduction. This type of deduction is reflected in the canon. One element of particular note is in 'A Scandal in Bohemia' when Sherlock manages to deduce from Watson's shoes that he had been out in the rain and that he has a careless housemaid. Watson, of course astounded by this listens to Holmes recount his brief cognitive process:

'It is simplicity itself ... My eyes tell me that on the inside of your left shoe, just where the firelight strikes it, the leather is scored by six almost parallel cuts. Obviously they have been caused by someone who has very carelessly scraped round the edges of the sole in order to remove crusted mud from it. Hence, you see, my double deduction that you had been out in vile weather, and that you had a particularly malignant boot-slitting specimen of the London slavery.'

This is a simple observation from shoes which tells us much information. So, we begin our study here with a combination of studies; that of the psychological study by an American university (you will find the full title to it in the references section) and the study done by your writers. Our findings of the most common shoes that are associated directly with specific personality types.

Firstly is the personality traits associated with shoes.

Extraversion: The more gregarious people will often have or be wearing high-topped shoes with a colourful or vivacious background.

Agreeable: The more agreeable people will shoot for practicality, non- pointy toes, affordability and no visible brand names.

Less agreeable: These are the kinds of people who have shoes that make statements and are often coupled with a narcissistic streak. They will often have pointy toes, look visibly uncomfy and will be expensive. These are seen more often in men than in women. Expensive shoes are seen in the 'nicer' people too though it will share the traits of that type and will be a luxury item. The cost can be seen as a view to the kind of salary/job they have or where their priorities lie.

Anxious/low confidence: These are often people who are meticulous in their approach to first impressions. If they are not brand new, they will be obviously cleaned and kept in good condition.

Sociable: worn in, soft sole and eye catching shoes.
Incidentally the brighter and more eye catching the shoe is,
the more indicative that is of an honest and open personality

No solid political views: Non-pointy toes, cheap, and getting toward being worn out. This would suggest a laid back attitude, relatively non-committal, the 'cool' guy as it were.

This material has been presented to you first, for the sole reason that you can observe these traits from afar, if the person with whom you are about to deduce is wearing the shoes. Allowing you to make inferences as you approach them or they approach you. So already, before you have made contact with the person in question, you have information about them. The other side of this coin is that you are presented merely with the shoes; let us say, for example, that you are the one who is working a case. You have been presented with a pair of shoes; Inspector Lestrade would like to know what kind of person he is looking for. You can now tell him about the owner's personality based solely (pun intended) on the shoes.

It is an excellent breakdown to begin your deductions with, as you can begin to delve deeper and deeper into their lives the longer you are talking to them. This gives you a personality framework to start with as certain personalities make certain choices, or go for certain jobs and can help light the way to solutions.

You can begin with the shoes and reason backwards from all that you see; this will give you the story that they tell. This chapter will therefore contain some of the most interesting, useful and frequent observations that can be made from shoes.

We do however give shoes away as presents and have to buy single serving shoes on the odd occasion. This then presents a new set of things to look out for, or to make you aware of.

Spotting a gift-ed shoe

Gifts, at whatever time they arrive, be they birthday or just because you need them, are subject to a couple of ramifications. They are as follows:

1.They are something that the recipients could not get for themselves.

2. They are sometimes, not always what the recipient wanted.

200

So let us take them one at a time then. The first point presents several mental items to put on a checklist of sorts but particularly concerning footwear. If they could not get the shoes for themselves then it may be then that they could not afford to buy them at the time. The logic here, being that if you wanted them/needed them 90% of people wouldn't wait for the special occasion just incase someone decided to buy them for the person in question. This then presents a new thought process to take care of and this is all coming from the footwear here so, if they could not afford them then there has been some kind of monetary hardship they have experienced recently. This could be anything from potential job loss, car trouble, or an extra child. I will leave you to your newfound deductive capabilities to find out which it is. So then they must have expressed an interest in them to someone, who is willing to spend the money on such a luxury item as this. That gives way to knowing information about immediate family and/or the people they care about. All inferences I grant you, but I will get in to how to chase down the information here toward the end of the chapter. The idea of not being able to purchase something presents only very few reasons, nearly all are economic.

This therefore becomes a luxury item then. Luxury items by their very nature have limited purpose and in shoes they are either that the recipient has few shoes and needs them for a purpose or they are for work. (We will revisit this in a moment)

Simply put then, want of an item, and in our case here, they are shoes, would indicate style/taste/personal preference and in following this trail of thought if the shoes stand out as the odd item out in the attire then would be cause for further observation. For example the 'Goth' who is bought a pair of Reebok classics will wear them when suffering duress from the person who bought them the shoes, or they will remain tactically unscathed buried in the owner's house somewhere. Either way, when you see them, you will be able to know by the fact that the owners legs are not in them and they still look brand new, or they will stick out like the proverbial sore thumb when taking the whole person into contextual analysis. This also works for hand me downs. Now then, it becomes slightly more difficult when the shoes don't break the bank but they are in fact gifts and something that the owner would genuinely wear. You could go about this in two ways. Ask them," Where are they from?" This question is ambiguous when examined but in the moment gives a double meaning. If they bought them, then, they will immediately tell you the store and if not, then, there will be a slight hesitation over them trying to figure out if you meant which store they are the from or something else. This will tell you then that they are in fact a gift, which would lead onto more inferences about the people closest to the person, as they would know the persons tastes well. Shoes (and nearly all things for that matter) are almost always a gift from a person who is very close to you and knows what you'll like. You are highly unlikely to receive a gift like this from a cousin due to the social distance and the implied social conventions of how much you can spend on what relative. Returning to the luxury item status, they will go through maintenance and/or at least some form of concerted upkeep. Again, what will tip this to you will be anomalies, highly whitened shoelaces on old trainers would indicate replacement and therefore care. Polished buckles on work shoes against the backdrop of ageing wrinkled leather would show pride in one's job and appearance and therefore the want to take care of them. This type of information would again spiral off into knowing the individual's mind and how they choose to live, all originating from someone's shoes.

This leads me on to what is expected wear and tear on a shoe, and what is not. The ability to separate between these two can often lead to a more detailed look at the individual's life at that particular moment. The first would be in relation to trainers/converse/loafers and all shoes of that nature, and, 95% of all cases of this specific wearing I have come across, have been on men's shoes. There is a hole that begins to form at the back of one of the shoes.

This indicates a base laziness on behalf of the owner. What is happening here is the shoelaces aren't being undone to remove the shoe, the dominant foot steps back and is used as a lever to pull the shoe off of the non-dominant foot

(Which is in itself another way to tell what handed they are). It is not as definitive on the dominant shoe because that is only being levered off with toes in socks and is therefore not as hard. You could put this down to a rush or a need for the speedy removal of their shoes, but in this instance, it is just mere laziness due to the fact that the shoes are made from coarse denim and would take more than a few times of quickly removing the shoes in order to rip them like this. This small observation alone can allow you to draw a number of inferences from it to pursue as part of your deductions, because let's face it, if you are walking around with holes in your shoes not only does it send an image of who you are at that time but the wearer would have to put up with all manner of discomfort, depending on the weather. This is because this is not really part of the expected to see wear and tear on a shoe. Here are some other things you can expect to see in wear and tearing. The more often the shoes are used, the more things like, wrinkling in the leather, fraying of and indeed the changing of shoelaces and erosion in the heel of a shoe are seen. All these are expected traits in the continual use of shoes. You would see them on the conscientious, the people who needed them, who valued them.

All is driven by the contextual analysis of your 'prey'.

JOB SPECIFIC SHOES

There are jobs that make a requirement for footwear; there are jobs that make a suggestion for footwear and then there are jobs that offer no choice, save the fact that you actually wear shoes and not wander in barefoot. This can allow us a great chance and stack the odds highly in our favour for being able to deduce the job role that somebody fulfills. The same can be said of hobbies and that will also be covered in this part of the chapter as well. Can you spot the Skaters from the freerunners? You'll be able to by the end.

When looking at the shoes and relating them to job roles it becomes about the unifying theory of this chapter, that unique ability to reason backwards. What is it that the shoes are capable of doing for the feet and then what job role would best suit that idea?

• BUILDERS/CONSTRUCTION SITE WORKERS- It is an expectation whilst on site and doing heavy manual work. The bones muscles and tendons in the feet are all subject to the potential risk of falling hazards and as they are quite fragile, this could cause the worker to be off from work for a while. So it is in their best interest to take care of them. Steel toecaps protect against most dropped objects from the hands. For protection of the sole of the feet there is usually a steel plate

204

underneath. This prevents against puncture and penetration from nails or anything sharp from underneath. A recent surge in the wearing of Rigger boots is caused by the belief is that they are easier to put on and more comfortable. They closely resemble wellington boots.

• Some companies have found that the people who choose to wear Rigger boots are much more likely to be subject to sprained ankles and twisted ligaments. As a result these companies do not allow them to be worn. Also

lace up boots are not allowed in places where there is licensed work with asbestos. There has also been a history of cement burns with the people who have worn rigger boots in the past due to the cement dropping down the side of the open boot• NURSES FOOTWEAR - With this job role there is no real pre-requisite other than comfort, as due to the very nature of the job these are the men and women who are on their feet for quite some time. Sometimes upward of 12 hours. So to make a solid deduction on the job role of a nurse you can combine it with other traits that will be mentioned in other chapters. A very popular choice in England is the 'croc'. This is because they are light, and don't cause the toes to become sore after wearing them for a great length of time. They are also very easy to clean.

• Most of the time the good men and women of the health service will carry their shoes to work, (sometimes their uniform too), to avoid any unnecessary germs leaking into the hospital. The same can be said of the shoes that Dental assistants wear.

• PLUMBERS SHOES - This is a job that is very physical in nature again, much like the builder. However there is more contorting of themselves behind sinks and toilets and into the small corners of the house wherever your pipes may be. So the shoes would need to be strong for protection, yet flexible enough to provide comfort due to the excessive moving involved. Timberland boots, Red wings, waterproof hiking boots, (hiking boots are also a popular choice in the field of technical theatre work) are the most popular choice for plumbers. As these tick the aforementioned boxes as well as providing a protective toe box and due to working with an excessive amount of fluid at times, are non-slip.

• Salesmen and women - Now then, before I go into detail I must tell you that there is no written work wear that they have to adhere to but there is a commonality at play that is representative of the kind of personality. This goes for both tele-sales, and sales pitches of all forms. It is the state of mind that it puts them in. Shoes will be black and shiny, which will mean that they are new or are cleaned regularly. The way to know if they are cleaned regularly is the ageing marks. These will be more vivid due to them actually being cleaner. This will also give you a timeframe of how long they have been in the job. The time frame is not a certainty, granted, but it is something that you can nail down with a question 'Have you always been in Sales?' Answer yes gives you the timeframe to work with, answer no would point to you to be more tentative in your inferences around this topic or just leave it altogether. The more aggressive/confident and by proxy successful salesmen and women conform to additional traits here. The shoes will come to a point at the end, and the heels will be made of the material that allows them to be heard when walking. There is a variety of materials that the heels are made of to make this noise but I will give you a particularly vivid metaphor to help you know what sound I mean. They remind me of the sound tap dancers shoes make.

• TEACHERS - In essence they share very similar traits to the shoes of nurses but they need to be suitable for a school so they will need to be smart and be able to work with a suit (unless they teach physical education, this is the red herring of the profession). Common choices are slip on loafers with a 1-inch heel or no heel at all for the men. These provide the comfort and professional look for a full day's worth of teaching. For women it's an almost identical choice however the heel does sometimes creep up two inches. You will be able to tell how they feel about their job by the way their shoes are maintained. The heel wear and tear mentioned earlier can often be a sign of someone that isn't really a big fan of their job and just can't wait to get their shoes off after the day is done. There won't be any holes but there will be excessive creasing.

HOBBY RELATED FOOTWEAR

There are many different hobbies in this world. Some make no requirement of what you wear. However there are many, and I would venture that nearly all make suggestions, to aid your success and enjoyment and therefore fulfillment within your field of choice. Listed here are the most popular choices and why.

• SKATERS - Skate shoes are designed to aid the ability of the skaters, though as previously stated you can actually wear whatever shoes you want to. They are designed to be flatter and wider than the average trainer, this is so they will grip the board better and therefore make it easier to complete the tricks. The widest of the skater shoes have extra padding in the sides and the tongue for protection of the feet whilst doing technical tricks. The thin classic skateboarder shoe is designed this way to allow you to feel the board more, when attempting very complex tricks/routines. Nowadays the more expensive brands even have reinforced side panels and lace protection for when they are completing Ollie's, and extra padding on the heel as well for even more help with the feet holding on to the board. They do have a small crossover in the field of BMX riding however there will be different wear marks. For example, of the midsole due to excessive pedalling and if you were to physically bend them in half they would also bend easier than the shoe of a skateboarder. Laces are very often not tied as tight as the skateboarders due to increased risk of getting caught in the mechanics of their chosen contraption, not that there isn't a risk in doing that on a BMX. It is just more intricately involved with the workings of the feet on a skateboard as well as being in a much closer proximity.

• FREERUNNERS - Also known as the sport of parkour, where acrobatic men and women run around at full tilt, jump off buildings and walls and consequently take a lot of pressure and force to the feet due to the very nature of the sport. So for longevity within this, the serious 'traceurs' will comply with standards regarding what they put on their feet. The study known as 'The Emergence of Forefoot Pathology in Modern Humans' has shown that the cushioning in trainers will prevent the feet from learning their natural ability to absorb shock and will shrink ankle muscles. So in order to avoid this, what you will find are shoes that have little support and a cloth upper sole. This is so the feet become naturally conditioned to the sport and will not affect performance. An unrelated tell for this sport is the combination of this with inordinately baggy trousers.

• BASKETBALL - A fast paced game of four quarters that sees the contenders constantly on the move at full speed changing direction at a moment's notice which can create a lot of exertion on the feet. Pro's and people who take the game seriously will only wear them at the game, knowing the true value of a solid pair of shoes in the game of basketball. Street ballers will typically walk to the game in their shoes or drive there. They are high topped with a thick covering of material from all angles, to protect from injury. The factors, which they will search for, are comfort and durability; this is subject to compromise though based on the position that they play. A point guard or the small forward. Is someone who requires speed so their shoes will be compromised in terms of weight and size of cut around the ankle, which will be either above or below. Where as someone who plays power forward or center will require strength and stability in their plays and will wear the type of shoe mentioned at the beginning of this segment, due to the nature of the position they play in. An interesting crossover in this style of shoe is when they are seen with small spikes at the front and/or rubber treaded heels. This is a sure sign of a cricketer's shoe.

• TENNIS PLAYERS - In the design of tennis shoes they have one major thing in mind, which is lateral support. This is due to the powerful and frequent lateral movements that the players endure. With each players shoes they take into account the style of court in which they are playing. Grass courts shoes will leave obvious traces behind, clay tends to rub off on to the toes or the outer rim of the foot due to the sliding that goes on during playing on the court and hard courts have the most wear on the toes. With this in mind you stand in very good stead of being able to deduce on which style of court the owner of the shoes play. In finding the right kind of shoe for the player there has been the creation of the three different types of foot due to the fact that nearly all tennis players fall into these categories. PRONATED, is the type of foot most commonly associated with injury and will therefore have extra

213

padding in the lining of the shoe. SUPINATED, is the type that is shown with excessive wear outside the heel of the shoe. These are the types of players that will literally burn through shoes and as such will have extra durable soles i.e. thicker. The final is known as the IDEAL foot type and has the freedom to choose from any style of shoe so long as they are comfortable and durable but they will keep in mind the style of court they are playing on. You will therefore be able to deduce the style and attitude with which they play their sport as well. Squash shoes are quite similar in the formulation of the sole due to the lateral movement involved, but squash can be played in any shoe as nearly all hobbyists, due it being merely for fitness. Add to this the fact that tennis shoes, a lot of the time, will have the word 'tennis' on the outskirts of the design somewhere.

There are far too many to enumerate here and many hobbies don't even require anything specific on the feet. I have purposely avoided shoes that you would only see in the places in which the hobby is played, as it wouldn't take much deductive analysis to be able to figure that out. For example seeing a man wearing the usually cream and comfortable shoes adorned with the spikes underneath and then see him actually stood on a golf course, does not take a great leap in thinking. Yet what has been provided is a look into many of the most popular hobbies worldwide that will take an interest in the kind of shoes that you wear on your feet. At all times reason backwards!

MEDICINAL TRAITS

There are many awful physical ailments that a lot of people are unfortunate enough to suffer from, but for what we are discussing here they will be reflected in the shoes. This is due to the overcompensation in most cases that the body has to go through in order to complete the desired movement.

There are also many cases of the use of Orthotics however, they are fairly self- explanatory and obvious of medicinal uses. Orthotics is the use of braces/splints and shoe inserts. They are there to aid the more severe of neuromuscular and skeletal damage and are literally add ons to help recovery and rehabilitation of the affected area.

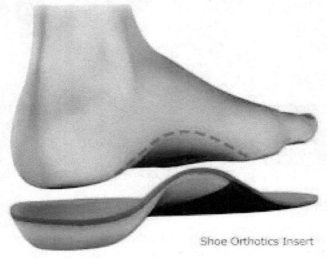

Shoe Orthotics Insert

So when the ailment is something of less severity that this, it can still be deduced by the trained observer.

Limping - When I say limping I mean actual painful limping and not the kind of limping you see the over compensating egomaniacal 'gangster' types doing. Limping, which is indicative of the pelvis having dropped on one side, most likely cause of this would be an osteoarthritic hip. This can be seen in shoes with an excessive wear on the heel of one shoe more than the other and for the detective, a consistently deeper footprint on one side. If the limp means they are tiptoeing on one side, this relates to medicinal problems with the heel and ankle of the foot and can be seen in excessive crease marks on one shoe more than the other, situated below the laces.

There are other medical conditions that can be noticed thanks to the shoes. Boston medical research centre found a correlation between a slow walking pace and the amount of

216

electrical activity in the brain. This basically means that fewer neutrinos are firing and it will function at a slower pace. This, can lead to a risk of dementia, poor performance on language' memory and decision-making. Speed walking relates to exercise and endorphin release. The heads of the National Institute on Aging's Behavioural and Systems Neuroscience Branch have stated that a walking change is an observable change in cognitive processing. A slow deterioration is the biggest indicator towards dementia and Alzheimer's sufferers. A note on this information would be that they consider a slow pace of walking to be 2ft per second and a fast pace to be 3.3 Ft. per second. A shuffling to the walk, much like the pace, this would need to be progressive but however would indicate Parkinson's onset. This is a progressive neurological disorder, which causes a deficiency of the brain chemical dopamine. Depleted Dopamine levels can leads to a loss of muscle control.

A stomping, which is consistent in the walk, may suggest a vitamin b12 deficiency. One of the functions of this vitamin is to help regulate the brain signals that give information about the position of the limb in relationship to the ground. This is called proprioception. Mentioning only quite briefly as well that any issues with walking up stairs, the most likely cause of this is bunions. There is also a tell for sciatic nerve damage in the leg specific to the illness. On the affected leg, the shoes' heel would be fresh. Like when compared to the heel of the other shoe it would look almost brand new, close to untouched. This is because it would cause agony to the owner to put the full weight down on the foot on the ground. This is also most likely to suggest the use of a cane.

Mentioning the idea of sound and relating it to shoes is something that is almost a fun game to play for the modern Deductionist. If you were only to hear someone walking up behind you, and with a little practice here is a list of the following deductions you will be capable of making.

• Judging solely from the pace of the walk you will be able to get a close to positive i.e. of the sex of whomever it is who is walking up behind you, or in the next room.

• You will be able to recognize the type of shoe and therefore get an idea about the type of person that might be in them. For example, trainers and shoes sound distinctly different. The recognizing the difference in the sounds of heels versus men's shoes is something I can only tell you will come with practice. So let's say for example (*Taken from a story from Bens life but phrased as a question*) you are performing in a hotel, that has all rooms reserved for the business function that you are working and you hear the quick pace and soft tread of a trainer shoe followed by a squeak as they turn on the marble flooring that you are standing on. Who are you likely to turn around and see?

1. The hotel manager coming to show you to your green room.

2. A man here to use the gym but cannot find the room he needs

3. A lady who, already dressed in her gym clothes, is looking for her room.

The answer is number 3, for the following reasons. You can clearly hear each footstep, which suggests someone walking fast and men are prone to a gentle jog or a run than walking fast. You can also hear the weight with which each footstep goes down suggesting a lighter person so most likely a female. The squeak suggests someone who is turning on her heel, which suggests frantically looking for something, and you know that every other person in the hotel will be staff (no trainers) or attendees of the function (i.e. dressed for business, no trainers). All deductions made from listening to the shoes and that is all.

218

• This brings me on nicely, to the point that was only touched on just, and that is that the pace and verve of each footstep that you hear can give you an idea of the mood of the approaching person. Quicker the pace the more heightened the mood.

There you have it then as an intro into the world of deducing a hell of a lot of information based on Shoes alone. Many things to practice and much to learn and store in your palace. Now it falls to the test of your new found knowledge, the questions again are 3 fold. REASON BACKWARDS.

• If you knew that the owner lived in either a flat/apartment, canal boat, house in the city. Which would you say that he lived in and why?

1. The answer is a canal boat, because of the old but frequent mud patches around the base. The owner would stand in

much higher sted for walking through patches of mud when mooring a boat on the canal side, than he would walking up an apartment high rise or a house in the city.

- Tell me the height, sex, and shoe size of the owner

- Tell me a bit about them, for example what they like/enjoy

- The average tile size for small squared tiles like the ones in the picture is between 320mm both ways and 150 mm both ways. Based on that and how many of the tiles the shoes cover, the shoe size can be approximated to between a 6-8, which puts the comparative height for someone with shoes/feet of this size at between 5ft 5inches and 5 ft. 10 inches. So for the sake of completeness in our work here I would go for the middle to garner a more successful hit and the shoe size be a 7, and the height 5 ft. 8 inches. (**When I was sent this picture for a challenge these were the exact**

thought patterns I went through. Turns out they were a size 7 but measured in at 5ft 7 inches) Chances are with the sizes involved and the fact that they are Harley Davidson boots that this is a woman (*it was a woman*). Given that the boots are of stern leather and appear well worn, it would be my deduction that they are a favoured shoe, so would go with the rest of her attire. Making her a rocker as that's the music most associated with this proclivity. She will also live in a suburban area and would walk a lot i.e. a place with streets and gardens due to the high mud covering and the well worn material. Given the fact that they are Harley Davidson boots and it is a very niche market appeal in clothes and they are quite expensive, would suggest the possibility of other bikers in her family (*She is a rocker, these are her second favourite shoes, she does live in a suburban area but walks a lot as part of her job and there are other bikers in her family*)

• Tell me the age of the owner and what hobby they do. Your only clue is, it is not a hobby/playtime activity they do at school.

• Building codes state that the minimum tread length of a household step, which is the bit your foot goes flat on to, must be 9 inches, and the minimum riser length must be at least 5 inches. Therefore the pumps become quite small, almost children sized. Due to the excessive nature of the wearing on the toes I would say this is a boy. Given the size the boy would be and the age most hobbies start in children, I said this young man would be 8,9,or 10 (*He is in fact 8)*. Now then the fact that most young boys and girls after learning to tie their own shoes only tie bows, some do double knots but not as tight as what is seen which would suggest they were tied tight by a parent. Parents natural inclination to do this would be because it would prevent them standing on their laces and falling. Putting that information into the context of a hobby, my deduction was that it would be some kind of martial art (*it was in fact martial arts he studied as a hobby*)

There you have it, you now you have the unique ability to be able to read shoes and the stories that they can possibly tell you. All you have to do is to look and remember to reason backwards.

THE SIGN OF PHONE

"I have heard you say it is difficult for a man to have any object in daily use without leaving the impress of his individual-ity upon it in such a way that a trained observer might read it."

Watson - The sign of four - 1890

MOBILE/CELL PHONE OBSERVATIONS

If we were to travel back to 1890 and tell Sherlock Holmes that in the future there will be a device that nearly everyone on the planet will carry around with them, in the pockets or briefcase. It will go to work and come home with them. It will contain some of their most personal details from banking to shopping and everything in between. You could also inform the master detective that they will dress this device in such a way that it is reflective of their personality.

I imagine, that being informed of all of this, he would be elated at the deductive possibilities. After reading this chapter, you will be too! There have been few objects that parallel objects carried around on a person in the 1890's but the mobile/cell phone is one of them. I liken it to the cigarette box that is carried around or the pocket watch, though the phones provide a plethora of deductive information.

Going into this chapter I was keenly aware that, thanks to the popularization of deductive technique through the numerous TV shows that use this approach, I had to ask myself some important questions, most of which fell along the same logical approach. Are the scratches by the phones AV socket just scratches or do they actually mean anything? How many times would someone have to repeat this action to get them? I basically set about testing every piece of research to the fullest extent, not only in this chapter but in everything throughout the book. This spans my life's work! Anyway, enough of the history of what I get up to in my free time let's get on to the good stuff.

FROM THE OUTSIDE IN

When approaching deduction with a mobile phone the best thing to do would be to approach it from literally what you can see from a distance and then to work your way in to the finer points. So from the outside what can immediately be deduced, thanks to where the person keeps their phone or how they operate it, is whether or not they are right or left handed. A standard deduction, but powerful nonetheless.

If the person keeps their phone on the left side of their body in the clothes this indicates someone who is right handed. Vice versa for the left-handed people, it will reside on the right side of the body. The reasoning behind this is that the phone comes out of the pocket in the hand that will support it, as the dominant hand operates the functions or at the very least most of the functions. There is an exception to this rule however and that is when the person has a lot of items in their pockets that they are using at any given time for important tasks at that time. The phones, themselves, rate higher on the list of importance than cigarettes and all the accompanying paraphernalia, so it is anything more than that i.e. post-it note pads, pens, wallets, business cards and their holders etc. As with all of this you will need to confirm your work through clusters of other observations but this is a good, reliable and sound observation that I confidently use on a daily basis.

Once the phone comes out of the pocket and is placed, say on a table or into a brief case, the habitual nature of doing this action takes over. For the righties, the phones tend to go down to the left and for the lefties they tend to go down to the right. This follows the same logical thought process as before. The left hand cradles the phone whilst being used by the right. So

224

when it isn't being used the right hand naturally moves off elsewhere and the left hand is free to put it down wherever the person wants it to go.

This brings us nicely onto the next visible clue....

CASING THE PHONE

The case, a person chooses to cover their phone in, is nearly always an extension of their personal choice and tastes. This is because nobody is forced to take phone covers and protection as part of the deal, so they get to choose their own. Even with the new IPhone 5C (which can still have a phone case on) that comes in a variety of colours. The customers will still choose the one that they feel the most comfortable with and therefore reflect a part of them.

The obvious fans here will not make any secret of their particular proclivities, as they will be there in plain sight for free viewing. To know what they relate too will rely only on what you successfully stored in your head to draw on.

225

Here we have an example of what we mean. This is a picture of my old phone case. Now if you Sherlockians have the right knowledge stored you will know exactly what this pertains to, or even if you simply have put in the time and the research to know who said it and where, then you will have a powerful deduction on your hands. It really only comes down to the knowledge that you have to draw upon. Others will not be as coy. The next page heralds an example of obvious personal tastes.

This is clearly a case that shows the owners affection for the greatness of the globally popular TV show '*Psych*'. So remember to store information wisely and to store it correctly away in your memory palace.

That takes us on to these types of phone cases:

These are the types of cases that are particularly emblematic of a person's day to day life. You won't see them on phone's that aren't at least somewhere close to top of the range models and you rarely see them in the hands of women but there are exceptions and I will get to this momentarily. They are emblematic of simplistic needs, in that the owner doesn't necessarily need all the other trinkets. Just the protection for the phone and their most used credit cards and that will get them through the day. The higher the quality, the obviously higher economic standing of the owner which will lead onto further questions regarding their income and job title. If you come across someone with a high quality case and other aesthetics but low quality income/job then these are luxury items and the reading then becomes about the way they project themselves to the world and their hardworking nature. Possibly a student looking to thrive after their course but currently in a low grade job. As previously stated these aren't particularly popular among women just because of the larger percentage of them keeping their day-to-day needs in their purses and handbags as they invariably need/want more. Now then, the women who do have them will suggest a hectic and busy job life that involves travelling and offices and people. This is because they may have their purses and bags and whatever else but they will leave them at whatever is their base for the day and when they go out they still require the high quality protection whilst keeping a few basic needs with them at all times. Other times the ladies who own the leather cases like this will have bought them for the designs on the back to reflect their tastes and personality and as such the card slots will not be used.

These are the other type of phone cases that are seen and are again emblematic of the owner's feelings toward their job. It's a status symbol in that sense. They are smart, stylish and expensive. These are predominantly found in the hands of majorly business minded people (bankers/salesmen and the like). If they aren't of this background then it indicates a similar standing but only more along the lines of how the people view themselves. Someone who maintains an image of himself or herself; someone who is technologically minded and well equipped to deal with the trials and tribulations of the 21st century.

The leather ones with a fold out cover will give you an idea as to how long they have had the phone case (and by default the phone itself) due to leather being what I call a very expressive material. If excessive wear has been placed into it then leather will reveal it. For example if the fold out front moves easily and almost lifeless then the phone is frequently used, if it still has some rigidity to it then it is either still new or it isn't used that much. The way to tell its age if it is leather, is in the wrinkles. If they are deep and obvious then it is of an age. Nearly all of the Samsung models of phone that have been released over the past few months now come with a built in case/cover. The same theories still apply to this model just as it does all of the other ones.

This brings us on to the next stage in this chapter and that is....

WEAR AND TEAR

This is the side of the chapter that really digs into the nitty gritty and what the media would have you believe is possible through the deduction, via the wear and tear on the phones and indeed the phone cases.

A lot of the wear and tear that you see on the phone cases is transferable in meaning and by that I mean that it reveals the same information when on a phone as it does on a phone case. So what we will begin with is something that is only unique to phone cases and in particular to IPhone cases but really any case that has the volume buttons on the side of the phone covered by the design of the case.

You will see an example of what I mean in the photo below. There is a segregated space for the volume buttons and what happens is, that these will snap.

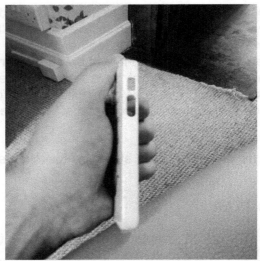

The little piece of plastic, which is on the outer edge that would be nearest to the phones screen, breaks in half with excessive use. There are a couple of reasons why this happens and this alone can be a moment of excessive deductive power when armed with other sources of the right information.

This happens a lot on the phones of teenagers and young adults. This is thanks largely to the YouTube generation in which we now live. Excessively watching and recording viral videos and vines, the volume is something that needs to be greatly controlled. As such, their fingers and fingernails are rammed in there consistently and so consequently the plastic will snap. The things that will alert you to the possible owner of this phone case and what they are like is the featured design on the case. This of course could be quite literally anything. Also be on the lookout for any visible screen damage.

Next suspect up, that is suggested by this kind of tell, is the person who uses their phone secretly in their job. They would use it secretly because it is either a job that they hate or they are the kind of person who enjoys slacking off. These two traits can work in tandem with one another as they breed off the others attributes. The reasoning and the research which went into this, provides quite an obvious answer. It is their escape at work, something they do secretly and as such the volume is something that will need to be tapered accordingly depending upon who is watching them and who isn't. Sometimes it will need to be immediately silenced, but more often than not the volume is in action whenever the phone is in use. The wear and tear in the form of scratches on the phone does absolutely come from what the phone is placed with, in the pocket. The more frequent the scratches then the less luxury the item is. This presents a new form of option here and is all about adding up the metaphors that are placed out in front of you. They can sustain scratches and marks absolutely, when they are placed into the pockets with other objects such as keys, coins and lighters for example.

However they are not sustained with any significance after only a couple of attempts. This is a misnomer. Repeated and daily groupings with these items will cause the damage. To gain an insight into how they view the phone and as a result, more about their character you need only put the price of the phone into context with how bad/visible the damage is. The more damage there is then the less luxury of an item this is to them. So if a brand new phone, which is top of the range, is covered in scratches and bumps of varying degrees then it is safe to say that this person is careless by nature and cannot look after their possessions with any great care. This leads on to inferences to back up about their day-to-day life. Hectic and taxing is at the top of leaderboard of possibilities here; this will be thanks to their jobs. Builders, plumbers and freelance labourers as well as carers of all sorts who have to deal with physical and threatening aspects of their job will often have top of the range phones so their business of choice can contact them at any given time with some reliability. The other possibility is the type of unappreciative person who doesn't know or understand the value of the world.

The tell with these types of pocket-related items is that they collect on either the top or the bottom of the phone. This is due to the nature of gravity and the items sitting in the bottom of the pocket and that the phone can go in there in one of 2 ways. The other telltale damage is caused by more obvious things such as dropping the phone, or dropping other items on to it. This causes the obvious things such as screen damage, button loss etc.

Screen dirt can often provide an interesting insight into what the person has done or been doing on the phone. This is only particularly prevalent with the phones of late in that they are nearly all screen, besides a button or two at the bottom of the phone. This provides a possibility here, for the deduction of pin/lock codes via the natural oils and greases and other substances that collect on the hand throughout the day (I will get on to the pin codes after though).

If we think of the screen in terms of a window, then what does it mean when we see straight streaks on the screen?

This is clearly a sign of cleaning but this happens because either something has been dropped on to the screen of the phone (which could be anything from rain to a beverage) or that something they have had on their hands throughout the day (which could be anything from chalk dust from working with pottery to the natural oils of the hands). The strength and colour of the streak that you see will tell you exactly which it is. Rain streaks that are rubbed will eventually decrease and disappear over time. Any other substance that appears on there will streak and move in the direction of the movement involved. They will stay on the phone for sometimes days until someone physically removes them. This is the most frequent and common streak mark that you will see. An idea worthy of note is that if the streaks curve in a line that looks like a stretched out letter c......

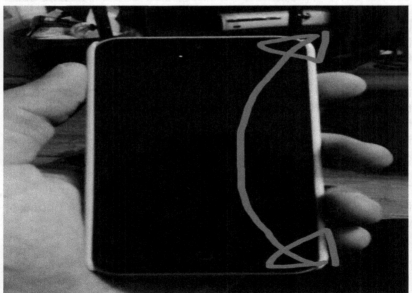

This points to action that was taken to clean it with the right thumb, or right hand. If the streaks curve the opposite way like so:

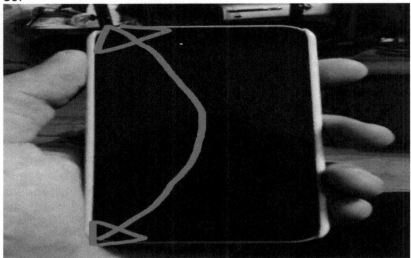

Then this points to someone who has taken measures to clean it with the left hand. As more people are right hand dominant than left hand dominant, the most likely cause here (if we follow Occam's Razor) is that the phone was wiped over with the thumb of the same hand that was holding it. Of course there could be other items that have touched the phone but there can be no accounting for every possible scenario that there ever will be. It remains for you to keep your eyes open for any telltale marks. This could be anything from mud, to hair gel to sauce from their favourite fast food outlet.

The natural oils and substances that stay on the hand throughout the day can also leave visible trails on the phone of what has been used.

You can see clearly that when holding the phone in the right light you can see what has been pressed the most frequently/recently. In this instance there is a swipe and 3 dots. Put this into context with what these dots hover over (apps) when you turn the phone on and you will know exactly what the most recent thing was that they did on their phone. This tells you a lot about the person in front of you. If the last 3 apps they touched were facebook, twitter and YouTube then this points in the direction of a younger person who likes to stay in touch with latest social media updates and viral videos. If someone has the weather, travel, currency exchange apps as the last things they touched then it is fair to say that they are planning on taking a trip overseas.

Which leads us on to a very unique aspect here, is it possible using this method to deduce someone's lock code for their phone?? Absolutely it is. Look at the photo above again. It could just as easily have been the swipe to bring up the numbers to enter the lock code for the phone. Now as you see only three dots, what logical inference can you draw from that regarding the code? That one digit in the code must have been repeated. The finger dots would be over the numbers 743. To obtain the code would be to simply try the possible combinations and you will then have it. Failing that, if you have the ability to observe the person entering the numbers into the phone then you have only to watch where their fingers move to when punching the numbers in. Combine this information with the knowledge you have gained via what you can glean from the screen and you will have obtained the persons lock code to their phone.

This is almost the same protocol for Samsung phones in the UK as well, apart from the fact that they have to drag their fingers across certain keys to form a pattern to unlock the phone. In fact the same technique can be applied to all touchscreen smart phones that have a lock code.

APP-LYING WHAT YOU CAN SEE

Much like the choice of cover for the phone or shoes that they put on their feet, the apps someone buys for their phone will tell you a lot about what they like to do with their phone and indeed their free time. First port of call would be to know and understand what comes already pre-built on to the phone with which you are making deductions from. It is much in terms of contextual applications of what you have in front of you. If you see a guy who has a sky sports app on his phone, as well as football scores and his phone case has the badge of his favourite football team emblazoned on to the side of it, then you know exactly what he does with his phone a lot of the time. He uses it to keep track of the scores and even to watch a few games. Now if someone has gone to the trouble of doing this to this degree on their phone, then a logical inference you can draw from this is that they don't get a lot of chance to watch the game at home on their television or at the bar. This could be down to their job and the restraints it places on his life, which then raises new questions for you to carry on your deductions with.

All this is information you can pull from the apps that they have on their phone. Particularly with the iPhones, there is a very simple approach to pull up the apps that are open as well, which will give you the same information that the screen marks will.

Another example would be, let's say, a top of the range Nokia phone with open apps featuring kids TV shows and there are games open as well. There are a lot of social media apps as well as a Job-Seeking app. It is most likely then, that this will be the phone of a single parent, who uses her device to help entertain her/his young one while they are trying to find a source of employment. This then becomes a luxury item in a low income family (as nowadays it seems to be the cultural norm to ply children with their own phones/tablets/ games consoles) thus negating the need to play on their parents. So it becomes something they all use.

This serves to further prove the contextual application of the apps, you can see, can be demonstrative of so much! Even though there are millions and millions of apps, the logos that are on the front and the names they are given will often tip you as to what they are about. Even with the iPhone, when apps are put into subcategories/groups of apps, these will be given a name by the owner so they know what apps are where. This also tells you exactly what they are about.

The same can be said of the choice of ringtone that someone has on their phone. It's a point of artistic choice, like most things of this nature. My personal ringtone of choice is the Psych theme song at the minute, and changes between that and BBC Sherlock's theme. Then when someone proposes the question for you to deduce the answer to 'what sort of TV shows does ben like?' you will have answers ready to go. In an age when you can quite literally have almost anything as a ringtone for your phone, it can and will accurately describe parts of the person's tastes and therefore personality to you. For example if you hear the sultry tones of Johan Sebastian Bach's Six Sonatas for the violin, then you would know that this would have to be a person of worldly knowledge. A person of age or at least deeply ingratiated in the world of classical music. If you hear ringtones which aren't music or polyphonic tones, then this tells you something about the model of phone that they would have to have in order to support the creation of such a specific tone and then further something more about the character of the person as they have gone to such great lengths to make sure they have that special piece of whatever it is that they like with them at all times.

Each specific phone model has a built in set of tones for people to make their selection from. What would be advised is to be familiar with what comes on a wide array of models as the standard tone that is switched on when the phone is simply set to loud. This will inform you of whether or not the tone has been changed for something else. Which in turn will raise the question of what kind of tone have they changed it to? What sound does it make? What emotion does this invoke? The answers to these questions will reveal information.

Something worthy of note that is often a reliable source of information when deducing 'out in the field' so to speak,(by this we mean anything that is not related to a paid performance) is that sometimes the silent function on the phone is engaged throughout the course of the day. When you find this on a phone it is indicative again of someone who has their phone on when they are at work and they want to keep it on secretively. This does lead to a variety of ends to this particular deduction, which will only depend on the owner of the phone. Statistically most likely is the person who doesn't enjoy their job and as such uses their phone as a source of escape from their shift. The other is the person who has a family and uses their phone so they can be kept in touch with all day, even though they shouldn't really have their phones on them. The silent function is engaged as a way to avoid the unnecessary embarrassment of having it go off when you don't want it to.

Apps, ringtones and sound functions will all tell you a tale; you just have to see it to read it.

THE ART OF THE SCREEN SAVER

Screen savers and lock screens are photos that can be chosen by the owner of the phone, and is another further extension of themselves and their likes. They are interesting as well because (and this applies more so to women than it does to men) they very often change with the events that have happened in their lives recently i.e. a birthday, a concert, a holiday and it is a way of being constantly reminded of the joys that they had on this specific day.

As with all, these come in a variety of formats. We have hundreds of them that I could tell you about but these are just the most popular ones and at times the most obvious. Birthdays for children in the photos are obvious ones. Just keep an eye out for signs like party hats, balloons, cakes, wrapping paper on the floor. This makes them recent, like within a few weeks due to the fact that doting mothers like to take a lot of pictures of their children and display them proudly when they get new ones. You can also put this into context with the weather, if the photo is outside. If you know that it hasn't rained for a couple of weeks and in the background of the photo there is an open window you can see it raining through or someone with soaking wet hair and clothes then you have a pretty solid idea as to the time frame for the photo.

You can start to put this into context with what you can glean from the woman in question. This isn't just particular to birthdays either. If the photo is of the child on their own then the child is more than likely an only child as mothers don't tend to pick one child over the other for pride of place pictures like on their phones home screen. If the child is of a very young age then this is quite possibly their first child. Again if it was just the new addition to the family then the other siblings are usually in the picture, and more importantly it is most likely that this is her first night away from the child so emotions will be running high and she'll be nervous and worried. If the woman in question has no obvious partner then look for signs of one rings, tattoos, the mere mention of one in off handed comments.

A single woman with children has a shift in perspective when everything they do becomes about their children. They are the focal point of their lives at that moment.

Now photos without children usually come in the form of partners or family members they are closest to due to whatever reason. If the woman has a picture of her partner on her home screen, this usually indicates that they are still in the honeymoon phase of their relationship because other aspects haven't crept in yet. Now if the woman isn't in the picture and you can tell from her countenance that she is reasonably quiet and at times even a little coy, she usually has issues with her appearance and insecurities about this. Now I'm not saying that you highlight it as this would display a clear amount of ignorance on your part. You can say something like 'there aren't a lot of pictures of yourself on your phone are there? You usually like to be the person behind the camera, which is a shame, beautiful woman like you'. This aptly demonstrates your skill without making her feel uneasy.

If she is in the picture with her partner then the reverse is usually true. With the males the same rules apply. However what is fast becoming a major commonality is that men only seem to put photos of their children on the home screen when it is a photo of a special occasion i.e. school plays, holidays, birthdays that kind of thing. If there is a picture of himself with his friends on, enjoying a night out, this speaks to a party animal personality, which could be for a variety of troubling reasons. What you can tell though is, that whatever job they do, it is usually just a paycheque and not something they particularly enjoy. Its either dead end or they are using it as a stepping-stone to something else.

In short, look for time frames, occasions, and people. Drink in every detail that you can and you will be well on your way to a plethora of information for deduction.

ARE YOU SMART? OR NOT?

In the age of the smartphone and the touch screen where you can sometimes get it to do anything it is quite an infrequent occurrence for the older models to be seen anymore. In particular, the ones with buttons, as these are often considered obsolete when considering the other phones that are on the market. Yet these do keep appearing from time to time and there are reasons for this.

The first is quite simply by far the most popular and that is from the concerned parent. For their children who are on the cusp of independence, they are slowly allowed some slack on the parental leash. The phone is a way for the parents to keep in touch with them, and make sure they are safe. So the average family will therefore reach an impasse on how to get a phone for the children but not have to pay through the nose for it. This is how they are given the cheaper phones, yes they may be a source for undue attention from some rowdy peers but they serve their purpose well. So if you ever see a phone like this in the hands of someone who is around the age of 10 then you now have a pretty solid inference with which to begin your reading of the situation.

The other is something worthy of note when making reference to being able to deduce possible job inferences. They are particularly apparent within the care system of your local neighbourhood. The reason for this is strikingly similar to the reasons that are previously mentioned. There is a sensationally small amount of government funding that makes it to the unfortunate few who have to live in residential care thanks to their learning difficulties. So as an unfortunate consequence of these disabilities they become prone to bouts of physically expressive behaviour and their phone (as well as other belongings) may get damaged. The idea behind residential care is for the person who is being looked after to be able to have as "normal" a life as possible. This means that they go out into their local community to do their shopping or buy things for their house that they need. They can't afford to keep replacing their phones so the cheaper ones are always considered first.

Secondary phones when needed as a source of extra business are often found in the cheaper end of the market as they are only needed for a small amount of things and would not warrant the purchase of something expensive. This will also allow you to determine the success of the business ventures they are involved in. Lets say for example that you see someone who has an IPhone 5s and a brand new Samsung s4 for their business. If they can successfully purchase these top of the line phones and successfully keep them running then you can successfully determine the quality of them by this small detail.

Keeping in mind the idea of buttons on a mobile phone there is a very niche market idea that we should simply make you aware of. The more frequent a button is used then the slacker it will become to push. I mention this purely for the sake of completion because it takes a practiced and gentle touch to tell the difference, particularly because it is rare find to come across a phone that is only used for one or two particular functions.

There you are then friends! Keep a weathered and practiced eye on these devices as they can feed you a gargantuan chunk of information! In this day and age there are few devices that are subject to as much personal impression as the mobile telephone.

The Grit In The Lens (A study in glasses)

'Wanted, a woman of good address, attired like a lady. She has a remarkably thick nose, with eyes which are set close upon either side of it. She has a puckered forehead, a peering expression, and probably rounded shoulders. There are indications that she has had recourse to an optician at least twice during the last few months. As her glasses are of remarkable strength and as opticians are not very numerous, there should be no difficulty in tracing her."

The Golden Pince Nez 1904

The glasses that people wear are of particular interest here as they are quite literally a vessel for how the owners of said spectacles see the world. They are designed with many purposes and ideas in mind from comfort to the removal of headaches when working. They are also an object that most glasses wearers will carry with them at all times, so in the same vein that a watch or a piece of jewelry or a person's clothes can tell a tale, so to can the glasses. A persons build and by inference, their height, their economic income, recent haircuts. Whether they are purely a fashion symbol or serve a prescriptive purpose, their upkeep. All give clues as to the person's personality. The difference in lenses will tell you how that person sees the world and consequently any problems they may encounter or ailments they may suffer as a direct cause of this. The list literally can go on and on and is why a separate chapter altogether has been given to the glasses, and they don't just turn up as part of the objects chapter. So let us begin with the first and most obvious observation you can make when using glasses for the purposes of deduction. This is to be done without the need of the owner present either.

A PERSONS BUILD FROM THE FRAMES.

The phrenological aspects here don't really apply as times have changed considerably and we are currently experiencing a growth in gym addicts and eating disorders of both kinds. What I mean to say is, to say that this person is intelligent purely because the person possesses a large head would be unwise. To ascertain the approximate size of the person's head you need only open the glasses. They are designed to fit snuggly and comfortably hug the face of the owner. So what I would suggest here is to put them on and then you can compare based on your own size. Often what will happen when you come across a pair of glasses which bends past the natural inclinations of the glasses themselves, is that they will be the only pair they own and as such have taken a bit of wear and tear due to the owners growth. There is of course an exception here and that is the kind, that are specially made, which of course speaks to a couple of things which are economic standing and specific prescriptive needs. There are specialist companies that will design glasses for the person with the bigger head such as Fatheadz but these will consequently come at a greater cost as it is with anything that needs to be made to specific requirements.

Here it begins then that the size of a person's head will correlate to their height so nothing seems disproportionate. This is just genetic normalcy working here. There is no real way of gauging disability, be it physical or otherwise from just the size of the head alone so the relationship between the size of the head and the size of the person is also inferred from placing the glasses on your own head. There will be no measurements here that I can give you as the glasses you come across will each be different and you all will be of a different size. So as you will know your own measurements better than I can infer I shall leave it up to your best judgments on this topic remembering at all times though to give a leeway of a few inches.

"For example, how did you deduce that this man was intellectual?"

Watson to Holmes in the Adventure of the Blue carbuncle 1892

This is not always the case :)

For answer Holmes clapped the hat upon his head. It came right over the forehead and settled upon the bridge of his nose. "It is a question of cubic capacity," said he; "a man with so large a brain must have something in it."

COMFORT AND THE CUTS

Primarily worn for great lengths of time and as such will have to provide some level of comfort for the wearer so that they don't cause more problems than they solve. This is why a lot of the frames will have a bridge with nose pads and occasionally have pads on the legs of the glasses themselves. These can provide a small insight into day-to-day activity. For example, as these pads are largely made from rubber based material which is designed in these cases both for its comfort and its ability to hug the face thanks to its properties it will naturally collect parts from the day. So anyone who has had a haircut recently and in particular this applies to males as we statistically have the shorter hair here, they will adhere to the pads on the spectacles themselves thanks to them being a huge recipient of the warmth and moisture created here. Dependent upon how worn in they are (anyone who has ever used a pencil eraser in school will be able to keep track of the amount of wear and tear that these things take) will give an inference to draw which will be idiosyncratic to each pair of glasses that you have in front of you. These inferences will be along the lines of the time that the person has owned the frames and/or whether or not they have another pair. This is due to the fact that the only excessive wear that this part will have on them is the wearing and removing of them. This is made even more apparent by any designs that may or may not appear on the pads of the glasses themselves.

Specifically referring to the nose pads here, the size and the upkeep of them (and by upkeep I mean whether the screws within them are

246

newer than the frames or if they are wobbly at all) will give an indication as to the genetic makeup of the persons face. Clearly meaning then, that the bigger the space between the nose pads are the larger, the nose will be. The wobblier nose bridge pads can mean one of two things; The first is that the owner may have a particularly bony nose which I know sounds obvious however I just mean a little less gristle and padding. The second is the direct opposite of this inference and that these may be the only glasses that the person owns. This is left to down to accompanying deductions that you make.

The exception of the pads on the stems of the glasses is that they will collect moisture from warmth, and length of wearing them, as well as any hair care products. The lack of pads even on the nose bridge is seen mostly on the frames with the hipster big black frames.

READING THE GLASSES

Reading glasses go by many names and prescriptions, the more popular of these type are the over the counter style of frames. These are primarily used in the treating of Presbyopia and Hyperopia, which are both forms of farsightedness thereby providing clearer vision. They vary in reading strength from 0.75 - 3.50 diopters. These are generally considered safe by ophthalmologists, but for long-term comfort a personal prescription and eye exam is the best way to move forward.

These particular reading glasses come in two styles, full frames and half eyes. For full frames the glasses will need to be taken from the face to clearly see what's in the distance whereas with half eyes the owner can look over the top as these frames sit further down the nose.

Bifocals are a different style of lens altogether and largely considered to be the most popular choice in corrective vision wear. This is due to the combination in the lens; the upper part of the lens is used for distance vision and the lower part of the lens to see clearly the things that are nearer to them. This allows the people that suffer with Presbyopia to see clearly in the distance without having to remove the frames. This makes it by far and away the most popular choice, just by sheer volume. One downside of the bifocal choice though is that they can cause headaches, dizziness and nausea. This is due to the owner having to get used to move the head or the reading material as opposed to the eyes thanks to having to acclimate to the small field of vision. Excessive use of computer screens (most likely down to someone's job) can lead to muscle fatigue. This is a list of ailments that is unfortunately shared with those that wear trifocal lenses. Trifocals are made in a similar vein to bifocals but they have an extra section in the middle of the aforementioned two (as if you hadn't already guessed by the use of the words bi and tri). The near and the far vision is covered within the lens but the extra portion of the lens is to take care of the middle ground i.e. the distance of arm length.

However the Trifocals are becoming rarer in lieu of the now popular varifocal lenses. These go by many names such as progressive lenses or corrective lenses and multifocal lenses. These are characterized by a gradient of increasing lens power. It starts at the top with the wearer's prescription and gets stronger the further down the lens you get. With this type of lens it avoids the incontinuities of vision and works better with natural movement of the eye. This will obviously cut down on the likelihood of discomfort as a direct result of the glasses here. A frequent disadvantage of this style is that they will be incorrectly aligned with the owners pupil and as such cause such things as blurred or distorted vision in one eye.

Now then, I have thrown a lot of information at you in the past few paragraphs. The question now becomes what do you do with it.

This, like everything else will depend on the glasses that you have in front of you as such what will follow is a lot of ideas and 'tells' as it were.

• The telltale red marks of the nose pads of the glasses. When these appear and there are no glasses on the face of the person, this is a sign of a couple of inferences. Moisture builds up under the pads due to them being in place for a long time. This will aggravate the skin underneath the pad due to the warmth and material the pad itself is made from. This is different to an indentation that can be left from the nosepads of other glasses that don't have actual pads and form part of a bridge. The red marks are made worse by rubbing and this is a sure sign of irritation of the eyes, headaches. This gives clues and inferences to possible job roles, which you can make further deductions on based on the person. However what this suggests is, excessive times of reading and concentration, which could be both paperwork and a computer screen. You can close down your field by a simple question of 'Do you work indoors or outdoors?' The indentation marks are indicative of time worn for a specific frame. The indents are born of similar idea just there is no aggravation involved which would suggest no discomfort; this in turn could suggest a more definitively prescribed lens. Also the nose bridges with no pads are more often than not found on the more expensive frames.

• Much like the infamous pocket watch deduction scene from 'The Sign Of Four - 1890', the nicks scratches and marks that appear on the frames and lenses can tell a certain tale about the owner. For example, any signs of small collections of tiny scratches on the lenses and the underside of the frames suggest that the most likely inference is that the owner has or at the very least did not use their glasses case on their most recent holiday. This is because sand is a granular material made up of very fine rocks and minerals. At the beach these will come off due to the buildup of moisture and sweat and the inevitable uncomfortable skin irritation. Primarily featured on the owners of people who specifically spend time there to get a tan, or the people who do tan whilst there but their main concern at that time is reading whatever book they have taken with them. This chapter concerns the glasses alone and as such I won't waste space by going into detail on the type. The material that the frames/lenses are made from make them very prone to small collections of scratch marks thanks to the rocks in the sand.

• If you notice that the legs on one side of the frames look slightly more worn than the other and is even slightly dented, this is often a sign of a chewer! In the same way that people chew pencils or pens in class when mulling over a particular problem that they are faced with. It will always be the same leg as the action is an unconscious response to a puzzling moment. Now you could take your deductions in a variety of ways at this point but it would again depend on the person and the other clues that will be presented here as every time you deduce the result will be different. It could be that they are of a nervous disposition, they have a particularly high profile job or it could just be that they are stuck in the first stage of Freud's psychosexual development the orally fixated.

That should be enough information to wet your whistle here but how would you know where they purchased the glasses themselves merely by looking at them? Read on and you shall find out....

NAME THAT STORE

Now, right from the off I should point out that this does not apply to all glasses, just the named/designer brands as only certain shops sell certain brands of spectacle. You will not find a shop that sells them all. So all you need to do is, something quite simple, and find out the names of all the opticians and places that sell and fix prescriptive lenses, shops that sell only glasses (as you can get over the counter reading glasses at your local supermarket) find out from them the list of their labels and store them inside your palace accordingly. So what I have done here is to give you the current ones from England and a handful from the state, the shop names and the full lists.

VISION EXPRESS

- *Emporio Armani*
- *Fat Face*
- *Gant Eyewear*
- Giorgio Armani
- *Givenchy*
- Guess
- *Hugo*
- Hackett
- *Heston Blumenthal*
- *Iron man*
- *Jaeger (Jaeger London)*
- *Jimmy Choo*
- *Levi's*
- *Lindenberg*
- *Marc by Marc Jacobs*
- *Max Mara*
- *Michael Kors*
- *Mont blanc*
- *Radley London*
- *Ralph Lauren*
- *Ray Bans*
- *Silhouette*
- *Sketchers*
- *Stark Eyes*
- *Swarovski*
- *Ted Baker*
- *Versace*

- *Alexander McQueen*
- *Animal*
- *Austin Reed*
- *Bench*
- *Bench Kids*
- *Beyu Eyewear*
- *Hugo Boss*
- *Bvlgari*
- *Carrera*
- *Caterpillar*
- *Chanel*
- *Christian Larcroix*
- *Converse*
- *Diesel*
- *Dolce and Gabbana*
- *Mister Men Little Miss*
- *Nike Vision*
- *Oakley*
- *Oasis*
- *Pepe Jeans*
- *Police*
- *Polo*
- *Prada*
- *Stepper*
- *Superdry*
- *Tag Heuer*
- *Tiffany and Co.*

- *Yves Saint Laurent*

There is a branch of the huge company in England called BOOTS (this is also devoted to the sale of over the counter medicines, make up and cosmetics, small electrical items) that has an optician and as such only stocks the following frames.

- *Givenchy*
- Police
- DKNY

- *Rayban*
- *Orla Kiely*
- *Nicola Farhi*

Then there is the ever popular Specsavers, who stock the following:

- *Boss Orange*
- Karen Millen
- French Connection UK
- *Roxy 25*
- Osiris B74
- Timberland
- Dyers

- *Gok Wan*
- *John Rocha*
- *Tommy Hilfiger*
- *Red or Dead*
- *Aurora 11*
- *Rhenium*
- *Quiksilver*

In the U.S.A there is the ever infamous LensCrafters.

- *Avant Garde*
- *Bulgari*
- *Carolee*
- *Coach*
- *D Viations*
- *Dolce and Gabbana*
- *Elizabeth Arden*
- *Essential Eyewear*
- *Liberty*
- *Maui Jim*
- *Oakley*

- *Armani Exchange*
- *Brooks Brothers*
- *Burberry*
- *Carolee Lux*
- *Converse*
- *DKNY*
- *Easytwist*
- *Emporio Armani*
- *Giorgio Armani*
- *Lucky*
- *Miu Miu*

- Persol
- Polo Ralph Lauren
- Prada Linea Rosa
- Ray Ban (jr)
- Sun Gear
- Tory Burch
- Vogue
- Zegna
- Occhiolini
- Polo Prep
- Prada
- Ralph Lauren
- Sferoflex
- Tiffany
- Versace

There is also Eyemart to think about as well:

- BCBG
- Ellen Tracy
- Jessica Simpson
- Rocawear
- Haggar
- Dana Buchman
- Kensie
- Vera Wang
- Calvin Klein
- Nautica
- Sean John
- Helium
- Phat Farm
- Carrera
- Jlo
- Nine West
- Valentino
- Dakota Smith
- Ted Baker
- Bongo
- Gant
- Guess
- Lacoste
- Cole Haan
- Izod
- Madden
- Sydney Love
- Peace
- Jhane Barnes
- Thalia
- Columbia
- Michael Kors
- Nike
- Float
- Baby Phat
- Banana Republic
- Claiborn
- Juicy Couture
- Saks Fifth Ave
- Andriano Franco
- Cutter and Buck
- Lulu Guinness
- Candies
- Harley

- *Sophia Laren*
- *Stetson*
- *Skechers*
- *Randy Jackson*

I could obviously recite list upon list but I have given you a very good place to start building your knowledge on the topic. It is a simple matter to find out what the current stock of designer frames is from your local dealer. If I haven't listed them, go into the store and ask for a list. They will be only too happy to help you as you will seem like an interested customer.

What can you do with this knowledge then, once you have obtained it? You can just by looking at the persons glasses (when they are a labeled make of course) and know where they have been purchased, which is a feat in itself. You then have the added bonus of being able to know within at least two possible locations where they live. To explain further, to keep glasses that cost that much in a high standard of maintenance they will require the glasses version of a tune up. They will therefore visit the shop that is the most congenial to them and unless they are travelling business person they will visit the nearest available outlet to their home. This is just basics of common sense! So in being familiar with the location of the shops and how they travel, it will stand you in great stead for being able to deduce where in the region they live. Let me cite an example to better amplify this point with a hypothetical person from the UK:

- A woman wearing Jaeger glasses.

- She is a mother pushing a baby in a pram

- There is no visible 'Baby Bag'

- You met her on the outskirts of Hanley.

- Weather is a mix of Rain and sunny spells

- She and her car are dry, her shoes show damp mud though.

Now then, what deductions can we make about this woman already? They will be listed after so what I suggest you do here is to test yourself and not peep ahead. As I cannot be sure where you, the reader, are from, I will give you the closest places surrounding where you saw her. Sneyd Green, Birches Head and Shelton.

- Car is likely used for the ease of transporting the large pram around.

- Glasses were purchased at Vision express.

- The child being so young will be prone to changing moods/temperament and above all needs. So the lack of baby bag is indicative of someone who was expecting only a short trip.

- Due to her and her car being dry and the fact that her shoes show signs of mud it is indicative again of the very short trip but the grass by her house is wet. Shelton is most a built up area with no grasslands by the houses, Birches Head has a mixture of both but Sneyd Green has the most houses that are directly surrounded by grassy areas.

SHE LIVES IN SNEYD GREEN.

So you can see that with a couple of other small deductions and knowing where she gets her glasses done you can have the possibility to deduce where she resides in this world.
So let us continue down this road here of labels. If you can see that they are in fact a designer label, then it is clearly a large economic purchase and she must have a bank balance capable of sustaining such a transaction. As such, what can we deduce from this? First of all you must remember that context will be key in driving home success. If you put it into context with the clothes you will be able

to ascertain as to whether or not the item is a luxury item or not. By that I mean if the person is wearing other expensive items i.e. jewellery, clothes and watches then this becomes part of their normal lifestyle and as such it isn't a particularly luxury item. This means then that they may have a well- paying job, or have an inheritance to dip into, basically a large sustainable income. There will be signs of which it will be, but as this chapter is strictly concerning spectacles, we shall leave that to the other chapters for you to acquaint yourself with. If the item appears to be the only 'expensive' item on the person at that time then this could mean that they treasure this item and value its use and purpose because their eyes need to be looked after due to what they use them for. Now this may be down to the specifications of their job or it could be that they are simply experiencing a laundry day! As previously stated it will be the context of your deductions that will narrow down the truth. There is also a way to spot the fake brands from the real ones. The real ones come with all of the paraphernalia with the correct logos on. The glasses case, the cleaning cloth etc. and the fake ones do not.

Now then, let me throw an anomaly into the wind at this point. That is contact lenses, and is there a way to tell if someone is wearing them just by looking and not having to ask? Of course there is and it is a remarkably simple task to complete. Soft contact lenses have a small blue ring around the outside of where the iris would be this can be visible on the right lighting conditions, which will be at almost any point during the day or with lights on inside at night time. Also from the side of the face you can see a small film over the eyes, which will be the contact lens itself.

The anomalies continue here with the next question. Can you tell if someone is wearing bifocals or reading glasses or basically know which lens is in their glasses just by looking and not having to ask them any questions about it? There is a very simple solution here. You don't have to ask them any questions about the lenses or even their glasses, but what you do have to do is ask them to read something and then watch how they react. You will need to be completely aware of how each style of lens is set up. Let us say for example then that you present the hypothetical person with something to read; they take it in their hands; gesture with it forwards and lean back slightly, looking down their nose through the glasses.

As you will no doubt be aware the split of bifocals happens to allow people to see clearly the things that are close to them in the lower half of the lens. The adjustment of whatever it is that they are reading and tilting their head slightly will give this away as a set of spectacles with bifocals. The irony of someone taking off reading glasses to read something you present to them will be astounding. The tell will reveal all by the way they react to new things to read. This is a remarkably fun thing to practice and is extremely powerful when demonstrated.

SPECIFIC EYE WEAR

This, though not completely devoted to glasses of a prescriptive design, does relate to the overall feel of the chapter. That is, that there are some jobs, which require specific eyewear and other occupations that have merely grown a specific style of glasses as part of their influence in the popular culture. For example the largely ironic and constantly changing frames of the hipster. A lot of the time these are ornamental and serve no real purpose but they will be large frames, often-wild colours. This type of glasses choice is most frequently associated with Baristas and people who work in Mobile (cellular) phones shops.

And the interchangeable lense of the jeweler, which allows for close inspection of jewels. For those unfamiliar with what I mean, I refer you to the Nicholas Cage movie National Treasure.

The protection that goes for Welders can range from full-face masks to glasses that cover the entire eye socket altogether. Consider the case and point below.

There are many jobs that will require a specific set of protective eyewear or in the case of jewelers, eyewear that further accentuates their vision in order for them to complete their job to maximum efficiency. To list them all for you would take a book in itself so this should be more than enough to get you started on your way. Practise, practise, practise!

KNOWING THE CARBUNCLES FROM THE CORONET'S

'It is an old maxim of mine that when you have excluded the impossible, whatever remains, however improbable, must be the truth.'

Sherlock Holmes - The Adventure of the Beryl Coronet 1892

In this chapter we will be taking a hard look at what can be deduced from the jewellery a person is wearing. Jewellery, much like watches, shoes, clothes are items that go with us everywhere on our day-to-day regiments. They are with us when we are at work and when we are at play. They come in the form of everything from gifts to heirlooms and everything in between. They can offer us an insight into someone's married life, their star sign, children, relatives, hobbies, personality. The list does go on and on. The advantageous aspect of deducing information from jewelry, when the person is wearing it, is that often they react to certain emotional stimuli, allowing us to combine our knowledge that we have developed about the person from the jewelry with their body language. Your accuracy will develop only in asking the right questions but the answers will come via the jewelry. We will explore this in depth later on in the chapter.

DEDUCTIVE RINGS AND OTHER SHINY THINGS

The styles of rings, available for consumer purchase, are astoundingly vast and each will offer their own insight into the person and why they have them on. Let us start with the simplest approach with deduction based on rings and this is something that has been mentioned in other chapters as well. Here the approach is no different. The style of rings will obviously have specific fingers that they go on which will allow you to further narrow down with the accuracy the size of the person. You begin by placing it on your finger and going from

260

there. Compare and contrast with how it fits you and you will have your answer. This brings us nicely onto being able to differentiate between the different ring styles that are available, beginning with the most popular of sorts and that is being able to tell the difference between an engagement ring and a wedding ring.

Historically, the engagement ring was given to the bride as a symbol of the groom's financial commitment to her family. He promised to marry her and "bought" her with an expensive ring -- which she then wore to symbolize that she would refuse all other offers. It was also a status symbol for the bride's parents/family -- that they had gotten a wealthy man to marry their daughter -- and the groom's family (that others would see how much money they had to spare on such luxuries for the bride). The wedding band, on the other hand, is a symbol of the bride (or groom, nowadays) having already made that commitment. It didn't have to be as fancy because the husband wasn't trying to "win" her from her family as with the engagement ring.

Although today is much more gregarious with their styles we still have similar styles of rings. The engagement ring is still typically more decorative, usually with one or more diamonds -- while the wedding ring is more functional.

The context of sight deductions here can give you all manner of insights. Weathered marks and signs of age (I will deal with scuff marks more in depth later on in the chapter) can give you an idea of the timeline between engagement and marriage. Weathering on the wedding ring (which is typically the newer ring in this situation) points to it being an heirloom of some sort, passed down from an older relative. The same can be said of almost any jewellery, if the style of it doesn't fit with the person/or the current fashion trend then they are wearing it because it means something personal to them. The balance of probability states that is therefore an heirloom or family gift from an older relative) Also the age and style of the ring can make you aware of heirloom gifts that are sometimes used as wedding/engagement rings. One will contradict the other one. Gold can fade as well. Not to mention the economic difference that can be visible here, an expensive engagement ring with a huge stone and a standard wedding band can often indicate materialism. Using the big rock to secure the lady in question so to speak and if they are reversed for example the engagement ring is silver and small and the wedding ring is a platinum band, this can be a sign of a promotion at work, selling a house etc. and he has chose to spend some of his extra money on a nice wedding ring.

Eternity rings are sometimes used as wedding rings/engagement rings but when there are 3 rings seen on the ring finger of a lady this is a sign of a healthy, happy long-term relationship. This is because traditionally speaking eternity rings are purchased after the birth of the couples' first child to signify that they will be together forever. The only real indication of eternity rings is that they are a stone set ring. This means they either have the same stones set all the way around or just half way around. Promise rings are a close neighbour of the eternity ring though they are a corporate/sociological creation and as such there is no defining characteristic about them. Thumb rings are invariably thicker sized both in length and in the size of the material.

Male thumb rings are reserved statistically for people who live and breathe the arts. These are people heavily involved in performance of all kinds, music, painting, writing. On rare occasions there will be items such as Championship rings for you to work with, usually presented for the winners of North American sports tournaments. So make yourself aware of the leagues that are involved such as teams from the NBA, NFL, NHL, MLS, and the CFL.

Bracelets, in particular charm bracelets are quite telling of a person. There are also cuff bracelets, friendship bracelets, id bracelets, leather bracelets and many others from which to gain insight and information via deduction. Friendship bracelets are telling due to them being from threads and fabrics and adhering to a pattern. There will also be matching bracelets which the other friends in the circle will have. The rule here being: the brighter the colours, the brighter the personality of the owner. ID bracelets are telling due to the engravings that accompany them. We can obtain nicknames and wedding anniversaries here. Cuff bracelets are stereotypically a high society piece of jewelry (popular with the elite who wear broaches) worn with this in mind. There are different styles that are more popular for work and some that are better suited to formal wear. They infrequently come with a space for engravings on and this allows us the same insights that I.D bracelets offer us. Leather bracelets are increasingly popular amongst the urban subculture. It seems to be style icons like Johnny Depp who have helped to skyrocket the popularity of these items. Charm bracelets though can be store-bought with a couple already attached, if the wearer of such an item has only a few mere charms on then they may not even signify anything. They are worth examining though as when they were purchased they may have been done with a specific intent in mind. For example hearts in an increasing size shows the person has more than one child, and then if they also have some male and female imagery on such as dolls for girls and teddy bears for boys you can then infer that this was bought as a representation of this person's children. However, many different charms can be purchased for these bracelets with each holding its own unique symbology. The more charms on a bracelet the more likely it is that this person believes in these alternative systems (Horoscopes, tarot readers, Homeopathy etc.,). The following is a list of charms and their meaning:

Acorn Charm: This charm symbolizes 'Strength from Tiny Beginnings'.

Ammonite Fossil: The symbolic meaning of the Ammonite charm is 'Long Life'.

Amethyst Charm: The meaning of 'Spirituality & Sobriety' comes from the ancient Greeks.

Angel: A charm for 'Protection'. □

Apple: The Apple charm means 'Knowledge & Health'. □

Artist: This charm symbolizes 'Creativity'. □

Ballet shoes: Ballet Shoe charms symbolize 'Grace'.

Bee Hive: Beehive charm symbolizes 'Co-operation'. □

Best friends: This unique charm symbolizes 'Together Forever'.

Bumble Bee: This charm symbolizes 'a busy bee'. □

Bunny: This charm has the meaning of 'Playful' □

Buttercup: Buttercup means 'Cheerfulness & Radiance.

Butterfly: This charm symbolizes 'Renewal'.

Caterpillar: Meaning Transformation.

Cinderella Shoe: Representing 'Rags To Riches'.

Cross: Meaning 'Faith'

Champagne Bottle: A classic charm symbolizing 'Celebration'

Chocolate Charm: Created for anyone with a 'sweet tooth'.

Clam Shell: Represents 'Fertility'.

Cupcake: A gorgeous Cupcake Charm means 'sweet nothings'

Daisy: In the Victorian era, each flower had a meaning and Daisies means 'Childish Innocence'.

Devil Tail: Perfect for the 'Mischievous' among us! Dice: Lucky 'Dice' charm□Dragonfly Charm: A symbol of 'Rebirth'.□Dog: This charm means 'Loyalty'.

Dove: A classic charm to spread the message of 'Hope & Peace'

Egg: The Egg charm symbolizes the 'Birth of Life'.□

Elephant: Meaning 'Never Forget'.□

Fairies: Meaning 'Forever Young'.

Feather: Represents 'Freedom'.

Frog Prince: Every girl looks for her 'Prince Charming'.

Flip Flop: a reminder of our summer holidays 'Travel & Carefree Days'.

Forget Me Not: Forget-Me-Not charm means 'Everlasting Memory'.

Four Leaf Clover: A wonderful 'Luck' talisman!

Genie Lamp: 'Rub to Make Three Wishes'

Gardening: Meaning 'Green Fingers'.

Heart: A perfect charm to start any collection – meaning 'Love'.

Horse Shoe: Symbolizes 'Catch Good Luck' and 7 holes are essential for luck.

Hummingbird Charm: A hummingbird charm symbolizes 'Flirtatious'.

Ivy Leaf: Means 'Fidelity & Optimism'.

Key: Key charm, meaning 'Awakening'.

Lily of the Valley: The elegant Lily of the Valley means 'Return of Happiness'.

Ladybird: Another whimsical charm, this little Ladybird means 'Luck is on its Way'.

Mortar Board: Mortar Board charm marks the 'Achievement' of graduation.

Monkey Nut: Monkey Nut charm to symbolize 'Good times'.

Oak Leaf: Oak Leaf charm represents 'Wisdom and Longevity'.

Palm Tree: Palm Tree charm meaning 'Sunshine & Holidays'

Peas in a Pod: Means 'Unity'. A quirky collectable perfect for twins, sisters or inseparable friends!

Pet: This charm represents 'Companionship'.

Pigs Might Fly: Realise the Impossible' and is enough to make anyone believe in miracles!

Pixie Shoe: The enchanting Pixie Shoe charm means 'Believe in Magic'.

Poppy: this Poppy charm means 'Remembrance'. ☐

Princess Crown: Everyone knows a 'Modern Day Princess'. ☐

Raspberry: Raspberry charm means 'Precious Times'

Rosette: Rosette charm symbolizes 'Success'. ☐

Sixpence: An enduring keepsake from your 'Christmas Pudding'. ☐

Snowdrop: Represents 'Hope & Purity'. ☐

Star: This Star represents 'Fame' and is perfect for any stars in the making!'

Starfish: Symbolism of 'Calm Resilience'.

Stirrup: Stirrup charms represent 'Taming the Wild'! Perfect for an adventurous horse rider!

Strawberry: Strawberry charm means 'Life's Sweet Pleasures'.

Sweet 16: To celebrate a 16th birthday! ☐

Treble Clef: Treble Clef charm symbolizes 'harmony'. ☐

Vintage Handbags: 'Retro Chic'.

Unicorn: Unicorn Horn charm provides 'Protection from Bad Luck' with a touch of magic!

Wedding Bell: An adorable commemorative gift for 'Matrimony'.

Welly: The humble Welly Boot has been a symbol of life in England for generations! 'Splashing in Puddles'.

Wishbone Charm: Meaning 'Make a Wish for Love'.

Wishing wand: To help you 'Make a Wish Come True'.

Earrings

Simply put, earrings are nothing more than fashion accessories to the public at large. They are bought because they look nice or go with the outfit that is needed to be worn for whatever special occasion is coming up. This is a predominant feature amongst women, men however when using earrings or any other kind of piercing jewelry put a little more thought into it.

If you see a woman who has earrings on that are of a matching set and work with the rest of her clothes (an example of not working would be pearl earrings and necklace on a skater girl) then you know she has put time and effort into the correct matching accessories so she is conscious of the image she is giving off. The flashier the jewelry the flashier the excursion, which is basic common sense really but is often over looked. It isn't until we begin to see the dangly earrings on women that insights can be drawn, as this is when they can be adorned with subtle images and talismans. The one thing we can be sure of with all large earrings is that they are a statement for attention. Now this can be taken in one of two ways and that is whether or not they are the abrasive, egomaniac type as seen with most of the 'Chav' culture of England or whether they are the demure type of person who is trying to gain confidence and feel better about herself. It is only when you meet each person that you will see the difference.

CHAV   **DEMURE LADY**

The dangly earrings can be adorned with dream catcher symbols and/or birthstones, and an intricate run of symbology (four leaf clovers, patron saints, are two extremely popular ones). It is only through knowing what symbols mean that you can deduce the information about the person. Let us say for example that you see a person who has amethyst set in amongst the gold. It is only from knowing that amethyst is the birthstone for February, that you can infer that that is when

269

she was more than likely born.

This brings us on to another fine observation, the birthstones. These are set in amongst all jewelry in some form or another and can be an invaluable piece for gaining information about someone without their knowledge.

BIRTHSTONES BY MONTH

January - Garnet

February - Amethyst

March - Aquamarine

April - Diamond

May - Emerald☐

June - Pearl☐

July - Ruby☐

August - Peridot

September - Sapphire

October - Tourmaline

November - Topaz

December - Tanzanite

Men's earrings form part of the more suburban life. Icons from the film and music have their ears pierced. Men in extreme sports get piercings and not just on their ears. Men's earrings frequently come with patterns of skulls and dragons, with fire and other such stereotypically masculine things. In the 80's and 90's it was popular for men to wear dangly earrings such as gold hoops with crosses dangling from them, this was a throw back to glam rock and rock and roll culture in general. Suffice to say (and thankfully) that that trend has long since died out. There were many urban legends and stories surrounding men and piercings in their ears in the early 90's, particularly in England. Were you to only pierce your left ear then that was socially acceptable, however if it was the right on its own then this meant that you were a homosexual and, if you were to get both ears pierced, then this meant that you were virtually a girl. All of which was the complete crap of childish name calling meant to aid in the growth of men. If there is a single stud of either black or an almost luminous colour, then this points to someone who belongs to the urban extreme sports group, everything from skates, to skateboards, and from BMX's to motorbikes. Then there are the spacers that are placed into ears (women have both these and the luminous ones as well, same rules apply). These leave a rather large hole in the lobe and 90% of the time are part of a pair. They look pretty much like a stud only the middle part that goes through the actual lobe itself is decidedly much bigger. These are found on (or rather in) the people of a much more alternative culture.

SCUFF MARKS AND SCRATCHES

There are many ways in which a piece of jewellery can sustain an indentation or a scratch, which will be explained, is a way for you to understand how and why these happen. It is quite rare to find necklaces that have sustained scratching and scuffs; what is most probable here is that whatever it is made from can fade and show signs of age and wear. However it is possible. So here are the most likely solutions to this cause. If there is no pattern/ collection or size then this is a sign of a person who has no real value for the necklace and when it comes off before they go to bed or to go back into the jewelry box or wherever they store there items it is just dropped/thrown/tossed in so that whatever it hits on the way there does its damage. The most popular of these is just dropping it onto the tabletop or a bedside table. Patterns of a lot of tiny scratches throughout most of the necklace shows someone who has just come back from their holidays and has spent time sunbathing on the beach. When these collections appear on bracelets this is someone who is manual labourer (most often this is man) and the collections of tiny scratches are where he has been handling bricks and putting up walls and such as well as having his hands in out of gravel. When it is a woman's, this indicate a cleaner in that they are scrubbing all manner of surfaces throughout the day and inevitably the bracelets will scratch along the tops of whatever they are working on.

It is rings, as they are on our most active of limbs, which will sustain the brunt of the wear and tear up on them. The same rules apply for rings as in the previous observations. The greater the collection of tiny scratches the more chance of it being sand from their vacation. Only when the lines become more sporadic does the idea of cleaners or manual labourers come in to the equation. Related to this point is when there is a collection, a small grouping of scratches in one particular spot on a ring. This is an indication of someone who uses tools as part of their daily life, which is most likely as part of their job. This would be people like plumbers, handymen, janitors, builders and to have their possible job narrowed to a small collection after only observing their jewellery is an amazing standpoint to be in. You will only need a few more deductive observations to nail it with pinpoint accuracy.

Another insanely popular job tell that can divined from someone's ring, is when it flattens out on the bottom of the rings that have stones set in them (therefore having a decipherable top and bottom) or just on one part of the rings that don't. This is due to an excessive amount of table tapping.

272

What I mean by this is tapping in boredom, tapping due to lots of work on counter tops, sometimes the ring constantly taps on the table during office work or when using a desktop keyboard because most people like to lean on the table when working. With jewelry being made from metal, though precious, still tough all the same. To wear the ring into flattening slightly on one part, will have had to be done with repeated use of the same actions for quite some time. This would therefore point to someone's job role. In this instance that would be someone who works in an office at a desk or behind a counter perhaps in customer service. If you see this, in conjunction with the scratch mark tell of a cleaner, then, this would further support your observations.

The other visible wear and tear that you will find on jewelry is aging and fading of the materials. This will give answers to the questions of, how old the piece is and how long the person has had it, which will in turn give inferences about heirlooms and hand me downs. Scuff marks and scratches and jewelry are to be treated as starting points with which to deduce backwards from. You will need to combine them with other observations you can make about the person. One tell is rarely enough to go on in the real world.

Rings, bracelets and necklaces can cause the skin some discomfort if they are either a fake a piece of jewelry (as in the gold isn't real gold) or an allergic reaction of some description.

Fake jewelry provides a telling discolouration to the parts of the skin where the jewelry has been. The most popular colour is a greenish blue colour.

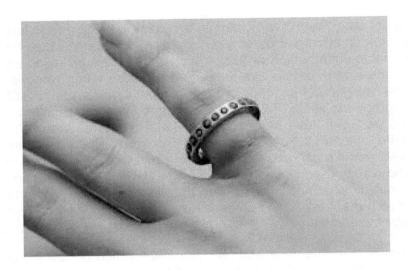

This is due to the fact that fakes are predominantly made from copper as its reasonably cheap considering the money they will make back on it and easy to cover up. When you perspire, the metals in the ring react with the acid in your sweat to form salts, which are green. These acids are essentially causing the copper to corrode on the surface of the metal, which forms a salt compound of the metal. These salts are absorbed into the skin and the result is a decidedly green digit. This happens with both bracelets and necklaces as well. Whenever it sits there for a while, it will inevitably create warmth, which will then lead to the reaction, the salts and the unavoidable green of a fake.

Allergic reactions can be in the form of anything from dry skin to acute dermatitis. They will be in the places that the jewellery has been. This is down to a reaction to the nickel in jewellery. It's such a popular metal for everyday objects as well, that is also in glasses frames, mobile phones and zippers in trousers. The same reactions can also happen here as well.

This leads me nicely on to the next point...

SPOTTING THE FAKE

With jewellery it is the simple manner of looking for the stamps that adorn the jewellery. 925 denotes a sterling silver piece that is 100% genuine. Gold will have the stamps on, of whichever carat it is (either 9k, 14k, 18k, 24k). Stamps such as HGE (heavy gold electroplate), gold filled, plated, RGP (rolled gold plated), and EP (electroplated). These stamps represent metal jewellery that is rolled, filled, or plated with gold. In some cases with jewellery of all precious metals, the brand/label will have their own personal stamp to adorn the piece with, to identify its genuine nature. Discolouration shouldn't happen in pieces which are genuine. With gold all you need to do, as well, is to hold a magnet against it, as real gold is not magnetic.

Items that therefore do not adhere to this code here are spurious and will react with your person in a variety of ways. For the Deductionist this makes them easy to spot as well as they are a physical anomaly that will stand out. This also gives us important deductive avenues to go down with questions that arise here.

• Why would someone knowingly wear fake jewelry? Proving a point? Fitting in with the crowd? Presenting an image of themselves that they need to present and have to do it on a budget?

• How would someone come to wearing fake jewelry, unknowingly? A gift from a partner, trying to cut corners? A gift, to a mistress, from someone who doesn't want to blow too much obvious money?

These are the questions that will arise and it will be the context of the piece of the jewellery that will give you its origin. Let's take one of the above examples and explain a little further then. If the piece is a necklace that is incredibly shiny and has stones, but the person who is wearing it clearly couldn't afford such a genuine purchase, (which would be made apparent by where it is being worn and the context of the rest of the outfit). Not too many people wear a diamond necklace to go to work, then this would point to extravagant gift, wearing it all the time to feel special and close to the person who gave the gift because they don't get to see them a lot. When this turns out to be a fake this then speaks to the idea of this person being a mistress to a terrible person.

PHYSICAL JEWELLERY

What I mean by this is the examining of jewellery in context with how a person reacts to it when questioned (not formally per se, just conversation), and the tells from the rest of the body.

A lot of the time someone will accessorize their body with items that reflect their own personal likes and tastes as previously stated but this takes the original point made earlier up a few gears.

For example, take the ring on the right hand of one of your humble author as an example:

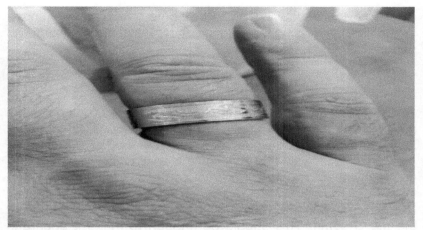

You notice an animal on the ring, what is it? Then look at this picture of my right arm:

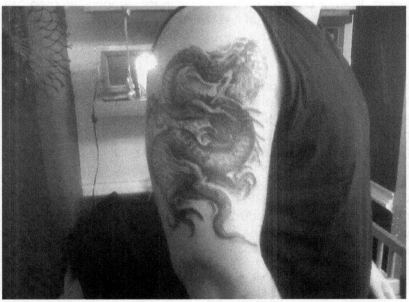

You notice it is the same animal as the ring. Now for these two to be a part of two aspects that I would carry with me all day everyday, there would need to be some personal investment in the imagery to be able to do that. What then, might we deduce is my favourite animal?

The answer is of course a Dragon

Jewellery provides an emotional connection depending on the piece. If you suspect an heirloom around the neck of a young lady, as it is a slightly older piece that has endured weathering and doesn't fit with the style of the rest of her clothes and outfit, she then (as part of normal conversation) mentions her Grandma and touches her jewelry. So a couple of minutes later you mention the grandma and she unconsciously touches the piece again. This should be enough to make it apparent that this was an heirloom from her grandma. Women have a tell when it comes to emotional stimuli and this is not to be sexist it is just that it is predominant among women. In particular, the touching of necklaces during time of heightened emotion, as this is around the suprasternal notch area of the neck, a control response and an unconscious one at that.

So observe anyway, in which the pieces of jewellery fit in with the rest of the person and their outfit/look and conversely be aware of the anomalies. The pieces that stick out always provide reliable sources of information. This will give you a greater and more reliable insight into their tastes, preferences, family, family members that may have passed etc.

With all this information in mind you will have enough to craft a room for jewellery in your memory palace and store all the pearls of wisdom that I have laid before you appropriately. It is a valuable source with which to work

TATTOOS▢

"Art in the blood is liable to take the strangest forms..."
The Adventure of the Greek Interpreter 1893

A STUDY IN INK

A few tattoos do in fact appear in the Arthur Conan Doyle's Canon of Holmes adventures: a blue anchor, a fish with delicate pink scales, a man's initials. Holmes even did some studies of tattoos himself. Add that to the popularity of Tattoo's today and I can't help but share my findings in, A Study In Ink.

The word tattoo was bought in to Europe, and indeed eventually the rest of the world and popular culture, by the explorer James Cook when he returned in 1771 from his first excursion to Tahiti and New Zealand. He refers to it as Tattaw and makes reference to the marking systems of tribes that were over there at the time, and signified rank and leadership, and above all else, power.

Tattooing throughout the centuries has appeared throughout most cultures and shares a lot of similar meaning. In China it was largely considered a barbaric practice of branding criminals and scum. However it has also made an appearance in their literature regarding Folk Heroes. Though they share similar origins with respect to habitats as the criminals from that time, these are the only stories in which it appears as a positive remark. This happened as late as the Qing dynasty and even then it was common to tattoo or brand the faces of criminals and slaves with the characters naming them as such.

In Egypt tattoos were found mostly on women and were used to indicate their power and status. They had tattoos for everything, from healing and religion to a form of punishment. Egyptian medics even used tattooing to treat medical conditions, scars on mummies of varying degrees of colour. It has been discovered that it was used to treat conditions in the pelvis, mostly likely chronic pelvic peritonitis.

In Japan as far back as 1603 tattooing was practised by the people known as the 'ukiyo-e'. Most often found on firemen, men who work in manual labour and even the ladies of the night and each group used it to communicate power and status. In Filipino tribes of the late 16th century they believed tattooing to possess magical qualities and gave the leaders more power.

As well as Indonesia, Europe, Samoa, New Zealand and in the U.K and everywhere in between, tattooing shares the same qualities of being made a part of the criminal culture and the lower forms of society, as well as being used to indicate power and status. It has only been throughout the past 80 or so years that tattoos have made their way into popular culture. Maybe this contributes to the way that popular society views tattooing of both visible and non-visible nature. This serves only the purpose of helping you understood the historical relevance to the permanence of tattoos as a whole. What is marked upon the subject and where it is marked upon them dually tell a tale about the person who wears them.

So then, let us begin. What is the first observation one can make on tattoos even before you have begun your encounter with them? Before even you can see clearly what form the ink actually takes? The answer of course being the placement of the tattoos themselves and what they mean in relation to inferences about thoughts and personality traits:

CHEST

A chest tattoo is more often than not emblematic of close personal affection toward whatever is there. Often emblematic of the fact that it quite literally crosses the subject's heart. The chest is also a part of the body that is not often exposed and as such romantic inclinations can be drawn from the ink wearer as it can be inferred that only the romantic interest would be able to see it. Often there is a cross-pollination of ideas with clothes and how they are worn and ventral fronting but this section is purely dedicated to the tattoos so I will keep it as such.

(An artistic personality type, who keeps this close to his heart for inspiration.)

(A punk rocker reveals his way of life to the world)
A young man emblazons his chest with an animal, indicative of his personality, at that current time in his life. Due to his age

and other tattoos, which I know you cannot see, however it is most likely that he has experienced some other trauma in his life which has forced him to revitalise this spirit within him.

FINGERS AND HANDS

Finger tattoos vary but are often commitments to a way of life both in respect to personality and jobs etc. This is because for the large part they cannot be covered up and, in today's modern business world, tattooing of this nature is frowned upon and heavily discouraged. The tattoos, seen on the fingers, range from jokes such as moustaches to personal mantras and acronyms. In either case the inferences that can be drawn are vast. A name that appears tattooed on the ring finger of the left hand is typically of their chosen life partner. If there is no ring however, we may draw inferences about their attitudes toward marriage but commitment to the relationship. If phantom bands are there then we may draw other conclusions about death/divorce. Hands are often seen to contain important images to the subject's life, which they can wear as a symbol of pride and of their open personality.

(Most likely a musician, displaying his lifestyle choices with pride. clearly visible for all. This right handed guitarist is showing the world what he is about.)

(A prime example of a Latino gang member tattoo. Literally letting his fingers do the talking here, showing you what it is they do.)

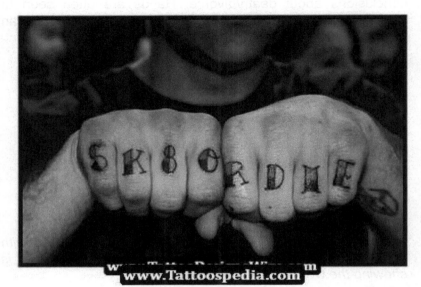

(A skater clearly, but demonstrating his creativity which would no doubt bleed over into his skating.)

FOREARM

In recent years, forearm tattoos have been a growing trend among men only, however women have decided to hitch a ride upon this particular body art band wagon as well. Reasoning and studies have suggested that tattoo placement here is representative, at least to some degree, of strength, but this can be of both the physical and psychological nature. Body types will give you a larger clue as to whether or not it is to call particular attention to their muscular definition or the meaning of the tattoo itself. i.e. pictures vs names.

(An unnatural folded arm position made to highlight the muscular definition and the tattoo itself, so either the model shoot was designed to highlight this specific aspect or the model himself is particularly proud)

(The roses, symbolic of the two most important flowers in his
world, his children. The strength of their relationship denoted
by the size and the fact that it is on the forearm itself.
SIDENOTE- flowers are a symbol of children and very, very
close immediate family so be wary when you see an
unopened flower bud or one that hasn't bloomed like the rest.
This has reflections in children who have died and still birth.
Dependent upon who you are and who you are reading this
may be quite rude go treading into this area without
permission.)

BICEP/TRICEP AREA

The most common place for tattoos among men, bar none, is
this area. It sees everything from the drunken mistake, to the
first tattoo, to the barb wires, to personal symbols of joy as

people very often enjoy wearing their heart on their sleeve. Body types would clue you in as to the proper meaning behind them. For example, a mesomorphic shaped person, with a barb wire band tattoo, will mostly likely have had it for a masculine status to accentuate the definition. This tattoo on a skinny person will likely have the opposite meaning.

(Dwayne Johnson's Tattoo depicting all that is personal to him in his life. Placement and design suggests his culture and ancestors, that of Samoa. Tattoos are placed here as a symbol of strength and leadership. As one of the most successful wrestlers ever and now a highly successful actor we can safely say this is reflected in the tattoo)

NECK-A neck tattoo is usually a major indication of personality, which of course can be used in conjunction with an array of other deductions. It's indicative of a daring person, forward thinking person who is prone to bold and impulsive decisions. Conforms to similar ideas as the tattoos on fingers and hands in that it cannot be covered by any clothing save for a scarf. Now, a tattoo on the neck will be painful, perhaps more than most. The sitter will know this, and for them to still get it done anyway says a lot about what the image/word is and what it means to them.

(I do not want to mention the actions related here, I will just say that this is around the time he was in a relationship with Rihanna. Due to its picture and placement one can clearly see the brash and impulsive personality he possesses, clearly a painful memory that he knows he won't be able to forget.

(English rap star Professor Green, had this tattoo on his neck mere weeks before he was stabbed. Ironic no? This tattoo crosses all the major nerves in the neck and with him coming from a modest working class background, this would be a symbolic reminder of his gratefulness and his work ethic, which we can then draw many, many more inference from.)

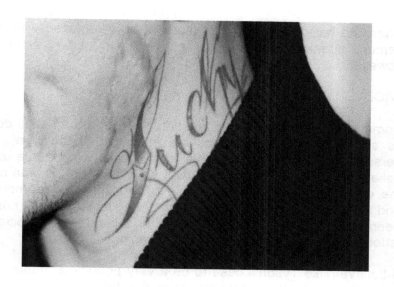

BACK

A back tattoo could give the impression of mystery or even a shy nature to the individual. These types of tattoos are not generally visible when out in the public, perhaps maybe in the summer months or when on a night out. Back tattoos often see symbols of past trauma or important life events, that they are literally leaving behind them, as well as affirming life mantras. This is likened to the way that many popular sports stars have numbers on their backs. They become known as their number, as in that is who they are, but in that game. A tattoo symbol of this nature displays heavy personal influence on how they conduct their lives. I have the words 'You see but you do not observe' tattooed across my back.

ANKLE

Since this can be pretty much hidden in plain sight it is suggestive of someone who is out going, sociable and mostly, when the hair is let loose, a little wild. It is replaced with a demure streak during the day and in their jobs of choice however.

FACE

Some may feel this an obvious point to mention but I shall do so all the same. Face tattoos are indicative of the type of person who flies in the face of all that society would have us believe and act like. Most likely their beliefs fall on the side of the extremist. Likely has a terrible relationship with parents and a very close circle of friends numbering less than 3. It has been noted however that some niche tribal leaders have facial tattoos that are demonstrative of their seniority.

(I believe Mike Tyson's case to be a very popular example of one, that of alcohol, possible rape the infamous ear bite. Conformity in every sense to the aforementioned description).

Getty File Photo

So already, without considering what the tattoos themselves actually say, we can already deduce a fairly sizeable amount of information.

☐

' When I was out working at a casino, performing my regular set I had noticed that behind the ear of a young lady in her early 20's, was the name Uncle Bill with a smiley face. What you could see about the ink was that it had faded so it had been there for a few years. She was wearing her hair down at the time and when I asked the seemingly random question of 'Do you ever wear your hair up?' She answered that she never did, it is always down. This led me to draw conclusions about her personality and the personal meaning of the tattoo. She was quiet anyway but this led me to be able to deduce that she had lost a great father figure in her life and wanted always to remember him, this had really had an effect on her psychologically and led her to almost be quite socially awkward at times. She had never had a real relationship with her real father, if at all. I drew an inference that Bill was not the man in questions real name, as Benedict Cumberbatch's Sherlock might say, it was a shot in the dark but a good one. The smiley face was the clue here, that even though the tattoo was on her neck right across the vagus nerve, and the caratoid artery which would be very painful to say the least. The face stood out as the emblem that didn't really fit with the theme so I deduced, that this may be to do with the personality of Uncle Bill the practical joker, the man who always had a smile on his face and in turn could put smiles upon the faces of others'

You can see from just the information of observing her countenance and the tattoo but in particular, the placement of it you can glean a lot of information indeed!

TATTOO IDEOLOGY AND MEANINGS

There is always going to be the time where the tattoos don't necessarily mean anything to the person that wears them but can mean something in the way of information for you. The obvious ones will be first tattoos, drunken tattoos, tattoos that were done just for the beauty of the artwork itself. So, the question then becomes how do you differentiate the ones with poignancy to the ones without and the answers are this:

The Drunken tattoos: These will contain several major characteristics, in that attempts will be made to cover them up at all costs. Even to the degree of making the person in question quite cumbersome with the extra clothing materials they have to wear in order to cover them up. It will also most likely be the only one they have.

If they do have more than a single tattoo however, this leads on to another point of how to be aware of the tattoo that is the drunken mistake in amongst the ones that are already there. Nowadays with tattoo's being a major part of popular culture most establishments will not accept drunks in to the tattoo chair for fear of ramifications afterwards. Adding to that the fact that alcohol thins the blood so they would bleed more and the unconscious moving around of drunken stupor would destroy the quality of the work.

So then it would be the quality of the work itself that would stand out amongst the rest and wouldn't be difficult to spot at all. Coupled with the drunken state of the image itself will be something that is clearly a joke or will not fit at all with the rest of the aesthetic of the tattoos.

(Case and point)

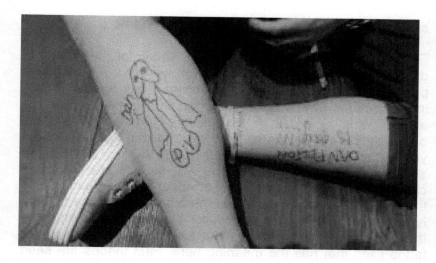

So since the only places that will accept drunks into their chairs will be back alley low budget type places, the anti-professionals so to speak. The quality of the work will reflect this, the colour and shading will have faded in places and look like a variety of shades when it is supposed to be the same and the outer lines of the design itself will be very shaky also. What this indicates then is personality traits and life experience. Partying to the point of drunken mistakes is always a clear personality indicator.

For example if there is a drunken tattoo on a lady that seems rather conservative and not the party type, this most likely points to recent trauma and 90% of the time is down to a break up. Where the woman has experienced much time of feeling oppressed and not like she can let loose, this is her letting loose. If she flashes shame on her face, if she catches you observing then this is a surefire reason in my mind. I would like to point out that to cover an explanation for every eventuality would be utterly impossible for one book, it becomes about feeling the moments and putting together enough of the clues you can see to detail a full deductive picture but we shall save this talk for later chapters.

First Tattoos: These are usually quite small, for men they are usually no bigger than 4-6 inches and women's are usually a pattern or some small repeating design. They appear on the inner forearms or just below the shoulder on men and on the ankles, wrist or small of the back on women. There will obviously be exceptions to this rule and that will depend on your niche preferences/likes/dislikes/hobbies which can successfully be deduced but you will have to see the other chapters for that information to combine with, to lead you to the answer. Anyway...These are the tattoos where the artwork has no particular meaning save for its being something that the person being inked likes the look of, however it is the tattoo itself that has the meaning here. First tattoos are seen on people from the ages of 18-25, and over 40's. The reasons are these; they are symbols of the transcendence into adulthood. They are beginning to step out from under the wings of the parents. Now I say over 40's but what I really mean is a group that is a collective of applied statistical research. The group of people it refers to is these:

- Men and women who have recently come out of long-term relationships/marriages.
- Men and women experiencing mid life crises.

The reasons are the same however and that is that it has been a long dream to get one done, and because they entered into a serious relationship where the partner was against the idea of them. A midlife crisis is essentially the same reason, the attempt to reclaim a part of their life that they feel has gone unrecognised and they wished to make it happen before it is essentially too late. These are the tattoos that mostly fall inside the barriers of just appreciating the artwork.

The symbolism of tattooing

The following are some of the major players in tattoo symbolism but of course anything can be tattooed on to the skin so it helps to have a good solid grounding in most contemporary symbols and pictures as well as some of the older ones as well.

Spirit guides: These have their historical routes in the Native American culture and the spirits of the totem. It was believed that the spirit guides came to them in dreams and were a metaphorical representation almost of themselves and their own qualities. You could in this sense liken these observations to Jung's archetypes. There are far too many to enumerate in this humble chapter so what will follow are the more popular ones and their meaning.

Hawk -⬜The majesty of a bird in flight mixed with power and directness of a bird of prey. They have been used in symbols of war as far back as ancient Rome and Greece, both Mars and Aries were depicted with both the hawk and eagle. It is representative of excellent vision in all the metaphorical sense, intellectual prowess. Someone who can easily overcome distractions and possesses high amounts of drive and determination.

Raven - Of course this is a tattoo seen mostly among fans of the work of Edgar Allen Poe for fairly obvious reasons, but the raven is also a symbol of mystery and intelligence. It is often associated with the darker side of literature and beliefs but the raven also stood as an ancient symbol of thought and of memory. It was said that the leader of the Norse gods, Odin, had ravens for both eyes and ears. In parts of Europe, though, the raven is a symbol of death. It was once believed, many centuries ago that if the raven flies away from the tower of London then England would fall.

Butterfly's - An insanely popular tattoo among women, due to the butterfly's short life span, is a reflection of impermanence and of the great transformative change. This change could be of a great number of things that I have detailed earlier. However, on the other side of this coin it has been known to have a contradictory symbolic meaning of materialism and the exploitation of their own femininity. To liken this to life it would be the way that the now beautiful butterfly travels from plant to plant seeking nectar. The reflection of butterflies with women and beauty can be seen as far back as ancient Crete and Mexico. They believed them to literally be the embodiment of beauty, and love and the spirits of the dead.

The following are no longer also spirit guides

Lions - lions have been recorded in texts all over the world and all most as far back as the history books actually go, places like the middles east, Africa and china and japan. The lion was most often seen as a symbol of royalty and regality, power and strength (Hercules was thought to have the strength of 10 lions and wore a cape made from lion skin). Every quality you would expect to go with the title 'King of the jungle', seen as a protector, the leader of the pack. Guardian lions were placed outside of the temples in china, and even statues of the lions were there to ward off evil. It is safe to say that anyone with a lion tattoo, particularly a large one will be a leader/protector of whichever pack they are in.

As we live in a deeply diverse culture I feel it very pertinent to mention some of the more religious tattoos, and so:

Buddha - A man who followed and preached about the four noble truths. All life is suffering, not nearly as bleak as it sounds but it reflects life's impermanence and everything moving on. All suffering is caused by attachments, everything from materialism to food. Suffering can be ended through the use of dispassion in the face of desire; Enlightenment being achieved through following the path. A religion of peace and being good to each other, you will see these qualities in the owner of such a tattoo. The same is said of tattoos of just Buddha's footprints. It reminds them that that their leader was a man like this, who walked the earth and still walks through their lives now.

There are a few less popular forms in which Buddhism appears in tattoos and this is the lotus flower, which is a symbol of purity and can be used in any colour except blue.

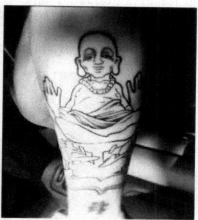

Christianity - For starters, approximately 20% of the American culture today have tattoos of a religious nature. This doesn't really contradict Leviticus 19:28 because at the time when the bible was supposedly written, there was no such word as tattoo and it came from a completely different part of the world. There are four of the most popular forms of tattoo in this sector and they are, crosses and will appear on everyone from military servicemen to the Latino culture and everywhere in between. This is literally a symbol of their spiritual connection, if it is seen by itself then I feel it fairly obvious to state the religious viewpoints of the owner, however to combine it with names and dates or other symbols could point in the direction of family ties and someone who is away a lot or someone who has died. Angels, which is a direct symbol of their relationship to their god. In that the angels were direct messengers of god. It can also be seen as a guidance symbol and is quite often found in the middle of a memorial piece. Doves, this became a powerful symbol of hope and peace thanks largely to the Noah tale, when the dove returned after being sent out to look for land with an olive branch. Praying hands (Note these are seen with rosaries frequently among the Latino culture) this is the original work of a German artist Albert Dührer, who believed his skill as artist was a gift from go., It, too, is most often seen as part of a memorial with Halo's and a name.

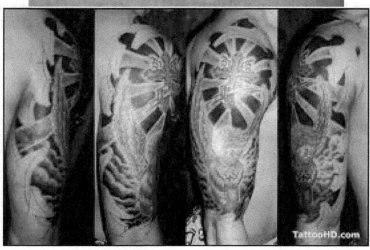

However, a close neighbour of some of the imagery seen here would be the Celtic cross. If you are either Scottish, Welsh or Irish then this cross will be seen as more of symbol of your heritage and national pride than of faith. Maybe even, in some instances Scandinavian, as during their initial art surgence, they often blended techniques. The cross' many internal Celtic knots and spirals reflect the complexity of life and the changing of the seasons.

The same could be said of this for nearly all religious based tattooing, everything from Hinduism to Judaism and more. The same inferences can be drawn if you see a six-pointed star or Shiva. It's about widening your knowledge base to contain the most possible and most useful information. Again what is contained within this humble chapter is only the most popular and I have a limit that I have to stick too!

Nautical Tattoo's - This is anything shrewdly associated with life at sea. Anchors, sailing ships, even mermaids. It has long been a symbol of service in the Marines or all Naval Careers. Highly closely identified with all sailors of the sea.

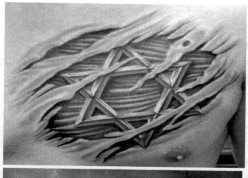

JUDAISTIC TATTOO

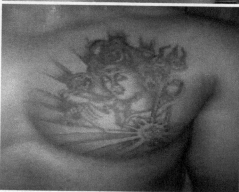

SIKHIST TATTOO

Decades ago many young sailors often got an anchor tattoo upon completing their first trip over the Atlantic Ocean. Particular to America, as far back as the civil war and right up to today, the forces have acquired specific tattooing marks for their services. The navy we have already mentioned. The army will have symbols of patriotism and the eagle mixed into a variety of patterns and styles. The Marines, traditionally the first people to hit the ground/beaches in times of war, so they have to carry all of their tags and equipment with them. They are infamous for having the fighting spirit of bulldogs and this will often appear in the designs of the tattoos they have, the bulldog very often wearing the given helmet. Even at the very least they will be adorned with the acronym for the United

States Marine Core. The U.S air force first started to appear with ink on them in the 50's and of course this would be a bird. It'd be silly not to. Right? But more specifically the bird of prey, the bald eagle, appearing in all manner of patriotic designs. It is representative of the pilot's dominion over the skies. With regard to the anchor and In relation to personality inferences, it can be that they are steadfast in the face of almost anything that comes their way. Strong and loyal and have the unique ability to be able to work well under pressure. The anchor cross however does have a slightly more religious twist to it, that tracks back through most of the ages. Romans, Greeks and Christians all held their own beliefs about it. It is an especially graphic depiction of religious belief, even more so when seen with fish and the palm. This is because it was deemed pagan and therefore forbidden. So if the owner of ones of these, then, they have an affinity to this way of thinking being true to their faith but acknowledging the forbidden histories behind it. Wise yet playful, and at times brash. The jolly roger symbol of the skull and cross bones, the common law symbol of the quote en quote pirate. What happens here is it is bought forward into the 21st century to show someone who doesn't enjoy rule following, huge amount of ego-centrism, creative, not afraid of concentration and could reside on both criminals and the artistic type.

A very popular tattoo amongst men pretty much exclusively, is that of the dragon. The mythology surrounding this fantastical beast is vast and a joy to read. They were seen as deities that would roam around the thunder clouds and each culture had their own beliefs based on the dragon lore, everyone from the Chinese to the Japanese and even as close to my home the welsh. The dragon appears on their national flag. In Chinese astrology if you were born under the year of the dragon then you were seen to be a leader, however, a bit of a bossy and domineering one, at that. A dragon tattoo is a symbol of nobility, the power of transformation, perseverance, loyalty and power. For those who have the tattoos of vanquished dragons it is a literal representation of all the human qualities needed to do such a thing, bravery, calm under pressure, leadership and strength. St George slayed the dragon and he is a treasured symbol of English pride.

Worthy of noting, is the growing popularity of the tattoo's relating to pin up girls. Pin up girls like Dita Von Teese, Sabina Kelly and the like. This is a nostalgic tattoo that has its routes in the era of the 40's and 50's in terms of style and flair. When found on a man it is often indicative of a chauvinistic nature, dog lovers, real working class men brand of personality. However, when found on women it is an entirely different kettle of fish. It is a symbol of strength and independence through femininity. Typical of women who know they are beautiful and, or at the very least know the power a beautiful women, can have over the pack of men who deem themselves masters of all they purvey. An interesting common denominator here is that the women with these tattoos will have jobs or hobbies that require a physical skill set and will be very independent in their nature. I've found these on women who do everything from burlesque dancing to wrestling.

www.Tattoospedia.com

Growing in popularity with reference to memorial pieces are tattoos of times and time pieces. The age of the watch will relate to the person in question i.e. pocketwatch-grandparent or someone of equal age. The surrounding accompaniments in the tattoo will indicate the sex of the person. If there are no accompaniments then it is more than likely a male. If the date doesn't feature as part of the piece then this will mostly be the actual time itself, for example if the clock shows 3:15 as in 15 minutes past 3, this is a symbol of the 15th day of the 3rd month.

Crime tattoos

Considering the history of tattooing and how a large part of their relevance to sociological interpretation has been to do with its back story with the criminal human, I feel it would be a great mistake on my part, if I didn't set you on your way to be being attuned to the symbology of the tattoos in circulation of the criminal system nowadays. They can be shown to depict individual gangs to which they belong, skills and specialties, as well as their own convictions. Some are even rife with a hidden code. However as they are often too complex for their own good, they are very rarely recognized or even interpreted.

British Crime tattoo's - ACAB is a very popular acronym that is found tattooed upon many who have been through the British legal system. It is thought to have meant either Always Carry a Bible or All Coppers Are Bastards. It is found between the knuckle and first joint of each finger. In some cases it is replaced by symbolic dots without the accompanying letters. Many homemade tattoos have been thought to be associated with the UK prison system as well but this has been proven to be just that, the case of it being homemade with a needle, a piece of cotton and some Indian ink.

The youth culture of Britain nowadays have adopted many of the tattoos from the old school criminal system to denote their tough exterior and the gangs to which they belong. Which is demonstrative of their willingness to go to jail for their respective gangs and beliefs.

Japanese Crime Tattoo's - Full body tattoo's or body suits as they are more commonly known are the most popular tattoo symbol to emerge from Japan, thanks largely to the visibility of them in popular action cinema. They are worn commonly by the Japanese Yakuza and are more commonly known as Irezumi. The bigger and more elaborate the piece the more the owner could show his affiliation with the cause, and his power through being able to sit through the pain. It was around 600 AD when tattooing began to be associated with the negative in Japan. It was a way to formally identify criminals to the rest of the world. Between the end of the 19th century and the start of the 20th Japan outlawed tattooing, specifically the Irezumi marks, to try and improve the worldwide opinion of themselves. It was legalized again in 1945 but retained its association with criminality, so much so that some of the bath houses and steam rooms will ban anyone with tattoos.

Middle eastern marks - There has only been one marking that I have come across that is specifically associated with the underbelly of crime in this part of the world and that is a tattoo of a raised arm holding a machine gun with Arabic writing underneath. Said to be associated with Hezbollah although their religion, Islam outlaws tattoos.

Russian Ink marks - The Russian criminal tattoo symbol system can be read to give quite a detailed description about the wearer of the ink. Both placement and the symbol itself

308

have a very specific meaning here. Gangland initiation tattoos more often than not feature a rose emblazoned on the chest closely linked to the Russian mafia. The ink specifically has a bluish grey tinge to it. Grins are tattooed on to the people who are deemed to require punishments even within the criminal society. Either grins or blatant and often graphic sexual imagery.

North American tattoos of crime - A triangular collection of three dots is seen on American criminals as well as Hispanic and Vietnamese criminals. With this though, in particular the Hispanic criminals will couple the dots collection with the Pachuco cross standing for Mi Vida Loca (my crazy life). A teardrop tattoo indicates that the wearer has killed, or that a friend of his was killed in prison. Shamrocks and the number 12 is closely linked to white supremacy and the Aryan Brotherhood, 1 standing for A and 2 standing for B, the initials of the Aryan brotherhood. The Aryan circle, a different white supremacy gang, use 13 as their symbol in tattooing and rather unimaginatively for the same reasons that the Aryan Brotherhood use 12.

However a number 13 on a Mexican person is gang related to the Mara Salvatrucha gang. The Mexican mafia use a simple MM and sometimes a black hand. The Ace of Spades as a tattoo symbol for gangs was adopted by the Asian boyz gang. It has transpired over time to be an 'A' in the middle of a spade. The A standing for Asian and the spade symbolizing thievery.

There are a slew of other symbols associated with crime and the things that go on within the criminal system worldwide. They are:

Spades: As in the playing card suit. This is the suit of thieves and is commonly seen upside down.

Diamonds: Again the playing card suit but within this context is known as the chummy suit. This is forcibly applied when people are discovered to be informants.

Hearts: The playing card suit again. The wearer of this inside a prison setting is showing to the rest of the world that he is a passive homosexual.

• A cross on the chest signifies the highest possible rank in their respective gang. It is known as the symbol for the 'the prince of thieves'. Snakes and tigers are also awarded to high ranking gang members, given for their reflective skills. Tigers being the enforcers, so to speak, and snakes being very devious and slippery. Continuing along the animal theme, a rare, but sometimes seen, tattoo is that, that have a feline nature. I feel it redundant to mention but for the sake of completeness I shall do all the same. This is representative of all those qualities needed to be a criminal, hence the title of cat burglar.

• Symbols of eyes are forcibly placed on the lower backside to indicate that this person can be used for sexual gratification.

• Barbed wire on the forehead indicates a literal meaning to life in prison, as in they will be the people who leave prison in a box.

• When a swastika is seen on the forehead of someone and it doesn't look stylized at all, and the artwork is terrible, then this is a symbol of someone who has been marked for death.

• When stars are seen as tattoos in the prison industry it is indicative of time spent inside each star represents 1 year. Churches are a very close neighbour here but for Christian prisoners, the number of towers indicate the number of years spent in jail.

Now that you have successfully topped up your knowledge of what it is to decipher the symbolism of tattoos, I propose a little game. What will follow is a short run of photos, nothing too strenuous. They will be accompanied with questions though. Unavoidable clues will reside in the questions but we are here to observe and deduce and this is part of the process.

- A fairly easy one to start if you're of British Decent. What can you tell me about this man's relationship with his mother? Solely based on this picture here.

- Answer - This man is showing a devotion and passion to his mother whom he is very, very close to. She had just survived breast cancer going through a full course of treatment and coming through on the other side. A devoted family man anyway though this scare would have bought him that much closer to his mother as the fear of loss will do this.

A slightly more challenging run now...

-Can you approximate the age of the wearer? -Describe her granddad?

Answer - The skin seems to be smooth, toned and unblemished. Most likely then it belongs to a young lady, not that this can't appear on an elder woman but the more likely is that it belongs to a younger lady. The photo is treated with the very popular social media Photo modification site Instagram. Most frequent users of this, who are female, are between the ages of 17-24. The middle of this being 20/21, which this person is, 20.

Which would make her granddad statistically most likely (given the average ages that people procreate) to be in his late 70's-early 80's. A very close relationship to the granddad is apparent here, given the size and placement it would almost be in the replacement of a father figure. The love is evident in the flowers. The overriding theme is the naval element, so given the granddads age, the most likely events for the navy to have been involved in would be around Korea and Vietnam.

All of which, is completely true, and can be seen just from this photo alone. And finally...

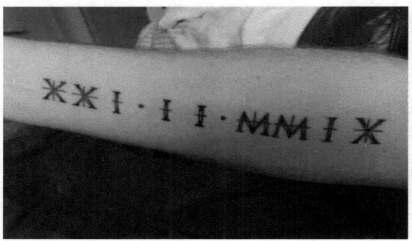

Tell me something about this person. The only thing I will tell you is he is English

Possible answers:

• Given that the tattoo is in Roman Numerals, means two things. One, that the date it translates to is a hugely important one. Secondly, combined with the placement and the fact that many important arteries and veins run down there, it is most likely either the date of birth of a child or a wedding date.

• The man has a fairly deep knowledge of Histories/wars and

feels national pride quite deeply. This is again due to the numerals. The owner would have to know them to change the numbers into the numerals. Given the popularity of Google this wouldn't be hard information to source but to commit to them in a tattoo shows an appeal of some kind. When dealing with possible items of weddings or children, the most likely age of the wearer is mid 20's. So a mid 20's English male, placement of tattoo in to consideration. Mixing the ideas of Roman and strength, gives them their great war skills, which isn't a big leap to infer a deep knowledge of histories in this field and given that we are in the 21st century that national pride is a given.

• He would be a football fan, given the masculine characteristics already gone. When I replied to this challenge I found that all the information I had deduced was correct! I had it confirmed that it was the date he got married which in turn told me a lot more about him, but I had no need to continue.

There are very few ways that can cause a tattoo to fade. In my studies, I have only discovered three. They are; that the tattoo has been out in the sun excessively. When the UV rays from the sun hit your skin they have tendency to bleach it, which is why our hair goes paler than normal and we often get a suntan, but this can consequently have an effect on the colour of the tattoo itself. The only thing you need to do, to look after it for as long as possible, would be to apply strong sun cream and regularly too, though this in itself can allow information to be deduced from it. We will cover tans and tan lines in a later chapter in great detail though. Water in general can affect the colouring in a recent tattoo. There are obviously many types of germs and bacteria that reside in any lakes that you swim in, but swimming pools and hot tubs and places that carry water with chlorine in can bleach out the colour of your tattoo, as they are chemicals that are in the pool designed to keep it clean. The same can be said of swimming in the sea, but the salt in the sea can dry your skin very quickly which can be detrimental to the colour in your tattoo if not allowed time to heal properly. I don't count the next thing as part of the list as it has an effect on all parts of the framework of the tattoo and is for want of a better word, unavoidable.

That is getting older. As you get older your skin ages also and thus can lose its collagen. Leaving the layers of the dermis in which the ink resides open to change. The final element is the quality of the tattoo artist who is doing the tattoo, we discussed shoddy workmanship in tattooing earlier in the chapter but this is another general pitfall of the amateur. As previously stated, the tattoo ink goes down into the dermis which is the second layer of skin (side note - we humans have 3 layers of skin) the reason is so that when we flake off dead skin cells from the top layer it will not affect the ink in the dermis. If the tattoo artist has not sent the ink down far enough then this will have an effect on the health of the tattoo itself.

So as you can see from something as small as a tattoo, it opens up a wealth of information for you to read! Combined with a few other smaller details you can deduce the impossible! Practice, practice, practise!

TOP 5 MOST POPULAR MASONIC TATTOOS

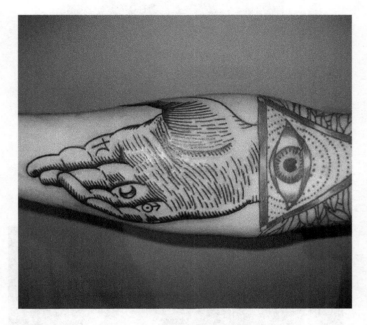

● Representative of the alchemy hand or the hand of mysteries is symbolic of the transformation of man into god!

● Forearm tattoos of this nature are designed to show some of the masonic symbolism, but designed to be only mysterious and leave the viewer of the piece searching for hidden meaning other than Freemasonry

• Skulls are not specific to Freemason imagery, however you will only see them contrasted between fiery orange and grey.

• Masonic tattoos of this nature are renowned for the design by geometry. One of the most popular symbols in freemasonry is of the compass and the square, also rumoured to be symbols of masculinity and femininity. Other fundamentalists have other theories on what they mean but the official freemason word is that they are mere tools

● Freemasonry often depicts the virgin interceding on behalf of god. Christianity has been linked to Freemasonry for centuries though nothing conclusive has arisen.

TOP 5 BIKER GANG TATTOOS

I have purposely not included images of people with the actual tattoos. This is because a lot of members extrapolate the imagery and use it in art so this is to give you the full sense of the image to store in your collective palaces.

GANGS FROM THE U.S.A

• Founded in Colorado and has spread throughout the states and now in parts of Europe and Germany. Their motto *'Donec Mors Non Seperat.'* It's Latin for 'Until Death Separates Us.'

● Started in Matilda's bar on Route 66 in 1935 it's one of the oldest biker gangs in existence. They use the imagery from the Marlon Brando film 'The Wild One' as their insignia and are now throughout the United States and parts of Asia and Australia.

Pagans

• Formed in Maryland in 1959, and has expanded rapidly from 1965. The imagery depicts the Norse sun god Surtr, wielding a sword with pagans written in Red, White and Blue. They also cut off their denim shorts and jackets to sport white supremacy markings. They are also accompanied with tattoo marks of the acronym A.R.G.O (Ar go fuck yourself) and the colloquialism NUNYA (Nun'ya fucking business)

• Also known as the Mongol Nation or The Mongol Brotherhood. It was formed in 1969, in California, from Hispanic bikers who were refused entry into the Hells Angels. Mostly in eastern America but has also spread to Canada, Mexico and Italy.

- Probably the most infamous gang in history, though information about their origin is unclear due to the Angels policy on secrecy. Their logo is the deathshead taken exactly from the 85th fighter squadron. It is believed that they are the most recognized, due to their infamous run ins with many other gangs over the years. The most notable of which was during the Altamont Free concert in 1969. It was also alleged that the rolling stones used Hells Angels' members as body guards.

GANGS IN THE U.K☐These are often chapters of Biker gangs that have originated in other countries and most likely the U.S. We have listed the most popular here and in the previous section based upon the gang's involvement in crime. The Hells Angels and Outlaws are in the U.K. These gangs are also sworn enemies. The Mongols is also another gang that has opened chapters in Britain as well. A point worthy of note is that there are many gangs not affiliated with crime at all, in any way. Though these gangs are a little light on tradition and codes because of it and as such will not bear any tattoo markings.

• The Vagos gang. An ally of the Outlaws biker gang and their symbol is the Norse god of mischief Loki riding a motorcycle.

• Most notable for Drugs and gun trafficking. According to Europol they are in the U.K but as yet do not know what they are up to. Seen on the next page

MILITARY TATTOOING! FROM THE U.S.A TO BEGIN WITH

• The Navy. The acronym is obvious and the navy tattoos follow major themes, anchors, ships and the like. Some of the lesser known is pin ups in nautical garb and roosters! The bird was thought to be a motif that protected the sailors from drowning.

• The Army. Again, the themes chop and change depending on the person who has it tattooed on them. Eagles are representative of the freedom they feel. The flag, unit patches, medals and dog tags which also feature in memorial versions for their buddies who have died in war. The meat tag is a permanent dog tag tattoo and is often inked on to them before deployment.

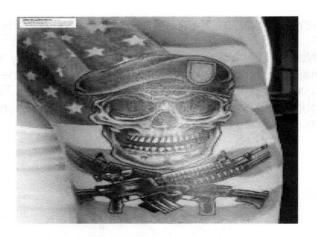

• The Marine Core. Again the acronym is obvious here and its themes to be aware of. The Bulldog is by far and away the most popular image of the marine core. It is often combined with either the marine core seal or a unit patch.

- The Air force contains images of the eagle and a mixture of wings with the American flag. These come in all shapes and sizes.

The U.K

The army itself has no particular tattooing motifs or themes but, there is a policy in place regarding the current tattoos on the person applying, and that is that they cannot be visible. The RAF and Navy share this outlook.

TO TRULY FINISH

Break up tattoos and family/loved ones, in tattooing are often completely idiosyncratic. To show you a top 5 here would be far too sparse a topic and we could not really qualify such a statement as that. However, they are considerably easy to spot as the one aspect they all share is, it will not be just a name on its own as this can appear plain and inartistic. Look for love hearts, dates and times, portraits, nicknames. Then the souring of the relationship can be seen in cover ups and oddities of placement, but other than that it will be quite clear and apparent what is happening or has happened as again tattoos of this nature that aren't cover ups do share a commonality in that they are not subtle.

Take the following example below. Deemed hateful or obscene, these are such as racist, anti-religion or belief, crude, homophobic, obviously sexist, drug- related or of an excessive political nature.

Other such affinities to be aware of and to store in your palace for use are, the popular team names and logos and nicknames of teams. This is also a very popular one. For example would you know what football team in the U.K this person swears allegiance to?

330

Band logos and album titles are also a popular choice as well, but the best thing to do would be to leave that your own research as these are niche market devices and we have begun with only the most popular. Have fun!

NOT JUST THE ENGINEER'S THUMB

"Beyond the obvious facts that he has at some time done manual labour, that he takes snuff, that he is a Freemason, that he has been in China, and that he has done a considerable amount of writing lately, I can deduce nothing else."

SHERLOCK HOLMES - THE RED HEADED LEAGUE 1891

One of the salient points that I could give from this book would be that whatever the item that goes with the person, it will leave clues to deduce its original meaning. It would be the hands that cover this point from beginning to end. They are quite literally everyone's vessels for doing everything; they open the doors we need to go through, hold the pens that we need to write with, help us to drive and the deaf to converse. They are everything we need to use for an easy and fulfilling life. In this chapter we will learn the ins and outs of reading hands and all the necessary information you will need, to make each deduction successful and accurate. As well as learning how to read skin conditions, hobbies and jobs, there will be a plethora of other deductive resources to pull. Now let me point out that you can use this for ethereal reasons, such as a more scientific approach to palm reading but let us be crystal clear when we say that is not our aim in divulging this information for you. It is a matter of hard reasoning that will lead you down your successfully deductive path.

REALLY GET UNDER THEIR SKIN

Whether it is dry, coarse, hard or oily the skin will always leave the signs. Each will be indicative of the kind of life a person leads. Let's take some other common conditions of the skin and examine them more closely:

TREMBLING OR SHAKING

This refers to a trembling or shaking all by themselves though most of our hands shake to some degree. But if the tremble is more than slight it could mean they are suffering from what is known as an 'essential tremor', a neurological disorder that tends to run in families. It could also be a sign of Parkinson's disease, which also affects the nervous system, or an over-active thyroid. Anxiety and stress can also cause hands to shake, as can drinking strong coffee and too much alcohol.

SWEATY/CLAMMY

Hot sweaty palms can be a sign of stress or an overactive thyroid, which tends to speed up your metabolism meaning you burn more calories and generate more heat. It can also be a symptom of hyperhidrosis, a condition otherwise known as excess sweating, which tends to run in families. Too much alcohol and stress can also make hands sweat. Typically though as emotions have a physiological response, clammy hands can point to someone who is experiencing an onset of nervousness. Permanence to clammy hands can indicate someone who spends their days in a particularly anxious state of mind. Someone who is really in touch with their emotions, not necessarily fear or nerves bare in mind.

COLOURED PALMS

One of the classic signs of liver damage in particular with people over 50 is a reddening of the palms. Called palmar erythema, this reddening usually affects the outer edge of the palms in a band from the wrist to the little finger. To modern medicine the cause remains unknown but the reddening is thought to be due to blood vessels dilating as a result of a change in the hormone balance caused by liver disease. Red palms can also be a sign of rheumatoid arthritis caused by the inflammation that is a major factor in the disease.

White, red or blue fingers

What it means when fingers that turn white, blue and then red with pins and needles and numbness is a sign of Raynaud's disease, a condition in which blood flow to the fingers is restricted. The exact cause is unknown but it often runs in families. It can also be associated with rheumatic conditions such as scleroderma, rheumatoid arthritis or systemic lupus erythematosus (SLE).

DRY

Now dermatologically speaking dry skin is dehydrated skin. This can translate to the body's water levels being low, which can mean a poor diet, in terms of not enough food at all being eaten or recent illness involving a lot of vomiting sessions. The other more dermatological analysis to be found here is an excessive amount of cleaning solvents being used on the skin. Mostly powdered bleaches or cleaning sprays. If their hands get to the point that they are so dry they become visibly cracked then this means that there is no obvious repairing regime which means no creams being applied as part of treatment or a nighttime regime or gloves being worn in their job. If it gets really bad then this points to a sign of an overactive thyroid gland, or in women when oestrogen levels drop below normal.

This type of skin also has parallels in other adjectives that could be used to describe it. They are coarse and hard. This points to someone who is physically minded and quite active on a day-to-day basis. The only way skin can become that hard is through physical exercises and repeated exposure at that. Contact with hard/rough materials will leave the tell-tale calluses and hard patches with which to gain a better idea of their reason. Bricklayers grab bricks in the same way builders grab their shovels and wheelbarrows. The handy thing with physically deductive marks is that they collect on the palms, just in different areas depending on what they are being used for. So what you need to do here is to compare what you see on their hand with the implements you have filed away in your memory palace. This means that you will need to make yourself aware of what is used in each manual labour job and how. A valuable deductive resource however you split it. In short the skin in particular on the hand will react to whatever it is subject to most often. Typically then with dry, coarse, hard skin these are byproducts of continual manual labour of some description, you will be able to further narrow these down with other deductions you make about the hypothetical person in question. One common profiling factor of the physical nature of the person is that it seeps over into parts of their personality in that they can be quite black and white with their opinions, as well as quite honest and forthcoming, really straightforward and to the point. This isn't a blanket term for everyone in this category but will apply to 90% of the people involved.

SMOOTH CRIMINALS

Not criminals per se just more of a catchy sub heading to explain the many traits of people with smooth skin. Not smooth as in hairless, but smooth as in what it would feel like to the touch. So this can also mean people who look after their hands with moisturizer and other such creams.

As you may have already deduced, people who have smoother skin to the touch are quite the opposite of the dry, coarse people. This is down to the obvious point that what they subject their hands to on a daily basis is nowhere
near as rough, and the balance of probability would state that it would therefore mean they spend a large amount of their time inside.

So conversely then this will mean that these people are much more people orientated as opposed to object orientated in their day today lives, people who work in offices and telesales, behind the counters of shops and in schools. A common profiling factor here is that smooth skinned people are the more sensitive creatures, however this doesn't refer to sensitivity in the terms of being incredibly in touch with your emotions.it is more the kind of people who would walk into a room and be aware that an argument had happened moments before, more aware of emotional shifts in other people (a salesman trait). Pale and smooth skin often eludes to the people who shy away from not just confrontation but people in general, shown in their skin as they like to hide away as much as possible. This has inferences that can be drawn about their personality clearly as anyone who shies away from people in general will be loners with passions in niche market ideals. If they have a stressful, people orientated job they will hate it and spend a lot of time day dreaming about other things and job-hunting in their preferred areas.

As previously stated, the smoothness of someone's skin can be a cause of their moisturizing regime. Now if this is someone who has dry skin or a need to look after the skin in general then this will show in the visibility of the ridges of the skin. Yes it will still feel smooth, but the 'wrinkles' will be more apparent, particularly prevalent in women over 40. This is a result from care trying to be taken of, hands that are prone to solvent and cleaning product exposure .which creates dry skin when left untreated or someone who just has a dry skin condition on their hands. A woman dressed in pantsuit and wearing 18k gold jewellery, will most likely not be a cleaner and will therefore have the skin condition. In many of these instances there will be residue of it on any rings worn on the fingers. It can be rubbed into the skin but is increasingly difficult with jewelry and just tends to leave streak marks, so keep your eyes open for this.

Now with men it can be a little more apparent as it'll be done to a more considerable degree. With men looking after their skin who have been working on say a construction site for example, it would be tantamount to social suicide. It is not for these wolf like pack animals to break out their Nivea cream in front of everyone, so they will instead swap it for something more industrial based and often have cleaning grains in the mixture. It has a distinct chemical smell like most laboratories have. The most popular brand in the UK is Swarfega, which will do for the men in this group. What this leaves is a handshake where you can feel the roughness of the skin, ridges in the palm as they have taken considerable wear thanks to the job but the skin will feel comparatively smoother. Now with the men who would use the Nivea this would be part of a much larger regiment of personal hygiene. Nails will be professionally managed (we will move on to the details on nails shortly) and clean, possibly even some fake tan as well as the moisturizing. This is most prevalent in Wall Street and international businessmen, or men who work with or managing a hell of a lot of money (This way it is the money and the possessions that became the symbol of their masculinity and indeed narcissism and will put the self-preening routine down to merely wanting to look good.)

In short, when regarding the skin on one's hands, it would be the smoother and more supple it is the less physical their day to day lives and then the opposite would apply to people with the coarse and hard skin. Touching briefly on handshakes for a moment (and this is very briefly.) When someone has a job of a physical nature and has done it for many years (10+) having to use a lot of strength on a daily basis for at least 7 hours at a time will result in a handshake that is effortlessly strong. This is because the body will have become used to exerting itself in such a way for so long that there will now be a latent energy in reserve that comes out naturally. This can be felt with ease, if your handshake is receptive to that of others.

NAILS

Though many people go through the time and the effort to have manicures and French tips, as well as all manner of polish and decorative nonsense, they can often miss some of the signs that can be read in to someone's health. For example large pale white patches on the nail can be a symptom of Anaemia. The low iron count in the blood thanks to Anaemia means enough oxygen doesn't get to the skin and tissues causing them to become pale, particularly inside that of the nail. In the more serious cases, for example if you see or hear someone comment on them growing then it can be a sign of the early stages of liver disease or diabetes.

Dark patches or vertical lines of a very dark colour on the nail are often mistaken for a dead nail that happens after trauma such as getting it caught in a door. However when nothing like that has happened these are most likely moles which many people consider not to be able to happen on the skin and can be an early sign of melanoma. Depressions and small cracks in your nails are known as "pitting" of the nail bed and are often associated with psoriasis, an inflammatory disease that leads to scaly or red patches all over the body. Individuals who suffer from psoriasis develop clusters of cells along the nail bed that accumulate and disrupt the linear, smooth growth of a normal nail.

Breaking a nail can be a pain in the neck for many a woman, but if your tips seem to crack at the slightest touch, it could mean your thyroid is amiss. This gland in your neck regulates metabolism, energy, and growth, and too little thyroid hormone often leads to hair loss, brittle and thin nails, and nails which grow slowly. Thyroid disorder also manifests itself by causing your nail plate to separate from the nail bed in a noticeable way. Lifted nails are thought to occur because the increase in thyroid hormone can accelerate cell turnover and separate the nail from its natural linear growth pattern. Stripes on your nails are only a good thing if they are painted on. Horizontal white lines that span the entire nail, are paired, and appear on more than one nail are called Muehrcke's lines. These could be an indication of kidney disease, liver abnormalities, or a lack of protein and other nutrients. A blue face is a clear indication that someone is suffering from a mild case of death or (and more likely) someone's lacking airflow, and blue nails mean the same thing—you're not getting enough oxygen to your fingertips. This could be caused by respiratory disease or a vascular problem called Raynaud's Disease, which is a rare disorder of the blood vessels. It could be just that someone has poor circulation, however if they were persistently blue then it would be wise to have them checked.

Persistent biters and pickers will reveal themselves from the uneven nail and sometimes-jagged tip as well as the broken skin at the side of the nail from where they have continued. Now, most people liken this to someone of a nervous disposition. This can only be inferred from context of seeing it in action. It may just be that they have a bad habit. The visible marks on the fingers are quite the same. If you see someone biting, one leg is tapping and they are sat outside an office waiting to go inside then you can make a reliable observation on the nerves however if you view it when they are sat on a sofa relaxing or reading, no tension in the facial muscles and sat in a comfy position then this points toward the habit side of the spectrum.

With manicure and the other glittery adornments that can be applied it is the only the designs that can have inferences to be drawn into the personality. Firstly though, with men, unless they are dabbling with cross dressing or the Drag lifestyle then any work that is done to the nails will be strictly in a 'Mani' style. So this will be things like filed and buffed nails for a smooth and natural shine finish. As seen in the next photo.

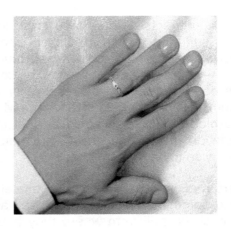

Women however will change nail style and colour depending on mood or preference, however they all follow that same personality guideline. The more outlandish and gregarious the style and design of the nail then the more this will reflect the persons personality. The more studious and subtle the design (freshly manicured, French tips) the more this reflects their personality in less obvious ways. The quieter ones and even the people who want to show the length of time they put in to the way they look for their job.

Conversely from here, any here dirt under the nails is suggestive of two things, either, recently finishing a manual labour task or poor personal hygiene. This applies when the dirt under the nails is dark. An accurate way to differentiate between the two is to look at the length of the nails. If they are short and the stuff still gets under there, then this is down to manual labour work and if they are longer, and not looked after and filled with dirt then this is a hygiene concern. Reflected in the fact that nails that are kept short, are done for reasons and would make the person aware of them. Which suggests maintenance so any dirt would likely be cleaned away, hence the recently finishing of manual labour. If the stuff under the nails is of a more sprightly colour, then this is indicative of someone who has been picking at something. It is not enough to say what that would be, based on the colour alone, but evidently it would be something that isn't man made and would therefore need to be picked at. The most likely cause is picking at old nail polish. To further help you narrow this particular observation down it would be nigh on impossible to pick a nail clean so there will be remains of the same colour on there.

SKIN AFFLICTIONS

In many cases, particularly deductive ones, it is wise to have a healthy knowledge of medical illness. This allows you to know more about the person through understanding how the illnesses they have can develop. This approach is quite 'Joseph Bell' in nature. As such, the following is a list of the most commonplace skin conditions of the hands and the reasons behind their appearance.

WARTS - They are basically flesh coloured lumps that appear, predominantly, on the finger tips. They are caused by infection with the human papilloma virus (HPV), which can be passed on through skin-to-skin contact and sometimes through surfaces such as floors and towels. If you have a wart, you can spread it to other people through close contact. You can also spread it to other parts of your own body. They are largely an hereditary condition but due to the fact that they can spread to all regions of the body, if they are not on the extremities i.e. hands or feet then they have been caught from someone else. If they are on someone that has them on their hands then the other areas that they have them will tell you where they touch the most.

IMPETIGO - Impetigo is an infection in the skin. Small blisters appear and burst, leaving yellow, moist, itchy patches that dry to a crust. The skin underneath can be red and inflamed. It is caused by bacteria that enter the skin through a cut, scratch or damage from an existing skin condition, such as eczema. Impetigo can be spread by direct contact and sharing towels or bedding with someone who has it. Not cold sores but the more extreme version, Impetigo, is developed in people who aren't particular about the hygiene of hands which is why it is more common amongst children.

PSORIASIS - Psoriasis causes flaky, red patches on the skin. They can look shiny and cause itching or burning. They can be anywhere, but are more common on elbows, knees and the lower back. Some of the body's antibodies attack skin cells by mistake, causing them to reproduce too quickly and build up on the skin. Certain things may make symptoms worse, including alcohol, smoking and some medicines, such as anti-inflammatories (for example, ibuprofen) and beta-blockers (used to treat heart problems). It is not passed on through close contact. Hereditary by nature though so isn't common to a specific person.

RINGWORM - Most common in children but can affect anyone. It is particular to the nails on hands but does show up in other parts of the body too. Ringworm is not a worm, but a number of fungal infections that grow in a patch or circle on the skin. It can be a few millimetres to a few centimetres across. The patches or circles look red or silvery and can blister and ooze. Fungal spores enter the skin through a break, such as a scratch or a patch of eczema. Ringworm can be passed on through direct contact and sharing items such as towels, bedding or combs. It can also be passed on from the floor of shower or swimming pool areas. Pets can pass it to people, the most common pets to do so being the household cat and dog. This again comes down to a cleanliness issue.

,

VITILIGO - Apparently the condition Michael Jackson was afflicted with. Vitiligo causes pale white patches on the skin. These patches can occur anywhere, but are more noticeable on areas that are exposed to sunlight, such as the face and hands, (apparently the reason the king of pop wore sellotape around his fingertips a lot), and on dark or tanned skin. On the scalp, Vitiligo can cause hair to turn white. Patches can be small or large, stay the same size, or grow. Vitiligo cannot be passed on through close contact. Any other form of hand-based malady such as scratches, callouses and burns are subject to context driven analysis of the person as well. Placement and further knowledge about the person combined with what you have filed away in your palace will guide you here.

For example hardened knuckles on the fist particularly around the bottom three knuckles (little, ring, and middle finger) would indicate someone trained in the art of Wing Chun as that is the area of the fist they are taught to hit with. Whereas any other marks on the knuckles that are not hardened and conform to no particular pattern suggest fisticuffs. Some press-up styles are done on the knuckles of the fist but these differ because you can see that the skin will have been rubbed away excessively much like a burn would do. Scratches to the hands would be consistent with a physical altercation of some kind but this could be with a tabletop and not necessarily another person. The way to differentiate between the animate and the inanimate is in the sheer volume of scratch marks that you see.

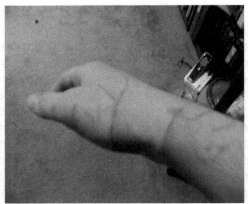

Volume of scratches points in the direction of the animate, the fact that each scratch is long and thin suggests a feline scratch. Were they in the same volume but short and thick it would have pointed to a dog and short, thick and accompanied by a bruise or two would suggest an altercation.

Hardening to the fingertips on one hand indicates a guitar player. If the hardening is on the left side then they are right handed and vice versa. If they are quite fresh then it will only indicate the recency with which the hobby has been taken up. A bass player has the hardening more on the finger pads than the tips. A violinist will endure diagonal lined callouses on predominantly the first 3 fingers, the little finger will be less apparent. The hands of a pianist have been synonymous for many years to be long and slender in the fingers and move with the fluidity of water and the precision of an eagle. For drummers there is the following photo to be aware of.

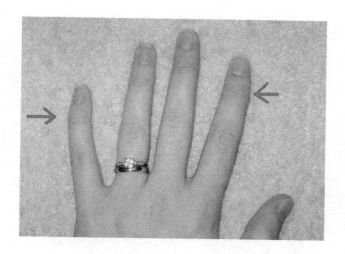

The first finger is prone to bruising and crookedness through heavy use of bass notes on the toms when drumming. The little finger is also prone to crookedness and scratching/indents all along the full side thanks to misfires shots to the tom and any part of the full side could and indeed does hit the metal rim of the drum. Golfers suffer from trigger finger which is where the thumb of their dominant golfing hand can become locked in a bent position. Also golfers have particularly strong thumbs and thumb pads.

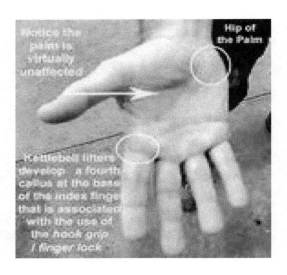

The photo above shows common tennis marks but could show signs of hammer work as well.

FINGERTIPS

There has been much research done into the analysis of fingerprints over the past century in forensic science. Dermatoglyphics, as it is more commonly known, is the process of studying the skin ridges and indeed the fingerprints. It is widely known that each person's fingerprints have their own individuality to express, which is how people are tracked down from crime scenes.

However people have recently inferred (in particular in the alternative fields) that there are personality inferences to be derived and throughout our study we have no evidence to substantially support these claims. It appears to us to be on the same level and standard as cold reading. Personality reading stock lines drawn from an arbitrary source, it could just as soon be parrot feathers as fingerprints. So what we will leave you here with, is the ability to recognise and spot the

346

differences in fingerprints by sight alone and for the sake of completeness the personality inferences too, for the reason that it will always do well for the performer to have a cushion to fall back on.

Learn to recognize each type of pattern. Each pattern is associated with a basic meaning. In order of commonality, the patterns are:

- Common loop (opens toward thumb) - go with the flow, like to fit in

- Radial loop (opens away from thumb) - put others before themselves

- Arch - practical, cautious, stubborn, traditional values

- Whorl - focused, independent, secretive

- Composite (two loops facing opposite directions) - difficulty making decisions, open to other viewpoints

- Tented arch (peak looks like a spike) - sensitive, impulsive nature, excitable

Read the meaning of the print type on individual digits. Not every pattern has specific meaning as some types are rarely found on certain digits.

- **Index finger** - how a person thinks about himself.

  ○ Whorl - very independent with a high preference to work alone

  ○ Arch - cautious and stubborn with dislike of change

  ○ Radial loop - very friendly people person who struggles to say no

- ○ Composite - uncertain what they want, have problems making decisions

- ○ Tented arch - intensive over-the-top personality

- **Middle finger** - how a person thinks about work and values

- ○ Whorl - original values who disregards conventional thinking

- ○ Arch - pragmatic, old-fashioned values

- ○ Radial loop - easily adaptable to other cultures and careers

- Ring finger - how a person expresses himself

- ○ Whorl - high interest in fashion, music and art

- ○ Arch - high interest in classic, physical expressions of beauty (i.e. architecture)

- **Pinkie finger** - how a person feels about communication

- ○ Whorl - love of specialized knowledge (i.e. ancient languages)

- ○ Arch - very cautious and particular about speech

- **Thumb** - how a person approaches doing things

- ○ Whorl - need to work by themselves, in their own way

- ○ Arch - thorough and persistent who concentrates on practical matters

- ○ Composite - difficulty making decisions, 60% certain is often the highest achievable

Identify any print patterns on the palm. It is common for there to be no discernible print patterns. Usually, if there is a pattern, it will be found in the lower outside area of the palm.

- **Loops** connecting digits exaggerate those digits' qualities.

  o Loop of leisure connects the pinkie and ring finger. Priority is placed on pleasure so be sure to enjoy your work and have satisfying hobbies.

  o Loop of industry connects the middle and ring fingers. This person takes their work very seriously, and is often a workaholic.

  o Loop of leadership connects the index and middle fingers. This person is a natural leader.

- Patterns found on the lower outside area of palm relate to the mind and psyche:

  o Loop of sensitivity - loop that opens toward the palm. This person is very perceptive and can often tell when a person is lying or hiding something.

  o Loop of nature - loop that opens toward the hand edge. This person loves nature and usually has a green thumb.

  o Loop of inspiration - loop that opens toward the wrist. This is most common on artists and indicates large flows of inspiration.

  o Whorl of isolation. This person is fascinated with the subconscious and other mind realms.

  o Composite pattern. Emotional ups and downs are common

and can result in difficulty maintaining relationships.

○ Arch pattern. This person has difficulty talking about their emotions and needs to express them physically.

• Loop of rhythm is found on the thumb ball and opens toward the hand edge. This indicates a love of music and great sense of rhythm.

• Loop of courage opens toward the outside of the hand between the thumb and index finger. This person constantly needs to challenge himself.

There you have it! A comprehensive work on how to read someone from only his or her hands. Differentiation in hobbies, jobs illnesses and the list goes on.

TELL-TALE TAN LINES

"Surely," answered Holmes, "it is not hard to say that a man with that bearing, expression of authority, and sunbaked skin, is a soldier, is more than a private, and is not long from India."□

SHERLOCK HOLMES - THE GREEK INTERPRETER 1893

We have all heard people say to some sun baked soul," Oh haven't you got a lovely tan from your holidays." Which begs the important question of, *'Is it the mere fact of someone's recent holiday, that we can deduce from a suntan alone?'* In short, the answer is no! And an emphatic one at that. We can deduce someone's job role, hobbies, how recent their holidays have been, and whether or not they drive.

It goes without saying the places that allow people easy passage to the browning of the skin, which seems so amiable to most. Failing that a simple Google search would allow you the knowledge of such, sufficed to say the closer to the equator the region gets then the hotter it will be. Then take into account the ferocity of the summer months in certain countries differs to others. For example, the people of Australia enjoy a much, much hotter summer than the people of the UK. This throws into the fray the idea of the time in which a tan can develop and whether the type of skin someone has can have any bearing on it.

HOW EXACTLY DOES ONE GET A TAN

In your skin there is something called Melanin. It is the very thing that gives your skin its colour. Darker skinned people have more Melanin and obviously then, lighter skinned people have less. The body will normally make Melanin to protect the deeper layers of the skin, and so when the skin gets damaged by the sun and its rays, the body will make more Melanin to try and protect the skin. This causes the change in colour we all know as tanning or burning. Darker skinned people will usually go a darker colour and lighter skinned people will usually go red or burn. In 1975, Harvard dermatologist Thomas B. Fitzpatrick devised the Fitzpatrick scale which described the common tanning behavior of various skin types, as follows.

Type	Also called	Sunburning	Tanning behavior	von Luschan scale
I	Very light or pale[11]	Often	Occasionally	1–5
II	Light or light-skinned[11]	Usually	Sometimes	6–10
III	Light intermediate[11]	Rarely	Usually	11–15
IV	Dark intermediate[11]	Rarely	Often	16–21
V	Dark or "brown" type	No	Sometimes darkens	22–28
VI	Very dark or "black" type	No	Naturally black-brown skin	29–36

So for a starter we can already begin to draw information here, based on the persons natural skin colour. We can estimate how long they have spent in the sun when we put it into context with how dark/red they have gone and whether or not they have used any sunscreen as well. This already puts us in a valuable position here as we are going in to the meeting with them with a lot of information already. If you follow it up with an arbitrary question such as how long of a flight they had, you can then narrow down to within a few countries the place they actually went to abroad. This is just accounting for the fact that you have that information stored in your head.

THE WHITE BITS

Once you know that the Melanin in the skin reacts to the exposure from the sunlight causing the change in colour, the white bits you see on a person can provide interesting tells as to where the person has been in the good weather. You would need to be asking yourself the question 'What would be there to create those white bits?' Then it is a mere matter of reasoning backwards from the other deductions you make about the person.

Say for example you see a man with a white patch outline where his watch used to be. Now he has obviously been committed enough to the wearing of a watch to get a tan around it. So why would it not be there now? You then notice that his hair is wet and smells nice, his fingertips are slightly shriveled and has a sports bag. Forgetting to put his watch back on after a session of swimming would be the most likely cause.

If you see a woman with sun bleached hair, slight curl to it, in shorts and with a smooth even diameter of a white patch around the ankle, like a bracelet, then she is most likely a surfer. The common ones that you may see are what I have affectionately entitled the 'Phantom bands'. These are the marks that are left behind when a ring has been worn for some time on the same finger. It goes without saying that the most common place would be the ring finger of the left hand. Pale and unblemished skin as a phantom band would lead to the most likely deduction of a divorce/broken engagement. When blemished however you would need to cross-reference this with the chance of Dermatitis or fake jewelry.

Only sundrenched hands, is a sign that a person has been out in the sun in full clothing. Now normally if a person has a choice then they will dress to allow themselves the most comfort with the given weather. Dressed in clothes, that cover the entire body, will not provide a lot of comfort in the blistering heat. So why would someone do this? Their job. Statistically most popular reasons in this area are the travelling salesmen and people in the forces. With all things in this area, it is the context that will drive home the accuracy of what the correct answer is. For example the salesmen will either be in their suits when you see them or dressed in normal clothing, in which case it will be their build, personality, hair cut, vernacular they use. With members of the forces (we are not counting seeing them in their military clothing as that would be just too obvious) their vernacular will be polite and much more courteous, their build will be much more athletic, their cut will be short trimmed and neat, and add in any tattoo marks you see you may also see the brief outline of any dog tag suntan marks on the neck/chest area.

Two tone tan marks are a unique find. Often found on the forearms of taxi drivers. This is because when driving in weather hot enough to develop a tan the windows in the car will be down and the driver's arm casually leaning out of the side. So one arm will be in the sun and one arm will be out giving the two tone tan line to the arms. On the arms as well, from the top of the arm at the shoulder and all the way down to the forearm, if there is a slow fade to the tan going from the normal skin colour down to the darker colour, this indicative of a person who changes their clothes quite a lot. This could be down to their constitution and/or perspiring frequently. So the shirts are always short sleeved but they vary in length so the sun doesn't have anything substantial to tan around.

SPOTTING THE FAKE TANS

Fake tans come in bottles, sprays, some gloopy liquids and all kinds of other madness. They are almost impossible to get right and pass off like a standard sun issued tan unless you have a team of stylists and makeup people to help you. They can create splotches in the areas where they haven't been applied evenly. Streaks can appear on the skin after a shower of rain. Many people fall foul of the unnatural darkness that came with being over zealous with the tanning solution. This can create what the media has affectionately entitled 'The Oompa Loompa effect'. Basically, when someone turns

354

themselves so dark that they would have then have skin cancer to make it a possibility.

So conversely the idea of spotting them doesn't take much thought and decision time. The closest to natural that is possible is sunbeds and sprays but they need to be real high-end places that do them as they inevitably charge more for the quality that comes with them. However, the idea of reasoning from here, will help you out with accuracy in this department. If they live in a place that is cold and wet with no signs of nice weather and no observations concerning a recent trip, then this will be the fake tan. Also look for smudges of darkness on areas that don't tan well or even at all, for example like the palms and the wrist.

What does a fake tan say about a person? Firstly and fore mostly it would be that they consider images to be very important to the person. This could be down narcissism or low self esteem as they can often work together to overcompensate in similar psychological areas. Bodybuilders go to excess with the tanning as well for a competition so this may be the difference in spotting an amateur and a pro. Secondly it would be that they have skewed sense of identity and they are trying to do things to fit in with whatever social group they are trying to plug themselves into.

In conclusion tans and the tan lines can come in all shapes and sizes, though a combination of your deductions, observations and reasoning's will lead you down the path to accuracy! Happy tan spotting!

"Precisely. And the man who wrote the note is a German. Do you note the peculiar construction of the sentence— 'This account of you we have from all quarters received.' A Frenchman or Russian could not have written that. It is the German who is so discourteous to his verbs. It only remains, therefore, to discover what is wanted by this German who writes upon Bohemian paper and prefers wearing a mask to showing his face. And here he comes, if I am not mistaken, to resolve all our doubts."□

SHERLOCK HOLMES - A SCANDAL IN BOHEMIA - 1891

There are many ways to tell where about in the world a person resides. Whether they live just around the corner and you have simply never seen them or 8,000 miles away is irrelevant. With the knowledge and ideas that have been presented in this chapter you will be well on your way to being able to do just that. There have been many ideas put forth on this topic in the previous chapter and this chapter is one that will focus intently on the topic.

To start, if you are performing/working in your local area then it is best to make yourself as keenly aware of it as possible! I am sure we are all familiar at this point with the many cases and references that Sherlock Holmes makes with his deductions to the area of London. The case of the tell tale mud on the boot which has its routes in the legends of Dr.Joeseph Bell, this mud would clue Mr. Holmes in to whereabouts in the city this person had been to or where they had come from. This is because he was intimately familiar with the surrounding area. If someone had a familiar smell about them, say from a popular bakery perhaps then Sherlock would be able to identify the bakery purely because he was aware of the ingredients that particular bakery used, which works in conjunction with his knowledge of London. We can put that into context with our local areas that we live in. It might just be that we know the areas that we use most frequently which would be the ones on the way to our work or to pick the kids up from school or wherever. It becomes then about expanding your knowledge of the area from this point.

Would you know where all of the grassy mainlands and fields are in your area? How many of them have a stables on the premises? Would you know where there is any building work going on? Would you know where the only place is that sell toasted bagels that is within a 5 minute walk from the local McDonalds? All these are possibilities that can arise in your work as a Deductionist.

Let us say for example that you come across a man in a suit, it is a smart and expensive suit but he is currently unaware that there is a small tear in the pocket on the right side of his trousers and, what appears to be grass stains. With one question you can have a good idea of whereabouts he lives and what he does for a living. I mention this here as a demonstration of my point about knowing the surrounding area with regard to deductions. It is something that came up as part of my work but not during a paid performance however. This was one of those times where a friend of a friend had heard about me and called me on my skills. That one question I asked was 'How long does it take you to get to work?' This gives a time frame from the moment the person leaves their house dressed in their smart suit until the time that they arrive at work. His answer in this instance was 'About 15 minutes'. So combine the tear, the stain and the time frame and he lives close to work and has to go through a field possibly a short walkway with overgrown bushes. Now because I was aware of my local area in such detail that I was able to come up with two possible locations that this could be but only 1 had any form of shops the other side. So I asked him if he came from a place called Birches Head? He did. Now then the closest establishments to the field that have their employees wear suits was a car dealership and a Solicitors. Since the salesmen and women at the car dealership will deal with people more directly there is a higher chance that the stain and tear would have been pointed out, so the solicitors was a more likely place of work for this young man. He was doing a legal internship. Now to quote the BBC Sherlock, *'A shot in the dark but a good one'*. As a more reliable indicator would have been a cluster of tells pointing to the same outcome. However it just goes to show that this type of deduction is absolutely possible in the real world and is not a work of fiction from the media.

So, first and foremost, begin to develop the ongoing knowledge of the surrounding areas that you each live in. Now a good test once you have a good solid working knowledge of the area is to ask for the assistance of a friend who drives a car. Give them the parameters of your knowledge and then ask them to drive you anywhere within them. You will of course be completely blindfolded and have to figure out where exactly you are. This will test the spatial awareness of your memory and the knowledge you have built up. You need to be taking the same journey in your head; it's just that you won't be able to see. It is a taxing challenge there is no doubt about that but it's one that will prove to you its worth.

So go as in depth as you can, restaurants, shops, fields, building work, petrol stations, culturally popular places, popular dog walking routes and bus stops. Make sure it is all stored sufficiently as you go.

GIVE IT A GOOD SHAKE

To continue on down the road of a working knowledge of the surrounding area, let us touch upon the handshake tell with reference to knowing where a person resides or even grew up. This began with the work of Barbara and Allan Pease and their remarkable body language books. In a nutshell, for the people who live in sparse, 'country' locations, such as farmers, they will begin their handshake greetings quite early. This is because in their home town they will see people coming from a fair distance away. To show the intention and their mood, the hand will come out as a greeting as they are walking toward the other person. This is a matter of opposites when referring to people who live in built up, industrial areas. Due to the hustle and bustle and sheer volume of people in these areas, greetings happen quickly and almost instantly. Therefore the hand comes out for the greeting when they are in normal conversational distance to the other person. When the person is in close proximity to the other, it becomes a learnt behavior, much like the handshake itself. We all know that the kneejerk reaction to seeing someone's outstretched hand is for you to do the same, almost without thinking. The speed with which you do it will also follow the same cognitive pattern. There is only a single anomaly here that we have found, that occurs with the handshake timing tell and that is someone's confidence level. If someone is of low confidence or self-esteem then they will invariably begin their handshakes early to avoid having to spend those extra few seconds looking at the other person in the eyes.

Now, to put this into context with our local areas. If you make yourself aware of where the different locations in your region, which apply to the two different types of settings, either the sparsely located or the industrial setting, then, when you see someone when you are out performing or working a case, who begins their handshake as early as possible and grew up in the same area. Go through the areas that relate to the criteria, put them into context with whatever other observations you can make and you will come up with where they live. Handshake timing and contextual analysis as you go will lead this to be a reliable deduction for you to make, time and again.

IT'S ALL GENETICS

What better start for being able to deduce where on the globe a person resides than their face. There are many parts of the world that have genetically different looks than others. Say for example, the Inuit people look completely different to the Native people of America. Here we will list some of the most popular places that get confused with others so as to make you aware of as much as possible.

This is information which is ignoring other possible sources here such as accent, clothing, behaviour, mannerisms etc., instead choosing to decipher information purely from physicality alone. Which sounds paradoxical to say when you know that these will be the more reliable and obvious pieces of information.

Most white Europeans are difficult to differentiate, from mere sight of face alone, it is the other 'tells' as it were. Things such as language, accent and clothing will tip you to the origin of white Europeans. The closest neighbourhood to this person is the Mediterranean. It was one of the sub races of the Caucasian population and was categorised by anthropologists in the late 19th-early 20th century. According to genetic testing from the National Geographic Society, the genetic component of the Mediterranean person references 43 different countries. The most popular of such come from the following places, Levant, North Africa, Southern Europe, the Caucasus and Iran – people from Sardinia, Lebanon, Egypt, Tunisia, Georgia, Kuwait, Greece, Italy, Iberian Peninsula, Northern Caucasus and Iran

The first social and indeed physical description of this race of person was given by William Rhind in 1851 he was a Scottish scientist who gave the following description:

*'The Celtic Race (**as it then was known**), are characterised*

360

by a well-formed ,well defined and elegantly formed; complexion dark; dark brown or black eyes; black hair turning early gray; form middle size, handsome; feet and hands small. Mental powers, quick, active, and energetic, rather than profound. Passions and affections strong. Fond of society, but not forgetful of injuries. Monarchial in their governments. They occupy the southern and insular parts of Europe.' head, elongated from front to back, and moderate in breadth; face oval;

According to William Z. Ripley who was racial theorist and a professor of economics at M.I.T in the beginnings of the 20th century, the marked features of the Mediterranean race were dark hair – dark eyes – long face – dolichocephalic (which means to have a particularly long skull) skull and a variable narrow nose.

http://en.wikipedia.org/wiki/Mediterranean_race - cite_note-Ripley_1899_p._121-11

http://en.wikipedia.org/wiki/Mediterranean_race - cite_note-30

C. S. Coon who was a professor of anthropology at the university of Pennsylvania in the 1950's wrote that marked Mediterranean features included skin color ranging "from pink or peaches-and-cream to a light brown", a relatively prominent and aquiline (known as a roman nose and likened to that of an eagle) nose, considerable body hair, and dark brown to black hair.

According to Renato Biasutti who was an Italian geographer and anthropologist throughout the early 20th century, frequent Mediterranean traits included "skin color 'matte'-white or brunet-white, chestnut or dark chestnut eyes and hair, not excessive pilosity (If something is pilose it refers to being covered with long soft hairs); medium-low stature, body of moderately linear forms; dolichomorphic (long and thin) skull with rounded occiput; oval face; with straight spine, horizontal or inclined downwards base of the septum; large open eyes.

Whether or not you believe Giuseppe Sergi's opinion that the Mediterranean race is *"the greatest race...derived neither from the black nor white people...an autonomous stock in the human family."* The further belief in Mediterraneanism is, that it is the greatest race because of its richly unique and diverse cultures and backgrounds, all of which are celebrated. This does not really have a bearing on our work here; we look only to be able to recognise the genetic traits and qualities that are visible from a person in order to be able to use that for our deductive needs.

Now then, this next part is considered largely to be quite a taboo question. Can you tell the difference between the Asian races? As Chris Tucker eloquently puts it in the hit movie Rush hour 2,*"All y'all look alike."* Now, let me be clear, this is purely from an informative standpoint and is passed on through my own research, as well as from the research online of many Asian men and women who have asked themselves the same question.

The people in question here are the Chinese people, the Japanese people, the Korean people and the Vietnamese people. So in short the findings here are based upon morphological and anthropomorphised observation as well as the genetic/anthropological histories of all.

JAPANESE - Japanese people tend to have a longer / oval facial structure with lower cheekbones, wider / larger eyes and more pronounced noses. Japanese people generally have larger eyes and many of them have poorly formed teeth. Japanese women tend to put on thick makeup so that they look palely white. Their behavior is different as well. They are more reserved and avoid physical contacts, bowing as opposed to handshaking as well.

362

KOREAN - Korean people tend to have flatter faces with higher / squarer cheek bones and smaller eyes with single eyelids (as opposed to double). Most Koreans are descendants of Northern Asians. Koreans generally have smaller eyes without double eyelid, with higher cheekbones and noses. Koreans are generally taller than Southern Chinese, Japanese and Vietnamese. (Actually, South Koreans are the tallest in Asia!)

CHINESE - Chinese people tend to have rounder faces than both Korean and Japanese people. China is a huge multi-ethnic country unlike Korea and Japan (which are more ethnically homogeneous) making it much harder to differentiate or generalize. China is a huge country and it is not a single-ethnic (ethnically homogenous) country as they are in Korea and Japan. Northern Chinese and Southern Chinese look quite different and they speak different languages which are not mutually intelligible. Southern Chinese are definitely shorter than Northern Chinese and they have larger eyes and darker skin colors. Southern Chinese look more like Southeast Asians. Mainland Chinese people don't dress well and less fashionable than Taiwanese, Koreans or Japanese.

VIETNAMESE - With regards to physical appearance, the Vietnamese are not very different from the Chinese. Both being Asians (duh) these two races share each other's looks. Nevertheless, Vietnamese people are often seen to have broader noses. They also have a smaller body frame than the Chinese. They are a quite short people, bearing a darker complexion and fuller eyes, as are those who live in Southeast Asia.

Conversely, Chinese people appear taller than most Asians. Their bodybuild typically ranges from small to average. Because China is a very large country, there are diverse cultural differences and alterations in physique that slightly vary from one Chinese region to another. For example, the

Chinese natives of the South are usually shorter when compared to those from the North. They also have bigger eyes, or are quite darker in complexion. Because of such, they resemble the characteristics of most Southeast Asian inhabitants.

This information we reiterate is to purely help to deduce the origin of the person in question and not to fuel the fire of any debates.

This touches on a mere pittance of the information that is available regarding the physical traits of specific cultures. To be able to recognise by sight alone is a difficult task to master given that our planet is richly diverse in many wondrous people.

THE WRITING IS ON THE WALL

With so many cultures raising so many different people, in so many different ways, it is almost inevitable that the way writing is formed, will change from country to country. This is particularly obvious when people from other countries are writing the same language as you. So in essence, this part of the chapter will focus on handwriting and not necessarily the language itself. So then, to begin with let us take a dive back into the Asian continent and its many diverse and difficult writing styles.

インプリメンテーション、フォント、テキスト表示、マルチ言語コンピューティングにおける業界の専門家が集まります。

Would you know where the person came from who wrote this?

And why? That is the point, there are not many who can and with accuracy, fortunately for us we are going to help you do this. With what follows we will look at the characters of China, Japan and Korea. This is due to the fact that as Vietnam gained its independence from China, scholars began to develop a logographic script, known as Chu nom (southern script) to represent Vietnamese speech. It is a classical vernacular script based on orthodox Chinese characters supplemented by a set of new characters specifically devised to write Vietnamese words. These modified Chinese characters usually consist of a phonetic part and a semantic part, both based on Chinese. The resulting look-alike Chinese characters, completely unintelligible to people from China itself, are considerably more complex than the originals and have never been considered as part of the greater family of Chinese characters. For nearly 1000 years after independence, the Chu nom script became widely used in daily lives and Vietnamese literature before the French colonial government decreed against its use in 1920. It is estimated that nowadays fewer than 100 scholars worldwide can read Chu nom.

Today, the Vietnamese use quoc ngu (national language), an alphabet based on the Latin one with some digraphs and diacritics. Based on a form developed earlier by Portuguese missionaries, quoc ngu was developed by French Jesuit missionaries who came to Vietnam in the 17th century. By the 18th century, quoc ngu had more or less acquired the form used today.

Modern Vietnamese is formed from the basis of 29 letters and looks like this when written out:

Cơ quan Du lịch Quốc gia Lào cho biết, năm 2004, Lào đã đón tiếp khoảng 900.000 du khá
nước ngoài, tăng 37% so với gần 736.000 người năm 2002 và 14.400 người năm 1990 và t
về cho nhà nước khoảng 113 triệu USD.

Ngành du lịch Lào, một trong 8 lĩnh vực ưu tiên hàng đầu trong kế hoạch phát triển kinh tế-
hội, đặt kế hoạch hàng năm thu hút khoảng 1 triệu lượt du khách nước ngoài.

Để đạt mục tiêu trên, các cơ quan và các ngành liên quan đang nỗ lực phát triển du lịch tới
Húaphăn (Bắc Lào), căn cứ địa cách mạng của Lào trong hai cuộc kháng chiến.

Hiện nay, Cố đô Luôngphabang, được tổ chức Văn hóa và Giáo dục Liên Hợp Quốc (UNESCO
công nhận là di sản văn hóa thế giới, là một trong những điểm du lịch di sản rất hấp dẫn.

If you find circles and ovals in the context of the characters in the handwriting then this is certainly Korean. This is thanks to the phonetic alphabet called Hangul. In amongst the circle and ovals is a large quantity of straight lines.

The Japanese writing system has 3 main components, Hiragana, Katakana, and Kanji. Most of the Hiragana characters are curved but do not have the neatness that (e.g. さっか) Korean has. Katakana uses straight lines for the most part but does intermingle slightly curved lines as well (e.g. チェンシ ゛). Chinese and Korean do not use either of these systems. Note that Japanese writing uses a mixture of hiragana, katakana, and kanji in the same text, so if you see either hiragana or katakana or both, you are looking at Japanese.

- Some common Hiragana いきしちにひみり
- Some common Katakana アルバイト

If you do not see the characteristic shapes of Korean Hangul or Japanese hiragana or katakana, then you are probably looking at Chinese. Chinese writing has complicated characters called hanzi in Chinese, kanji in Japanese, and hanja in Korean. Although these characters are also found in Japanese, if there are hiragana or katakana, it is Japanese. So if you are looking at a small block of text that has only complex hanzi characters, you cannot rule out that it is Japanese. However, if you are looking at a large block of text and see no hiragana or katakana, then you can be pretty sure that it is Chinese.

It is decidedly difficult to pinpoint someone's ethnic background based solely on their handwriting. I myself don't fully ascribe to the laws set down by graphology textbooks and there are people who say it is faultless and people who say it is poppycock. If you worry less about the trizonal dynamics and loop sizes, and focus on the writing more as a series of pictures that tells stories about the person, then more can be deduced from it. So if you take for example the idea of deducing someone's background or where they grew up based on their handwriting you need to keep in mind a couple of ideas as you go. Let us say that you have a handwriting sample that is written in English. Pay close attention to the words that are written as quite frequently someone who has learnt a foreign language will speak it and therefore write it differently to the indigenous people of that place. This is down to how they have learnt to speak the language, which would be through education and schools. Therefore it is learnt properly. The indigenous group pick up the subtle nuances and sarcasm and tones and slang through their natural conversational habitat. This will reflect in their writing, properly taught people still go through life using the cursive joined up writing they were taught. It may be written quite slowly and with pressure on the paper therefore signifying their concentration on getting it correct. What will inevitably happen, from time to time, is the mixing up of words or adding in small words that don't need to be there. This is the same with the spoken word as well.

Particularly prevalent in eastern Europeans, who have learnt English is the missing out of small words like will, to, the etc. Which turns sentences like '*I will bring that to you,*' into, '*I bring that you*'.

It might something as off hand as a phrase or saying from that particular place that catches your ears. Would you be able to pin down the location of this person based on something like that? Well, as with all information in this book and particularly this chapter if there is something that you feel we have left out it is only because it is insanely hard to cover the entire globe in one book.

With each country having its own culture and set of people, it is almost inevitable that there will be a set of stock phrases from said place. So what will follow is some of the more popular phrases and sayings and where they are from in the western world of today.

THE SOUTH OF AMERICA (TEXAS ETC)

● *So foggy the birds are walking, So dusty the rabbits are digging holes six feet in the air.* These are popular due to the South's (particularly Texas) powerful seasons of weather, drought, flood, blizzard and twister. On a nice day it may be that it's *Hotter than a honeymoon hotel.*

● *He's got a 10-gallon mouth, She's got tongue enough for 10 rows of teeth.* Most of the south is prone to be able to spin a good yarn at the drop of a hat, developing into the stereotype that some just keep going irrespective of whatever is happening.

● *Happy as a hog in slops, I am cooking on a front burner today.* A particularly prevalent phrase to describe happiness or any other positive moment is to make reference to food in the statement (*fine as cream gravy*) or to an animal and the thing it enjoys doing the most

As you can see from this short batch alone, the south of America is particularly fond of its descriptive metaphors and similes. The accent will no doubt clue you in as well but as accents were described in another chapter, they won't be making an appearance again here. There are many words, sayings and idioms that have crept out of North America and in to today's modern language throughout the world so there is no real tell for the words alone here, other than the accent. The only thing it will demonstrate is knowledge of Americanized language and a deft, affluent vocabulary.

OH CANADA

10 Key words and phrases to single out someone who has spent a lot of time in the great white north.

1. Eh? Add at the end of your sentence as a friendly short-cut for "don't you agree?"

2. Double-double: Coffee with two creams and two sugars. A triple-triple is cream and sugar times three, made popular by famous Canadian staple, Tim Hortons.

3. Pop: If you're craving a Coke, don't say "soda" or you'll find yourself with a glass of carbonated water. "Pop" refers to the bubbly soft drinks you love, which is the same as in England

4. Loonie (Toonie): A loon on the Canadian dollar coin led to it being nicknamed the "loonie." The Toonie or twoonie is the tongue-in-cheek nickname for the two-dollar coin.

5. Poutine: A Canadian dish of fries, gravy and curd cheese.

6. Washroom: Bathroom, or toilet. □

7. Zed: The last letter of the alphabet.

8. Chinook: A warm wind that blows from west to east. It starts in late winter and goes to early spring.

9. Whales tail: This is a fried dough pastry. It is also known as beavers tails or elephants ears.

10. Canuck: This is a nickname for a Canadian.

DOWN UNDER WITH OZ

1. Aerial Ping-Pong: A slang term for their famed Aussie rules football.

2. Billabong: an oxbow lake cut off by a change in the watercourse. Billabongs are usually formed when the course of a creek or river changes, leaving the former branch with a dead end.

3. Bludger: A lazy person, or sponge in the sense that they are always after using other people's belongings. Also related is a 'dole bludger' who is someone unjustly receiving government handouts or benefits.

4. Built like a brick shit house: A very big and strong person.

5. Brizzie: Brisbane, which is the state capital of Queensland.

6. Chook: A chicken

7. Digger: A soldier

8. Exy: Expensive

9. Franger: Condom

10. Garbo/garbologist: A garbage collector

As you can see many words are shortened and/or then jazzed up to sound better. Due to the fact that in the 18th century, Britain thought it would be a good idea to use Australia to house most of its prisoners, the language inevitably went with it. Which still holds true today and you can see some it in the parallel's in the Aussie slang. They have dole Bludgers and the English have dole dossers, they have standard Bludgers and the English have people who are bone-idle. English also uses the term built like a brick shithouse as well. This is only to make reference to a few, there are of course many more.

SOUTH AFRICAN☐

1.**Aikona** - not on your life / never

2.**Aita** (Pronounced 'ai-tah') - a greeting

3.**Akubekuhle** (Pronounced 'aako-beck-hoole') - meaning cheers, to cheers a drink or thanks in Zulu

4.**Arvie** (Pronounced 'rve') - afternoon☐

5.**Bobotie** (Pronounced buh-boor-tea) - served with yellow rice and raisins, this is a spicy traditional Malay mince with an egg custard topping.

6.**Babbelas** (Pronounced 'bub-elaas')- South African Afrikaans for tender the morning after the night before, hangover

7.**Bakgat** - (Pronounced 'buck-ghat') - when something is done correctly☐

8. **Bru** - Male friend☐

9. **Braai** - a BBQ☐

10. **Chow** - means eat - this can also mean sex, so be careful how you use it.

I have given you some phrases and terms and have purposely not gone in to any other languages due to the fact that the sound of the language itself will tip you to the origin of the person and not any key words or phrases that you manage to pick out.

MONEY MONEY MONEY

To make yourself aware of as many currencies that are available in the world today can also point you in the direction of someone's place of origin. For example if you overheard someone say;

'God, I haven't lived there since the Drachma was still being used'

Would you have any idea where they lived for a while? The answer was Greece by the way but this points to yet more knowledge and help for the ability to deduce someone's homeland or where they have recently been on holiday or done business.

There are presently 180 currencies in use at this time. So what follows is an excerpt from that list for countries that have the largest tourist spots and people traffic.

1. Afghanistan - Afghan Afghani

2. Argentina - Argentine peso☐

3. Australia - Australian Dollar

4. Austria - Euro

5. Bahamas - Bahamian dollar

6. Belgium - Euro

7. Belarus - Belarusian ruple

8. Brazil - Brazilian real

9. Bulgaria - Bulgarian Lev

10. Canada - Canadian Dollar

11. China - Chinese Renminbi

12. Costa Rica - Costa Rican Colon

13. Cuba - Cuban peso

14. Czech Republic - Czech koruna

15. Denmark - Danish Krone

16. Egypt - Egyptian pound

17. Hong Kong - Hong Kong dollar

18. Indonesia - Indonesian rupiah

19. Japan - Japanese Yen

20. Kenya - Kenyan Shilling

21. Pakistan - Pakistani Rupee

22. Romania - Romanian Leu

23. Russia - Russian Ruble

24. South Africa - South African Rand

25. Tunisia - Tunisian Dinar

26. U.K - British pound sterling

27. U.S.A - United states dollar

28. Vietnam - Vietnamese Dong

29. Venezuela - Venezuelan bolivar

30. Turkey - Turkish New Lira

There are many countries in Europe that use the single currency, the euro. These countries are:

1) Andorra

2) Austria

3) Belgium

4) Cyprus

5) Estonia

6) Finland

7) France

375

8) Germany

9) Greece

10) Ireland

11) Italy

12) Kosovo

13) Latvia

14) Luxembourg

15) Malta

16) Monaco

17) Montenegro

18) Netherlands

19) Portugal

20) San Marino

21) Slovakia

22) Slovenia

23) Spain

24) Vatican City

There are many other ideas to throw at you, for you all to store sufficiently away in your palace but this book would then turn into a mere list upon list of information. So in the interest of keeping your interest here, the ideas and situations are as follows.

Flags are representative of many things from how patriotic a person is to the country that is in the world cup final. They appear on all kinds of materials such as clothes, luggage, promotional items, tourist spots and some flags have nicknames too such as the stars and stripes or the union jack. Now I aren't going to suggest that you begin to study Vexillology immediately but only to begin to build your knowledge database of the flags themselves. So the next time you are on a stakeout in an airport and your mark is an Estonian mercenary, the only thing you know is he has a tattoo of the flag on his forearm (A hypothetical stretch I know, but this is just a for instance) could you spot him? In short, flags are a direct link to someone's place of origin or, something that they are a fan of, that the country is synonymous for.

Make yourself aware of popular companies which only reside in certain places. It is quite a niche market idea but proves useful nonetheless in our work. Take Holmes' observation from the beginning of the chapter regarding the recognition of paper from Bohemia. This served to further solidify in his mind where this person would be from. A good place to start would be car companies and the license plates. The car companies go worldwide, and also the license plates each have a specific way to be made up depending on where they are from. A California license plate is easily distinguished from a Miami license plate, just as a license plate from eastern Europe is easily distinguished from an English one.

Current events and the people it relates to will only bother a certain type of person or only give a certain person reason to talk about it with any kind of passion or gusto. The exploits of Vladimir Putin will only affect specific people, The Right Honourable Tony Abbott will only incite passion in certain people and events. Certain state officials who are spoken about will only be spoken about by people who are from there. Certain clothing labels only sell in certain areas of the world. It genuinely depends on how in-depth you want to go, as the more information you hold on anything the more accurate you become when wielding it. So we look to be as well rounded as possible in our knowledge.

There are many thoughts and ideas and deductions that have been laid before you here and with them you will be able to deduce where someone is from, where they are going and maybe even where they have been! Remember to observe carefully and deduce shrewdly! Also to store your information efficiently! Can't really say that enough!

You Hear But Do Not Listen

"There is no part of the body which varies so much as the human ear."

The Cardboard Box 1917

Conversational and Auditory Deductions.

Conversational deductions by their very nature are the art of talking and listening. From this and this alone, much can be gleaned. Listening, in all its many forms and splendor, can provide so much glorious detail about a person from which we can deduce a vast array of apparently unknown information. It can provide the Deductionist with almost anything from pin codes, to pet names, from the present they always wanted but never received to the names of the people they dislike the most in their office.

For as simple as it is, many people overlook this and, to a degree where it is quite shocking. Take, for example, the cliché Husband who is forever being accosted for not listening to his wife and therefore (to her) not caring. The power that goes with over hearing her mention a big meeting she has that week when she is talking on the phone to one of her girlfriends and then when she comes home from work that day, for him to merely ask how it went? Is something that will mean a lot and will only take the slightest of input to be able to do. Granted, this is taken slightly out of context for what we are doing here but the underlying point still stands. For the mentalists to be able to deduce someone's safe code by only listening to the key pad entry, or for the detective's (which could apply to any of the heads of companies in sticky situations) to know that one of your employees says they are ringing sick because they don't feel too good but you know it was their birthday the night before, all because you kept your ears peeled, so to speak. This is where your observational skills can be honed in a new light as well. It is an additional string to your deductive bow.

What this chapter will cover is the idea behind language and slang and what these can indicate, as well as Freudian slips and the ability to differentiate between accents and much, much, more.

ARCHIVE TALE FROM MY WORK AS A MENTALIST

' Its in the middle of my casino residency, and I was enjoying a drink with some of the bar staff before I started work that evening, clearly a soft drink as I am a professional here and would save that for afterwards. In amongst chatting with some of the staff who I knew there, I had kept listening to what was going on around me. This is so the staff would have no clue as to what I was doing because in their minds I am talking to and at times performing for them and to anyone else watching. This is totally how it looked. I simply kept my ears peeled and the work was done. I could commit to memory who had travelled from where and what kind of a day they had. What they ate, where they were from, and as it happens on this particular day there were a group of women celebrating the news that a child would be on their way in the group. '

It's not a matter of simply listening and regurgitating because each time it presents a new issue from which to deduce information. You hear an accent, can you recognise which one and why? You see a group of women celebrating, making a fuss over a particular woman, why? It is this chapter that will help you figure out what is going on and why?

We will begin with phrases and context.

URBAN PHRASEOLOGY

There are certain groups within our society that use certain terms in their natural everyday speech pattern. This applies to everyone from certain social and urban groups like the punk rockers or the local hip hop collective, to people in specific job roles. If you hear someone say," I upped the guy at the front and then took him to the first Rat." This is terminology that only car salesmen use. It is niche market ideas but very handy when working in the trenches. All of this information is quite easy to source as well. Most of the time it is information that you will already know but we need to present it for you to cut down the cognitive time you use to retrieve the information.

There are of course many different ways to tell a punk rocker from a hip hopper but 90% of these tells are visual i.e. clothes or hairstyles but there are idiosyncratic terms in each group. This comes from knowing the groups to which you listen to as well. In particular you may fall foul of stereotyping. As it seems, a lot of these stereotypes are born from the ideas put forth and perpetuated by the media and most 80's movies. Not all surfers are stoners who say gnarly and awesome, though some do. Not all hip hop fans wear their trousers below the waist and say 'Dawg' and call people G. These are things that you need to be aware of when out working.

Skaters share some important terms that describe their art form that they practise:

• **Sick** - this means the same as "cool" or for you older guys, "rad". Pretty much anything can be sick. You can pull off a sick trick, have a sick board, or a skate park can be sick. It's one of those slang words like "bad" was a decade ago, meaning the opposite. Along with "sick", something really cool might get called "ill", "insane", "gnar" (short for "gnarly"), or even "rad" or "righteous".

- **Stoked** - to like something or to be excited. I am stoked that you are reading this. I'm stoked I can land a tre-flip. The word comes from making a fire bigger - when you add fire to it, or fan the flames, you are "stoking" the fire.

- **Sketchy** - not well done, or not trustworthy. A sketchy trick looked badly done ("clean" is the opposite - a clean trick looked flawless). A sketchy person is someone who you don't want to bring home for dinner. A sketchy skateboard is a piece of junk that might break. I think it's funny that the shoe company "Sketchers" tries to make shoes that LOOK like skate shoes, but are, in fact, sketchy.

- **Bail** - to bail is to either fall, or to jump off of your board right before falling. It doesn't get used all the time though - some people just say to fall or crash. The word "bail" is more traditional in skateboarding, but if the people you are around don't use it, you might sound like you're trying too hard if you insist on saying "bail" all the time!

- **Poser** - this is someone who looks like a skater, or who claims to be one, but who doesn't know anything about skating. This term can be pretty hurtful, so don't use it lightly. And it's tough to know if someone truly IS a poser - read **Posers Vs Slow Learners** for more.

There is a particular movement that seems to be growing in the UK at the moment, and it is to do with Hip Hop and other affiliated genres. They have their own unique language and accent that will identify them in seconds.

https://www.youtube.com/watch?v=ympl2mdABUM

This is a link to a standup comedian from the UK but to the uninitiated or people from overseas it will also be of great help in explaining the slang as it were. However some of the affection for hip hop can and will leak out in speech. Such as

382

referring to houses as cribs, or announcing their immediate departure by informing all that they have to bounce. If someone is acting crazy, then they are said to be clownin'. Fly is a popular word that many an awkward wannabe has adapted in film and television. Affectionately entitling someone as their Home Skillet is a term of endearment for their best friend.

This is something that can provide a unique insight into a person tastes but they don't just have to stem from musical tastes, it could be sport or a particular author's work. You can use deductions like this to forge relationships, particularly helpful in the business world as well as the social.

To use this in terms of job roles just requires listening to the friends who you know, and inquisitive research on your own part. We will give you the most common starting points but it will be up to you if you wish to continue down this road in detail. When revealing someone's job role, the more information you have on this topic the better, and the speech can let slip some reliable information. The information will require proper storage in the palace in your head.

SALESMEN (CARS)

Cream Puff - Car on the lot that is in good condition.

Sled/Rat - Car on the lot that is in poor condition.

Bogue: A customer with bad credit. *Also: Get Me Done.* 312

Back End: The profit from financing a vehicle, including the products sold in the Finance Office, such as extended warranties.

Bolt-action: Manual transmission. As in: "Was that an

automatic, or a bolt-action?"

Bone Thrower: Sunroof.

Buried: To owe more on a trade-in than it's worth. *Also: Hooked, negative, tanked, upside-down, etc.*

Car Attorney: Someone a customer believes to be knowledgeable about cars and is presumed to have negotiating skills, brought along to help the customer avoid being taken by the dealer. *Also: PIA, Third Base Coach.*

Dehorse, or **Unhorse:** To hide a customer's trade-in so he/she cannot leave the dealership.

Filet: To make a big profit on a customer. *Also: Bend 'Em Over, Rip 'Em a New One, Tear Their Heads Off, etc.*

First Pencil: The first set of numbers a sales manager gives the salesperson to present to the customer. Usually represents the greatest profit to the dealership. (It only goes down from there.)

Flopper: A customer who buys on the "first pencil." This is taken from fishing, as in a fish that doesn't even wait for you to drop your line but jumps right in the boat and flops around until you hit it with an oar and put it in the ice chest. *Also: Laydown or Mullet.* Every salesman's Ideal Customer.

Front End: The profit from the negotiated purchase price of the vehicle.

Green Pea: A new, inexperienced salesperson.

Ghost: A customer with no credit history, usually a younger person who has never bought on credit before.

Laydown: A customer who walks through the door and "lays down," i.e., offers no resistance to the salesperson and pays full price or above.

Mooch: A customer who attempts to prevent a dealer from making a profit; someone who wants something for nothing.

One-Legged Shopper: A husband without his wife, or a wife without her husband. One of the prime decision makers is missing, hence the buyer has only "one leg."

Puppy Dogging: Sending a customer home with the vehicle he/she is thinking of buying so they can think about it overnight. The idea is that when the customers show it to their friends and neighbours, they will make such a fuss over it-- just as they would a new puppy-- that the customer will have no choice but to buy it. Sometimes it works; sometimes it doesn't.

Skate: To try to get around another salesperson to steal his/her customer.

Take It in the Brown: Does not refer to the customer's choice of color.

Tire Kicker: A customer with no intention of buying a vehicle.

T.O.: Short for turnover. To introduce a customer to a manager, or "turn them over" to a second person, such as a manager.

Two-Pounder: A deal with a two thousand dollar profit. Two-pounder, three-pounder, four-pounder, etc.

Up (noun): A customer. Or, as a verb, "**to up someone,**" meaning to walk up to a customer and wait on them.

There are few job titles that come with their own unique slang, but truck drivers have theirs for the radios they use. This is most globally popular in the U.S. As previously stated we won't list the entire language as it will just go on too long but we will give you the important points. **Bears** in whatever form they come in will be officers of the law, with their **disco lights** on top of their cars. **Leo**s aren't describing anyone's particular star sign but is a literal acronym for law enforcement officer. **Kojak with a Kodak** would refer to an office with a radar gun or a mounted camera doing the same thing. In Australia, these differ slightly when it comes to describing officers of the law. **Candy car** and **camera car** both refer to police patrols but only one clearly has the mounted camera. **Double one** would refer to a marked patrol car. **Meat wagon** is the affectionate title for an ambulance as well.

Bears are popular again in the UK terminology but we English call them 'lorry drivers'. **Bagging** is a term that refers to trapping speeding motorists. **Blood wagons** is the term for ambulances, following this line, a hearse is referred to as a **bone box. Burst balloon** is not an unfortunate story from a children's birthday party but referring to a flat tyre.

Aside from physical and personal traits that can be deduced from ones speech and its patterns, it is also possible to gain an insight into someone's behavioural make up by how they speak.

For instance, take the sentences below: □

' *I feel that this project will be a great adventure.*'□

' *I think that this project will be a great adventure* '

Now in just changing one word, of this example sentence, you can get two different meanings from it. The first demonstrates a person who is led by their feelings with passion and gusto, and will be looking forward to the experiences they are going to have and all the new feelings they will get in this hypothetical project. The other demonstrates someone who operates under their critical mind, they have one or two extra thoughts about the project and are conscious of the undertaking they have to do.

This can also indicate someone's emotional stress peak and a change in their baseline, if the way they speak usually comprises of a lot of feeling based words and adjectives then on one particular topic they turn to using thinking words and adjectives, this can represent a seed of doubt and uncertainty. In the same way someone who talks with their hands (illustrators) may decrease the amount used and use more pacifying behaviours to indicate their uncertainty and emotional stress. There are far too many words to enumerate here that will fall into either category so you will have to keep your ears peeled in order to pick up on the subtle changes and decipher their intended meaning.

I mention this following point merely as food for thought as, well, the research has currently not been conclusive on the topic. Multi-linguals and bilinguals are currently demonstrating different personalities with each language that they speak. It is believed that this is down to the learning of the languages that happen in different ways. Our native language, the one we are raised speaking is how we also pick up all of the colour and intonation. The others we learn in a more structural manner. So we fall foul of things like cognitive traps, and it slows down our thinking time and in our native tongue we will inevitably feel more loose and free to be blunt and decorative with our speech. In short, the different creation of languages makes for different feelings when speaking them. For example, in Greek, they begin their sentences with verbs and the form of the verb which includes a lot of information so you have a good idea as to the meaning after the first word. Some Germans believe that putting the verbs at the end of the sentence makes the language especially logical.

PSYCHOPATHIC SPEECH

Is there a way to differentiate this personality type purely from how they speak? The results here are the results of extensive testing done through police forces and the interviews therein. A number of psychopaths and non- psychopaths were interviewed and a couple of very important indicators arose.

The psychopaths shared an affinity for the past tense more so than the present tense when speaking, which is in direct contrast to the non-psychopaths. This is a form of psychological detachment from anything based in the present.

Dysfluencies of language are more apparent in psychopaths as well. These are the 'uhs' and the 'ums' that occur naturally in speech. It is believed that this is merely the mask of sanity that is being placed on. This is likened to the idea that liars will not look you in the eye when lying when actually, it is the opposite that is true, so they over compensate by holding eye contact more so. To appear "sane" the naturally occurring Dysfluencies have to be forced and therefore appear more. Also, when these occur in non-psychopaths they are accompanied with an emotion on the face and when the psychopath uses them there is usually no emotion or a fake version of it. The language of a psychopath also contains more subordinating conjunctions, otherwise known as 'cause and effect' words. Examples of the most popular are "because" and "so that". This suggests that they view their actions as the logical outcome of a plan or something that had to be done. Further analysis revealed that psychopaths used about twice as many words related to basic physiological needs and self-preservation, including eating, drinking and monetary resources than the non-psychopaths. This topic also includes the 'sociopath' label as they are merely a different breed of a psychopath.

388

For further study on this topic, we would suggest that you source the studies that the FBI have carried out on the written\typed word of the psychopath as well, in light of the global popularity of social media and the grooming that goes on.

A histrionic personality is much more easy to spot, as the very nature of their personality (*often verging on the strength of a disorder*) is to seek the attention of others. This is down to grandiose and over the top metaphors to describe illnesses and occurrences that often don't exist. This can reflect in the tone of voice they adopt as well, often making them come across as the stereotype suggests 'whiners'. A higher pitch will often accompany the more 'emotional metaphors. It is largely a massively impressionistic way to speak but it just lacks in any great detail.

Facial adornments and dental work are easily recognizable as well during someone's speech. A tongue stud that has just recently been inserted can take a few days to settle in. There is chance of swelling and can often need to a temporary lisp, it has an audible rattle at times as well. As well as that, when someone has recently had a false tooth and or a crown put in, there is an audible clink when speaking.

PREVARICATION OF SPEECH

Now to be too over informed on the subject of lie detection (it is my belief that one can never be too informed) but aside from the usual suspects of behavioural analysis with regard to lie detection, there is in fact a list of things to be aware of that liars and those who mishandle the truth will adhere to. When those that plan out their lies do exactly that, they plan and try to come up with answers to every possible solution to their story. It is for those reasons that they fall foul of something most common in normal speech pattern (which is what we term as telling the truth). Repeating questions back , verbatim is often a sure sign of emotional stress in a situation:

POLICE CHIEF : *Did you murder John Doe??*

SUSPECT: *Did i murder John Doe?*

This is a common tactic that is employed to stall for time during a question. It is not an admission of guilt on its own, more a stifling of the current anxiety, they are trying for whatever reason to suppress, and prepare a deceptive response. In normal conversation a person would only repeat parts of the question or re- word it in their own manner, but repeating it verbatim is a sure sign of stalling.

Guarded tone to the prevaricator in question will usually be adopted. For example if someone had replied to a simple and direct question by lowering their tone and saying something along the lines of,"how do you mean?" it is characteristic that a lie that is on the way. Tone of this nature isn't needed and is therefore emblematic of concealment of some sort. It could be the truth, his feelings toward you asking the question, or simply the question itself.

People who have taken the time to plan out their lies will inherently forget to use contractions in their speech of choice as well. Bill Clinton's infamous speech regarding his dalliance provides what is known as a 'non-contracted denial'.

'I *did not* have sexual relations with that woman'

The extra emphasis on the denial is the point of interest here as it is unnecessary if it were the truth. Yes it could be indicative of his outrage at the allegation itself, however his face and body language convey the true nature of that. Simply *'I didn't have sex with her'* is the most likely way an honest person would have phrased the denial. Good ole Bill said a lot more than he wanted to here.

390

Over adherence to chronology and the timeline of the situation: To keep their stories straight and practise the necessary intonation where it counts, liars will often stick to their stories to the letter. They can't be thrown off by a random detail, as they are concentrating on more than enough as it is. This isn't the way that people recount tales when being truthful; they are regurgitated as we remember them, which is often much like the narrative of a Tarantino movie. This is because there is an inherent emotional part to the true telling of a story. More often than not we will open with what pertains to us the most, emotionally and then jump around in the time of the rest of the tale.

Its human nature and frankly Darwinian to not want to implicate ourselves when there are misdeeds afoot, it is for this reason that liars love euphemisms. It helps them to take the heat off of any part they had to play in the sordid affair of whatever it is that went on. Language softeners are a way to do this.

Normal denial: *I didn't steal the money*☐

Same line with softeners: *I didn't take the money*

If the answer to a simple and direct question involves them changing their normal speaking pattern to include more softeners then we would heartily recommend that you keep your ears peeled!

The over emphasis on the truth in their statements, 'I swear to god' 'to tell you the truth' 'Honestly'. These are unnecessarily emphatic on the elements they want to be concentrated upon. Truth tellers do not need them.

Pronouns make frequent appearances in the statements of liars as they are used incorrectly. These are most often used in normal conversation and are a sign of someone engaged in comfortable speech. To see them or rather, hear them disappear or be misused is a sure fire sign of someone who is actively monitoring their speech.

LIE: *You don't record time that you didn't do*

TRUTH: *I don't record time I didn't do*

That latter is a clear first person statement.

There is one thing that a liar does that is quite obvious when you look at it objectively, which involves the not telling of the truth in any situation. Which is exactly what we just did here and that is to give a long introduction that says nothing and skips over main points. This is a way for the liar to build some sense of credibility with the interviewer by fattening up the tale with as much truth as they have to give. There has been some study done in this area by an Israeli researcher Avinoam Sapir and he found that liars will add more detail into the prologue of events than the main part of the story which they just gloss over as here is where the lies are based.

Specific denials are something that again relates to the way in which a liar will phrase their denials and their willingness to shine a light on to themselves. Someone who is telling the truth has absolutely no problem with a categorical denial:

'I haven't stolen anything from anyone in my entire life'

A liar will choose their words more carefully.

An attempt to hedge their statements, which are often heard on TV and in court and are the attempt to give themselves a built in/out to what they are saying. Some popular phrases are *'As far as I recall'* *'If you really think about it'* *'How I remember it is'*. These aren't a sure sign of deception, merely low confidence in themselves and their words, which could be

392

down to the makeup of their personality. However, repeated use of these should definitely give rise to concern.

FREUDIAN SLURPS...ERM I MEAN SLIPS

This is in essence a verbal and/or memory slip-up that leaks out in one's speech. It is believed that it is directly linked to the person's subconscious mind and this is why they are seen to be deceptive, and a link to their hidden thought pattern. Some common examples of this would be calling your current partner by the name of an ex, or saying the wrong word in a sentence that gives a totally different meaning, even misinterpreting the written or spoken word.

It wouldn't take a Deductionist to realise that these were discovered and placed into print by one of the godfathers of psychology, Sigmund Freud. He wrote up a variety of examples and explanations in *The Psychopathology of everyday life* released in 1901. They have also been given the title of Parapraxis.

These are interesting, more so, to watch how the person reacts to them afterwards. Do they immediately panic and backtrack or do they calmly explain themselves, or genuinely muse over why it is that they said that? Whatever the outcome here, it will give you information with which to deduce from.

A common, and indeed very popular example of this is when George Bush Snr. stated:
'*For seven and a half years I've worked alongside President Reagan, and I'm proud to have been his partner. We've had triumphs. We've made some mistakes. We've had some sex -- setbacks.*'

After the statement you hear the audience just explode with laughter, and poor Mr. Bush appears to have a coronary. You've only to watch his chest to see how much he panics.

Rather than revealing that Bush unconsciously wished to have intimate relations with Reagan, as a Freudian interpretation might suggest, this slip was more likely an example of a speech error called a *deletion*, which involves omitting a word or part of a word. In this case, "ba" was inadvertently omitted from "setbacks." Speech errors like this are common (though generally less embarrassing), and they are especially likely to occur when people are tired, nervous, or otherwise not at their peak level of cognitive functioning. Linguists argue that speech errors reflect the complex way that language is organized and produced, and are unlikely to reflect repressed desires or conflicts. This doesn't mean that errors and slips are always psychologically meaningless.

In this instance Mr. Bush was concerned about the impression he gave, and it conflicted against his nature being rather old fashioned, and thus it was embarrassment we saw creeping across his body. If someone makes a slip of this nature and then begins to panic and stutter, emits some pacifying behaviour and uses a statement such as '*erm what I meant to say was*' this is a sure sign of immediately attempting backtrack. A leak in their true nature at that moment.

The extent to which a given thought happens to be on one's mind, conscious or not, can bias subsequent language production and comprehension. Word completion tasks, for example, are often used to assess the cognitive accessibility of a construct, particularly those that individuals are likely to lack conscious access to, such as death or suicide. In an older study conducted by Motley and Baars (1979), male participants who believed they might receive an electric shock were more likely to make shock-related slips (e.g., misreading "shad bock" as **"bad shock"**), whereas those who were in the presence of an attractive and provocatively dressed female experimenter were more likely to mistake phrases like "lood-gegs" for **"good legs."** These findings, as well as a handful of others from the same time period, are aligned with Freud's observation that slips of the tongue may reveal more about a

394

speaker's internal mental state than whatever it was he or she intended to say. More recent research also supports the idea that avoiding certain thoughts may make them even more apparent: Daniel Wegner's theory of ironic processes of mental control suggests that efforts to suppress unwanted thoughts or behaviors can, ironically, increase the likelihood of their resurfacing, in dreams or other forms.

These slips are still frowned upon in today's modern cognitive psychology but are accepted in today's modern urban culture. For example, why doesn't Emily immediately forgive Ross when he says Rachel's name at their wedding in the hit TV. Show *'Friends'*? It may because, even if he can convince Emily that he has no feelings for her, at the very least it shows that she is on his mind.

So the real key to knowing what to deduce from Freudian slips is in the follow up behaviours. They work much in the same way as reliable reading of body language. It is the clusters of tells that will point you in the right direction. The same here with the behaviours after the slip up, in that it isn't just the slip ups and the Freudian fails that are the indicator to meaning so look for the clusters.

Accents and training

We all have our own recognisable style and tone, to how we speak, that are indicative of where we have spent a large portion of our lives. These are our accents. There are hundreds throughout the globe. The recognition of each of them, or as many as you can find, provide an ample source of information regarding where the person has lived and/or grown up.

These may sound like generic pieces of information to glaze over but they can be quite unsettling in a powerful sense when the Deductionist knows where you live or the many different places that you have lived. Especially when it comes to accent blending. As there are so many, particularly when it comes to the different regional dialects or the different accents in the different states it is considered quite impressive. One way to get to know the many different accents and 'twangs' with which they speak is to learn how to speak them. This will also better help with the storing of them in your palace. One of the things you will realise, when studying these is, that each accent and region has its own unique twist on a few of the English words.

Take for example the midlands in England. In the midlands the three meals are referred to as Breakfast, dinner and tea, but when you get further afield the three meals then become breakfast, lunch and dinner. This is merely a for instance, there are many to research.

First things first, here is a basic guide of getting to grips with an accent and understanding them, thus helping you recognise them when you hear them later.

It isn't just about the pronunciation of the words. There is a musicality to any dialect and accent. It's happened many times with the British actors trying to be American and vice versa.

Learn the slang! This is how you learn to become comfortable with a new accent. Take for example the Irish slang word 'crack'. To the Irish it is not a class A drug.

The thicker the accent you listen to, the quicker you will understand and get to grips with it. It is much like the memorization techniques requiring the imagining of certain things to a ridiculous degree. You take the normal and exacerbate it. The same theory is at play here.

Overconfidence is not key here, so practise practise practise.

The other choice you have is to track down as many accent training cd's for actors, as you require for your own research. These will give you stock phrases, sentences and key words to allow you the ability to imitate an accent successfully. Which, if you were Sherlock himself would be an incredible asset to have to any disguise that you were using!

What will follow is a brief breakdown of some globally popular accents to make yourself aware of as a Deductionist. For the readers from the U.S.A in particular but this applies to anyone looking to know a thing or two about the British accent, there are a few things you can do to know how to recognise this. They have a similar approach to the previous method but with one or two small changes.

Immerse yourself in the English language and at all times ignore Dick Van Dyke's attempt. This way you will become aware of all the subtle nuances involved in the proper dialect and tone. There are plenty of soaps available to Google at your leisure so you can hear the more regional tones. Not everyone is posh or speaks with an RP accent.

It is widely considered in the states that the British accent has a more elegant feel to it. This is down to the vowel sound 'aw' (a) and it being replaced with an 'ah' or 'uh' sound. This doesn't ring true for the entirety of the UK, however for an estimated 80% of the population it does.

With words that end in 'rl' like girl, it is pronounced as just the one syllable, but with words that end in 'rel' an extra sound is heard. For example Squirrel would sound like squih-rul. Another similar example would be mirror, and in England it would be pronounced 'mih-ra'

The u sound changes. For example, words like duty, stupid would be pronounced DEWTY and STEWPID.

The a sound in words like father comes from the back of the throat and makes and 'ar' sound. So father would be pronounced 'farther' which is the sound that is exaggerated in an Rp accent. However a twist on this sound appears when you hit the divide between the south of England and the north and parts of the middle of England. This is particularly apparent around words like bath, path, and bastard. In the south of England you would hear them pronounced like B-ar-th, and P-ar-th and B-ar-stud. Then when you start heading north from the centre of England these words and others that sound the same are pronounced b-ass-stud, p-a- th, b-a-th.

When you are more aware of the regional tones you will notice that Londoners/cockneys drop the 'h' sound at the end of the words that have it there. There are many buzzwords that will alert you to the English accent or a great deal of time that has been spent in England. This is of particular relevance for the difference between the U.K and the U.S.A:

English	American
Anti-clockwise☐	Counter clockwise
Barrister	Attorney
Block of flats☐	Apartment building
Boot	trunk
Chemist	Drug store
Crisps	Potato chips☐
Drawing pin	Thumbtack
Flyover	overpass

Nappy	diaper
Lift	elevator
Postcode	Zip code
Waistcoat	Vest
Solicitor	Lawyer/Attorney
(Car) Saloon	(car) Sedan

This should provide you with sufficient enough detail to spot the British in anyone. What will need narrowing down from there onward is, whether they just lived there for a while, or are a tourist or even recently immigrated. It is listening that will give you the clues.

THE LARGER THAN LIFE APPLE ACCENT

The good people of New York speak a little differently from the generic U.S speech in both the way it sounds and the words that are used. There are certain vowels and consonants and again a few buzzwords that you will need to become keenly aware of. New York English is always pronounced forward, as if throwing it from the mouth take for example the following:

• Tomorrow becomes te-ma-ro (te is like a mix between a and o)

• Sunday is simply sun-dA

• Tuesday is Twos-dey

• Thursday is Therrs-dey (err being kind of rolled r) □

The consonants are often dropped or rolled. The 'Y' sound in a

New York accent, at the end of a word is almost never pronounced. In some cases it sounds like a slightly rolling 'r'. The 'g' at the end of '-ing' isn't pronounced either. The main twist is in 'Long Island' which is pronounced 'Lawn Guyland'. So 'going' is pronounced 'goin' and 'here' sounds like 'hea'. The hard 'th' at the beginning & middle of words has a sound something between 'd' and 'th' it is in fact more like a rolled 'd', but if you're unsure, speak with the 'd' sound. The soft 'h' sound, in words like "both", has a "t" sound, as if the "h" was dropped, so "both" sounds like "boat" & the number 3 becomes "tree", rather like the Irish way. This might be the singular most popular attribute to the New York accent and that is learning how to effectively recognise their pronunciation of vowels. In particular the letter O. The best demonstration of this approach is found in the word 'new', to a New Yorker or someone from New Jersey this is pronounced 'noo'. There are a few words that adhere to this, though 'stupid' and 'due' spring to mind, 'few' and 'queue' are still pronounced with that same 'ew' sound in the middle. Many words that have the 'o' sound in the middle such as 'dog' and 'coffee' are pronounced with the 'o' as an 'aw' sound. This make these words sound like 'dawg' and 'cawfee'. The inflection of the accent is particularly noteworthy as well. As a mass, the New York accent is quite a deep but soft accent, though it isn't without its blends. Brooklyn and Staten Island are still 44% Italian, as such this will show in the accent. Think of Sylvester Stallone for those who are unsure of what we mean. There are also a great number of Jewish people in New York, this means their version of the accent takes a different tone. Think of Fran Drescher, or Mrs Wolowitz from the TV show 'The Big Bang Theory'.

DO AS THE BOSTONIANS DO

Another of the hugely popular accents from America, it is frequently mocked in film (see the movie TED for details) and standup comedy and as a consequence many are aware of it.

It will take a great deal of time to master talking in the accent (though you should at this point only be considering this for one of your disguises when you are out working a case) it is quite straight forward recognising it. Let us first begin with the pronunciation of the letter 'R', the word 'park' pronounced with a Boston accent would become 'Pahk' and 'car' would become 'cah'. 'O' turns into more of an 'ahhhh' sound and as such Boston would become 'Bahhhst-inn'. Over correcting where none is needed is something that frequently happens with the letter 'R'. One of the more popular words that this rule happens upon is 'drawing' making it turn into 'drawring'. John F Kennedy would be someone to listen to for an almost cliché accent. Cuba = Cuber and vigor = vigah.

BRUMMY ALL THE WAY

Though the United Kingdom is quite small in comparison to the rest of the world, there are a lot of different cultures and regions and places and therefore dialects. London is by far and away the most popular place in the United Kingdom with it being the capital. Also what we proffer here, are two other accents from two other regions of England. First up is Birmingham, the birth place of Ozzy Osbourne and to those who reside in the U.K they are affectionately known as brummie's.

There is no collection of specific words to this region of England. It is only the way that the words are pronounced and the overall sound of the accent itself.

Beginning with the way in which the vowels are formulated. The vowel sounds are often the key. In Brummie, **'oy'** is used instead of **'i'**. For example: 'Oy kwoyt loik it' (I quite like it). This sound is similar to the 'oy' employed in most Irish dialects. The **'u'** as in 'hut' is lengthened to become **'oo'** as in 'took'. **'ar'** as in 'star' is also lazy. In some forms, the vowel shortens and becomes **'a'** as in 'cap'. The **'i'** as in 'pit' becomes **'eel'** as in 'feet'.

With regard to the consonants Brummie employs a mild form of the stereotypical Spanish **'r'**. This is a rolled variant, formed by vibrating the tongue at the top of the mouth4. Not every written 'r' is articulated. Here, the Birmingham accent mirrors RP quite closely. With a word like 'Centre', the 'r' sound is completely ignored. This differs from standard North American English, where every 'r' is pronounced if it appears in the written word. **'H'**'s are dropped wherever they occur, except when emphasis is required. The word 'Birmingham' therefore, has a silent 'h'. It also has a strong 'g', and the 'r' is not pronounced at all. The following statement is taken from a tourist website about the city of Birmingham and underneath I have translated it phonetically to how it would sound when it comes out of the mouth of homegrown Brummie:

Birmingham is one of the largest cities in the United Kingdom.

berminggum is wun uv the larges citays in the U-nyted Kingdem.

Probably most famous for the Bull Ring and Spaghetti Junction, but it has

prrobebLay moest faymus fer the bullrringg und spegettee jungshun, but ittas

A lot more to offer. The National Exhibition Centre is a great source of

eLo- mor to offa. The nashnel eksibishun senta is a grrayt sawss uv

Pride to the local inhabitants and steps have been taken in recent years to

prroid te the lowkel in-abitents und steps av bin tayken in rresunt yeers to

improve the appearance of the city.

imprroov the appeerents uv the citay.

NORTHERN YORKSHIRES

Yorkshire is the largest county in the United Kingdom and it is situated in the north of England. There are a considerable number of sounds that are pronounced differently such as the differentiation between 'right' being pronounced as 'raight'. 'Oh' sounds are pronounced 'or'. For example, No would be pronounced 'nor' and just remember that there is no emphasis on the 'R' - if you say it like that, you'll sound Irish. Words ending with and 'ee' sound are pronounced as 'eh' sounds. Example: 'Nasty' would be 'nasteh'. Yorkshire folk sometimes say 'aye' for yes, and 'nay or nah' for no.

The words 'nowt' and 'owt' mean nothing and anything. The word 'right' is often pronounced 'raight' and has many, many different uses other than correct or the opposite of left! It could mean 'really' E.G - 'It's really good'/'It's RAIGHT good.' Another use could be 'Alright' - 'Are you alright'/'Are you all-raight?'

This is more than enough pieces of common conversational words for you to be able to recognise the Yorkshire accent. Nowadays the most popular man with a Yorkshire accent is Dynamo the magician.

NEW ZEALAND VS AUSTRALIA

There is no easier way to annoy a kiwi than to ask what part of Australia they are from and vice versa with the Aussies. This is why I have given you some of the details of the subtle

403

nuances that can help you to differentiate between the two with almost relative ease. The film 'Once were warriors' would be something that you could source to further your research however the main difference between the two is that the New Zealanders clip their vowels when pronouncing them. By this we mean that they become short and concise.

For example, take the dish that is loved the world over, fish and chips. For a kiwi this would be pronounced 'Fush and Chups'. When someone talks about their kids this word would then become 'Kds'. 'Quickly' becomes 'Quckly, 'sheep' becomes 'ship'. Words like Chair and cheer sound the same in the Kiwi dialect. Not that I am only about describing the Kiwi dialect here but these are things that New Zealanders do and the Aussies do not. They have been listed for the simple reason that they are the most frequent sounds to pop up in general conversation, which makes your deductions twice as powerful when the information isn't directly focused upon. The most casual greeting of G'day is something only an Aussie would say and if you hear the familiar tones to the words of that particular region of the world and are unsure but also hear the overuse of the term of endearment 'Bro' then this will most likely be a New Zealander.

Many accents get confused with one another: Canadian and American, Scottish and Northern Irish, Jamaican and Barbadian, but the granddaddy of all of them? The three-way mix-up between Australian, New Zealand and South African English.

The South African dipthongs are also quite different than for the other two: the vowel in KITE is pronounced similarly to the way it is in American Southern English–'Kaht'. The dipthong in words like MOUTH, meanwhile is even more unusual–'mouth' is nearly homophonous with American English 'Moth'.

Those are really the only things that make the South African accent stand out and easier to recognise. Watch Lethal Weapon 2 for your homework on this area as my gift to you. There are countless more accents to master in the world, even in the United Kingdom alone. There is the welsh accent with its many regions, Scotland with its many regions and Ireland also. Eastern Europe often gets tarred with the same brush. Most people cannot tell the difference between a Polish person talking to them and a Russian person. Then there are all the different states in America, and the list for the rest of the planet goes on. What I am. saying really is that someone's accent is often overlooked as a vital piece of information but that would be far too much for one book maybe there will be some more in the next edition.....who knows???

URBAN LISTENING

Listening can quite literally get you almost any information you desire, as almost everything makes sound with which to reason backwards from. Let us set up a rather obscure hypothetical situation.

'You're a detective in a room with three viable suspects and you know one of them has committed a heinous crime. The only thing you know for sure is that the criminal takes 2 sugars in his drink.'

Now then if they are made in china cups and given a metal spoon to stir did you know that you can actually hear which one has the sugar in. This is just down to the volume of it and how quickly it dissolves in the liquid so there will be the inevitable crunch on the bottom as the spoon hits some of the undissolved pieces of it. This sound is made even more apparent if the drinks are made in cardboard/take-away cups.

Mood is very clearly indicated by sound. Going back to the aforementioned hypothetical you could hear if someone was in a heightened emotional state based on how fast they were stirring compared to the others. Footsteps can be indicative of mood also. A fast stride or even a run can be clearly heard against the backdrop of people milling around at the same speed. Toe tapping on the floor when sat still can at times suggest nervousness or impatience.

You hear three people go upstairs, for example, let us say that you have a daughter and it is her and her 2 friends going upstairs. 1 has high heels on, the other sounds like an elephant as she goes up the stairs stomping her feet and your daughter is the more energetic and goes up the stairs two at a time. An hour later and you hear a door slam followed by the sound of the heels moving quite quickly toward the stairs, a fast paced step moves in the same direction as the heels. Muffled words can be heard. What can we deduce from this incident? It would seem as though the elephant walker has offended the lady in the heels and she was going to leave. Your daughter chased her down to try and appease her or settle the argument.

This is only a hypothetical situation, granted, but the techniques remain the same. Because of the information you picked up via listening, you were able to deduce exactly what has gone on in a place that you weren't even close to being in.

Car's need to be subject to regular maintenance and as such there are certain noises that they make when there are certain and specific things wrong with them. You can clearly hear when a car is in need of new brake pads or an engine failing. You can hear learner drivers approach by their excessive and overuse of the clutch pedal. New brakes needed, can be heard in the scratching sound the car makes when the pedal is engaged and the car draws to a halt. Engine fails can be heard in the audible almost kangaroo bounce to cars usual noise. Excessive exhaust pipes can be heard because they are loud and abrasive; these are heavily featured on the people who like to 'pimp out' their cars. Similarly over use of the acceleration pedal can indicate this particular proclivity as well.

The onset of everyday illness such as cold and flu symptoms can be heard in the back of people's throats and the change it makes to their normal voice. When your child goes into the kitchen to get a drink of a juice and you hear the rustle of the bag of sweets that you know are in the cupboard (this is an incredibly simple example but serves to further prove the simplistic power behind listening). You know precisely what is going on because of the information you have.

To conclude this chapter and the abundance of information I have given you to play with, you have been left with one solution and that is simply to practise and store the information accordingly. Listening and conversational deductions is a treasure trove of often overlooked information. So as I have said before, be sure to keep those ears peeled.

SCENARIOS

"You must be shapeless, formless, like water. When you pour water in a cup, it becomes the cup. When you pour water in a bottle, it becomes the bottle. When you pour water in a teapot, it becomes the teapot. Water can drip and it can crash. Be water my friend."

— Bruce Lee

What has been thrown at you in this book is awesome! But besides my humble and modest opinion, the information is also quite varied and plentiful. So dependent upon where you are sitting in the work spectrum you might be thinking, well how I can apply this to my job at the minute, what situations could apply it to? I have tried to be as thorough as possible in the explanations of how to use it. Though just on the off chance, this chapter is trying to illuminate some of the possibilities

So what I lay before you here is a series of possible scenarios and granted, the list of scenarios could be infinite but I only have so many pages with which to play. The scenarios will be followed by how a different job role may use the information they gather via deduction and relate it to their work. For example, how a performing mentalist might use the information, how a policeman might, a tarot reader and so on.

Scenario 1

FOR A MENTALIST

' A group of women sat at the next table you are going to be performing for, they are all drinking. You hear one say 'Congratulations' and just the words 'any plans yet?'. As you move over to the next table you see a direction in the feet of all women pointing to only one woman. She is holding her own hand and

smiling in a coy manner. You notice her phone has a picture of her and her obvious partner on. She is in a nurse's uniform and the partner is wearing a blue polo shirt, combat trouser and steel toe capped boots. His knees are wet and they appear in the photo on a driveway with a big garden behind.'

Now a mentalist is geared toward performance and entertainment here. It isn't wise to be seen as a smart ass when trying to give a performance that people are going to remember. So the 'news', the hand can't be seen for confirmation but as all are drinking then this feels like an engagement celebration. The partner would have had to have stayed at home with the child (children) as is shown by the big garden and the driveway in the photo. This is statistically most likely, that a big house, with people of an age to marry, both work full time and have a garden that there will be children there. So as you are there performing as a mind reader you ask the person whose hips everyone is pointing at if they have any news on the horizon that is positive in nature? They will confirm, as you heard 'congratulations' before you got to the table and everyone is showing the importance of one person at the table thanks to their hips. Open ended question follows 'It's not anything to do with your job is it?' which could be taken both ways. If they say yes it is, then you know what she does for a living thanks to the photo and if she says, no it isn't, then you still know what she does for a living. Look at her for a moment and then ask her if her partner is involved? If she tightens her grip on her hands then she knows what you are driving at and is enjoying it enough to test you. If she takes them off the table she may be just a little unsettled at your accuracy. Congratulate her on the impending nuptials, and mention that it'll be difficult getting time together to plan the wedding with you having such different shifts, making reference to her being a nurse and her partner of course being a plumber. The plumbing is shown in the durable yet malleable clothing and the wet knees. This is a direct presentation of mindreading and why people could misconstrue the skills of the Deductionist for a clandestine psychic.

Scenario 2

FOR THE POLICEMAN/WOMAN

'In an interview room, interrogating a murder suspect about what has happened and gone on during specific times on a specific date. You notice he has the number 13 tattooed behind his ear but no other visible tattoos, he is leaning forward protesting his innocence, you also notice he isn't wearing any socks and tips of his right shoe have been visibly cleaned to the point where it is obvious and they have become flakey'

So what can you as the officer do with this kind of information? It is clear that he is a white supremacist. It is also clear that he has paid specific attention to one shoe more than the other, which if it was both would indicate that they could have been cleaned for innocent reasons but in this situation to clean one is more indicative of getting rid of something that he does not wish others to see. You can talk to him arbitrarily about the man who was killed and read his reactions. Any reclusive behavior, such as leaning backwards and or hands coming off the table shows an emotional stress peak. Check for masking of hate and anger. Then you can make reference to his shoes and ask why he isn't wearing any socks? which is odd for anyone to wear shoes and no socks. Continue to monitor his behaviour again and if the same emotional stress peaks are there then you have enough reason to go and look for his socks, as he clearly does not want you to see them. As with police work there are rules to follow, and you will find that it is in your best interests to tread carefully when gathering information and make mental note of the pressure points to go for. This is because there are the rules to follow, you know, the law and rights and all that.

410

Scenario 3

FOR THE ETHEREAL READER - Authors note, it is not my intention to help people use this information to take advantage of people as our own opinion of this is that it is downright sickening! However a pen in the wrong hands can be an instrument of murder or used to write the most beautiful of poetry. I am merely showing how best to use your newfound skills of awesomeness!

'A woman is sitting in your waiting room, clutching her necklace with a look of sadness on her face. When she is called in she looks almost stony faced. On her necklace is a bald eagle that she is pulling at and rubbing. You approximate her age to be 23. She hasn't had much sleep clearly and judging from the smell of her clothes has only put a cigarette out seconds before she came in through the door but there no other visible signs and the only thing she seems to have on her are her phone and purse. You notice her index fingers are bent and have a curve to them and during your reading you notice a Mike is calling her on her phone. She cancels the call in anger'

You already have plenty of information for a successful reading at this point. She is clearly looking for help but does not know who to trust and open up to. As shown in her sadness being seen when she thinks she is on her own and keeping a poker face when in front of other people. The sadness is clearly related to the necklace and is therefore recent. You know that eagles relate to the marines and the most likely outcome here is that she lost her father in the most recent war. Mike is therefore most likely to be her boyfriend. What would be most honourable in this situation is for you to say something along the lines '*I know you feel like you have lost your way due to recent events (merely point at the necklace) but you can't shut your family out, least of all mike as he only wants to help because he loves you. Picking up smoking again after you did so well (no smoking paraphernalia, no other signs in the skin/teeth/fingers shows extensive time off but she doesn't seem under any duress because of smoking so she hasn't done it for a while.) won't help, you should be around people and your family who love you and if you do need that time on your own then go and sit at your drum kit and bash out a few songs'* The drumming being shown in the curvature to her index fingers. You have given a noble reading and encouraged her away from you and into her family.

You can now therefore see just how malleable and interchangeable deduction can be. Also its reliability and accuracy with practice can be seen clearly. You just need continual practice and application of the skills I have hammered home at you.

CONCLUSION

I am going to keep this brief and to the point as you have a considerable amount of information to think about. Take heed of all of the lessons that have been imparted. Play the games, do the practice drills. Above all, engage all parts of your brain in what will be the biggest adventure yet, becoming an expert Deductionist!

Thank you all for your time. You can find me on facebook, twitter, Instagram or visit my website to read my blog which has free lessons on deduction as well www.bencardall.com

Be sure to find me on YouTube for new episodes of my hit web series 'The Deductionist' as well as keeping up to date with pioneering Deduction experiments!

My eternal thanks to my partner in life and all this madness, Charley Hannon! I love you so much! Thanks for putting up with all the midnight experiments, drills, week long games and all the madness that is no doubt to come!

Also from MX Publishing

MX Publishing is the world's largest specialist Sherlock Holmes publisher, with over a hundred titles and fifty authors creating the latest in Sherlock Holmes fiction and non-fiction.

From traditional short stories and novels to travel guides and quiz books, MX Publishing cater for all Holmes fans.

The collection includes leading titles such as *Benedict Cumberbatch In Transition* and *The Norwood Author* which won the 2011 Howlett Award (Sherlock Holmes Book of the Year).

MX Publishing also has one of the largest communities of Holmes fans on Facebook with regular contributions from dozens of authors.

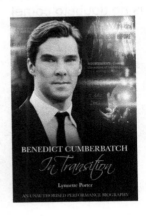

www.mxpublishing.com

Also from MX Publishing

Our bestselling short story collections 'Lost Stories of Sherlock Holmes', 'The Outstanding Mysteries of Sherlock Holmes', 'Untold Adventures of Sherlock Holmes' (and the sequel 'Studies in Legacy') and 'Sherlock Holmes in Pursuit'.

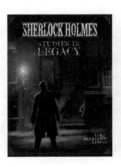 

The Amateur Executioner

London, 1920: Boston-bred Enoch Hale, working as a reporter for the Central Press Syndicate, arrives on the scene shortly after a music hall escape artist is found hanging from the ceiling in his dressing room. What at first appears to be a suicide turns out to be murder . . .

The Enoch Hale and Sherlock Holmes series continues with *The Poisoned Penman* and concludes with *The Egyptian Curse*.

Also from MX Publishing

"Phil Growick's, *'The Secret Journal of Dr Watson'*, is an adventure which takes place in the latter part of Holmes and Watson's lives. They are entrusted by HM Government (although not officially) and the King no less to undertake a rescue mission to save the Romanovs, Russia's Royal family from a grisly end at the hand of the Bolsheviks. There is a wealth of detail in the story but not so much as would detract us from the enjoyment of the story. Espionage, counter-espionage, the ace of spies himself, double-agents, double-crossers...all these flit across the pages in a realistic and exciting way. All the characters are extremely well-drawn and Mr Growick, most importantly, does not falter with a very good ear for Holmesian dialogue indeed. Highly recommended. A five-star effort."

The Baker Street Society

Lightning Source UK Ltd.
Milton Keynes UK
UKHW02f0737070118
315674UK00005B/105/P